The Line Between Us

The Line Between Us

Teaching About the Border and Mexican Immigration

BILL BIGELOW

A Rethinking Schools Publication

The Line Between Us: Teaching About the Border and Mexican Immigration
by Bill Bigelow

Rethinking Schools, Ltd., is a nonprofit educational publisher of books, booklets, and a quarterly journal on school reform, with a focus on issues of equity and social justice.

To request additional copies of this book or a catalog of other publications, or to subscribe to the quarterly magazine *Rethinking Schools,* contact:

Rethinking Schools
1001 East Keefe Avenue
Milwaukee, Wisconsin 53212 USA
800-669-4192
www.rethinkingschools.org

The Line Between Us: Teaching About the Border and Mexican Immigration, by Bill Bigelow
© 2006 by Rethinking Schools, Ltd.

Cover design: M. J. Karp
Cover photo: Rick Reinhard
Page design and layout: Joanna Dupuis
Project coordinator: Barbara Miner

ISBN 10-digit: 942961-31-5 13-digit: 978-0-942961-31-7

Acknowledgments

All Rethinking Schools books are collective endeavors, and this one is no exception. *The Line Between Us* begins with the patience, humor, and brilliance of the four individuals who were my main guides and teachers on the Rethinking Schools–Global Exchange trips to the border, and to whom I dedicate this book: Carmela Castrejón, Xiomara Castro, Jaime Cota, and Claudia Rodriguez-Zinn. None of the border trips or resulting curriculum would have been possible without their wisdom and kindness. Other guides I learned from in Tijuana include Lourdes Lujan, Gilberto Martínez, Carmen Valadez, and Luis Castro; in San Diego, Benjamín Prado, Christian Ramirez, and Fernando Suarez del Solar; and in Chiapas, Eva Schulte, Jutta Meier-Wiedenbach, and Miguel Pickard. Thanks, too, to Ryan Zinn of the Organic Consumers Association, who is a NAFTA encyclopedia and led several workshops for teachers in Tijuana. In the Global Exchange office in San Francisco, Tanya Cole and Malia Everette helped make the border trips possible.

My 2003-04 Franklin High School Global Studies class is the subject — or guinea pigs, as they might complain — of much of this book. They were a lively and cooperative group and I'm grateful that I had such a forthright collection of individuals to work with. My student Abe Figueroa read and commented on much of the manuscript and kindly allowed me to reproduce his metaphorical drawing. My colleague Aníbal Rivera generously invited my class to interview students in his Spanish language humanities class about their immigration experiences. Sandra Childs and her then-intern Tim Swinehart taught much of the curriculum described in the book, allowed me to observe and participate in their classroom, and made valuable contributions. And thanks to Aníbal's students and Sandra and Tim's students for allowing the intrusions.

Rethinking Schools editors Linda Christensen and Bob Peterson co-led the Rethinking Schools–Global Exchange border trips, and graciously agreed to contribute chapters to this book. Many other individuals and organizations have allowed their work to be included in this volume, and I thank them all: Sarah Anderson, Connie Aramaki, David Bacon, John Cavanagh, Martín Espada, Danica Fierman, Arnoldo Garcia, Elizabeth (Betita) Martínez, Amalia Ortiz, Rick Reinhard, Luis Rodríguez, Pam Muñoz Ryan, Kevin Sullivan, Heidi Tolentino, Howard Zinn, the Environmental Health Coalition, the San Diego office of the American Friends Service Committee, and Witness for Peace.

Over 60 teachers have traveled on Rethinking Schools–Global Exchange trips to the border, and all of them were part of the process that contributed to this book. The Mexico trips and work on this book were supported by the entire Rethinking Schools editorial board and staff: Wayne Au, Susan Bates, Terry Burant, Catherine Capellaro, Linda Christensen, Stan Karp, David Levine, Larry Miller, Bob Peterson, Kelley Dawson Salas, Rita Tenorio, Mike Trokan, Stephanie Walters, and Kathy Williams. Other friends and colleagues who contributed ideas and critique include Robin Blanc, Norm Diamond, Marty Hart-Landsberg, Leon Lynn, and Deborah Menkart. I also would be remiss if I didn't acknowledge the many quick-witted and entertaining baristas at Peet's Coffee and Tea on N.E. Broadway in Portland, and Quinn and Katherine Losselyong at Foxfire Teas; both establishments should charge me rent for the long stretches I worked there.

Special thanks to Mary Jane Karp, who designed the book's cover; Joanna Dupuis, who designed and laid out the book; and Jennifer Morales, who proofread the book. Barbara Miner coordinated the book's production. Her editorial insights (and scalpel) were a huge help. Barbara put up with my whining and foot-dragging, and with good-humored determination kept the project on track.

Finally, thanks to my wife and best friend, Linda Christensen. Linda is the most creative and compassionate teacher I've ever seen. She has been my inspiration for much longer than I labored on this book. ∎

CONTENTS

STRUCTURE OF THE BOOK

Section 1 of *The Line Between Us* is a narrative that describes a curriculum on the U.S–Mexico border and Mexican immigration that I taught to my Global Studies class at Franklin High School in Portland, Ore. Sections 2 through 5 contain lesson plans, readings, and student handouts that flesh out and add to the descriptions in the narrative.

Following these, in Section 6, are thoughts on additional teaching ideas; related articles and lessons from *Rethinking Globalization;* and book, video, organization, and web resources. All the resources are posted at our website, www.rethinkingschools.org/mexico.

—B. B.

ABOUT THE AUTHOR

Bill Bigelow has taught high school social studies in Portland, Ore., since 1978. He has written or co-edited a number of books including *Strangers in Their Own Country: A Curriculum on South Africa* (1985), *The Power in Our Hands: A Curriculum on the History of Work and Workers in the United States* (1988), *Rethinking Columbus* (1991; 2nd edition, 1998), *Rethinking Our Classrooms, Vol. 1* (1994), *Rethinking Our Classrooms, Vol. 2* (2001), *Rethinking Globalization: Teaching for Justice in an Unjust World* (2002), and *A People's History for the Classroom* (2008). Bigelow currently works as an editor for *Rethinking Schools* magazine. He can be reached at bbpdx@aol.com.

Introduction

I was born and raised in what was once Mexico. The county courthouse was in *San Rafael,* we did our shopping in *Corte Madera,* I went to seventh and eighth grades in the neighborhood of *Del Mar* on *Avenida Miraflores,* and we looked across the bay to the closest big city, *San Francisco.* I grew up surrounded by linguistic memories of Mexico.

Mexican place names have always been welcome here. But the U.S. attitude toward Mexican people and Mexico itself has been more ambivalent. And these days, the border between Mexico and the United States has grown increasingly tense.

Since the mid-1980s, I've traveled to Mexico 12 times. The most recent trips — five to Tijuana and the border, one to Chiapas in southern Mexico —

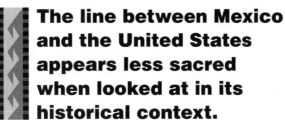

The line between Mexico and the United States appears less sacred when looked at in its historical context.

gave rise to the lessons in this book. This curriculum project, in turn, grew out of work on the Rethinking Schools book *Rethinking Globalization: Teaching for Justice in an Unjust World.* Throughout, I've sought to engage students in a search for connections: between Third World debt and rainforest destruction, between food exports and sweatshops, between free trade and global warming, between social analysis and imagining alternatives. And it's been a search to discover which lessons resonate with students, which touch their hearts, which make them want to dig deeper.

The relationship between Mexico and the United States is a good place to focus a rethinking globalization lens. These days the anti-immigrant rhetoric is growing even more shrill — from quasi-vigilante groups like the Minutemen, to think tanks like the Center for Immigration Studies that mask their nativism in a statistic-dense scholarly discourse, to congresspeople who demand, "We need to get serious about enforcement." Our students are surrounded by a culture that exposes them to some very bad "teaching" about Mexico and immigration. Too often, the conversation is abstract and centers on immigration disconnected from its history and from its root causes. The questions commonly asked — e.g., Does our economy benefit or suffer from immigration? Should border security be tightened or should there be a new guest worker program? Should bilingual education be banned? — tend to be narrow and ahistorical.

In *The Line Between Us,* I offer my own classroom experiences, as well as teaching reflections of Rethinking Schools editors Linda Christensen and Bob Peterson, to suggest the importance of a *connected* inquiry. Thus, the book features lessons and readings on the history of the border itself — the product of a war pursued by a slave-owning president, James K. Polk, who misrepresented intelligence, lied about his intentions, and provoked and invaded a sovereign country. The line between Mexico and the United States appears a bit less sacred when looked at in its historical context.

As lessons on the North American Free Trade Agreement (NAFTA) reveal, the line between us has become less of a barrier to investment and trade. But the huge number of migrants seeking to cross the border is inexplicable without analyzing the impact of this so-called free trade. "The NAFTA Role Play" activities in the book aim to lay the groundwork for students to connect these phenomena. The link between trade and immigration may be news to some in the United States, but not to observers in Mexico. Three years before NAFTA took effect, José Luis Calva of the National University of Mexico, predicted, "If the governments and legislatures of the three countries [Mexico, the United States, and Canada] agree to liberalize trade in agricultural goods, U.S. citizens should be prepared to receive some 15 million Mexican migrants. The Border Patrol will be unable to detain them, and even a new iron curtain, rising on the border at a moment when the Cold War has given way to economic warfare among nations, will buckle under the weight of millions of Mexicans thrown off their lands by free trade." Prescient remarks. Students need to explore these kinds of connections.

"Reading Chilpancingo," "The Transnational Capital Auction," and "Border Improvisations" encourage students to consider how intimate details of people's lives are framed by the imperatives of a global economic system. The jobs that people have or don't have in *maquiladora* zones along the U.S.–Mexico border, the wages they receive or, for that matter, the quality of the air they breathe and the water they drink, are connected to investment decisions in a global game of profit maximization.

This is the kind of historical and contextual inquiry that students need to engage in if they are to avoid the immigrant scapegoating that distorts so much thinking these days. It is also the approach that informs the lessons in this book.

The Lines Between Us

The book is called *The Line Between Us*, but in fact, the material here traces many lines between us. The most obvious are the multiple walls between the United States and Mexico. However, the lines inside Mexico are also growing more pronounced — between men and women, between countryside and cities, between rich and poor. When Bob Peterson and I were in Chiapas in July 2005, people told us that villages there increasingly are being emptied of the men, who are fleeing low prices for their crops and seeking work in sprawling Mexican cities or in the United States. Entire villages are now mostly women and children, the lines slicing relationships and families. Mexico's gulf between the haves and the have-nots is also growing. Mexico has long been one of the most unequal countries in the world, but it's getting worse.

The line between the rich and poor in Mexico mirrors the inequality between the United States and Mexico. The typical U.S. *hourly* wage equals the typical Mexican *daily* wage. It's a line that separates people who have a right to organize a union (albeit with significant limitations) and those who, for the most part, have little ability to secure authentic union representation. And for too many companies, the line between the United States and Mexico signifies the line between

environmental regulations and a toxic free-for-all, highlighted in Linda Christensen's "Reading Chilpancingo," and Kevin Sullivan's "A Toxic Legacy on the Mexican Border."

In the United States, the border legitimates lines between legal and illegal residents, and all that these categories entail. I explore these lines in "Teaching About 'Them' and 'Us,'" recounting my students' reactions to my curriculum. It's a line between those who live in fear of deportation and those who don't, between those who risked their lives to get here — like Marco and his father in Pam Muñoz Ryan's "First Crossing" — and those who didn't.

But these are human-made lines, so they can also be *un*made. It's easy to focus on the negative, because the injustice seems infinite. Yet the curriculum itself is an expression of hope and features people of courage and conscience: cross-border environmental justice organizers, collectively owned *ejido* communities that refuse to sell or leave their land, the American Friends Service Committee activists who monitor the U.S. Border Patrol, poets and artists who speak truth to power, and ordinary people trying to live dignified lives.

The material here is still a work in progress. For instance, I'm in the early stages of writing lessons on the history of U.S. immigration policy. Much more could and should be written about how students here can themselves contribute, however modestly, to putting the relationship between Mexico and the United States on a more just footing. I still struggle with how to get my non-immigrant students to resist fearful responses to immigration and to see their own self-interest more expansively. But in the face of proposals to criminalize immigration as never before, to build more and bigger walls, and to "develop" Mexico and Central America with even freer free trade, the issues discussed in this book have taken on greater urgency; the benefits of waiting to publish would have been offset by the costs of staying silent at a critical time.

These issues aren't going away anytime soon. To the contrary. So long as the line between us marks such dramatic inequality, and so long as the models of development that predominate in Mexico mostly benefit the rich on both sides of the border, the south-to-north migration is here to stay. Teachers of conscience will need one another as we fashion our response. This book is Rethinking Schools' contribution to a curricular conversation that we hope will find a wider audience. It's our attempt to erase some of the lines between us. ∎

BY LUIS RODRÍGUEZ

Running to America

For Alfonso and Maria Estela Rodríguez, migrants

THEY ARE NIGHT SHADOWS violating borders,
fingers curled through chain-link fences,
hiding from infra-red eyes, dodging 30-30 bullets.
They leave familiar smells, warmth and sounds
as ancient as the trampled stones.

Running to America

There is a woman in her finest border-crossing wear:
A purple blouse from an older sister,
a pair of worn shoes from a church bazaar,
a tattered coat from a former lover.

There is a child dressed in black,
fear sparkling from dark Indian eyes,
clinging to a headless Barbie doll.

And the men, some hardened, quiet,
others young and loud — you see something
like this in prisons. Soon they will cross
on their bellies, kissing black earth,

then run to America.

Strange voices whisper behind garbage cans,
beneath freeway passes, next to broken bottles.
The spatter of words, textured and multi-colored,
invoke demons.

They must run to America.

Their skin, color of earth, is a brand
for all the great ranchers, for the killing floors
on Soto Street and as slaughter
for the garment row. Still they come:
A hungry people have no country.

Their tears are the grease of the bobbing machines
that rip into cloth
that make clothes
that keep you warm.

They have endured the sun's stranglehold,
el cortito, foundry heats and dark caves
of mines, swallowing men.

Still they come, wandering bravely
through the thickness of this strange land's
maddening ambivalence.

Their cries are singed with fires of hope.
Their babies are born with a lion
in their hearts.

Who can confine them?
Who can tell them
which lines never to cross?
For the green rivers, for their looted gold,
escaping the blood of a land
that threatens to drown them,
they have come,

running to America.

Luis Rodríguez is the son of Mexican immigrants. He has been a journalist and children's book writer and is author of the memoir *Always Running.* "Running to America" first appeared in *Poems Across the Pavement* (Sylmar, CA: Tia Chucha Press, 1989). All rights reserved. Used with permission.

Teaching About 'Them' and 'Us'

ONE

The Border

On a gray February afternoon, I stood on U.S. soil next to the "fence" of enormous concrete pillars dividing the United States and Mexico. About a hundred yards away, a second fence, this one of corrugated iron, kept Mexicans on "their" side of the border; giant stadium lights towered over the dusty no man's land between. Just beyond, cars raced along a Tijuana highway.

Without these barriers it would be impossible to determine, simply from the landscape, where the United States ends and Mexico begins. There is nothing natural about this border.

I was traveling with 16 other teachers on a four-day tour, a collaboration between Rethinking Schools and the San Francisco-based human rights organization Global Exchange. Our mission was to explore life at the border and learn how globalization plays out in this corner of the world — and to bring our insights back to our students. We were based in downtown Tijuana and took day trips to working-class *ejidos* (collectively owned communities), migrant shelters, a squatter neighborhood, *maquiladoras* (foreign-owned assembly plants), and the toxic site of a former battery recycling plant abandoned by its U.S. owners. We talked with labor, environmental, and women's organizers, as well as factory managers and U.S. Border Patrol agents. Our Tijuana-based hosts were Mexican labor activist Jaime Cota and artist-activist

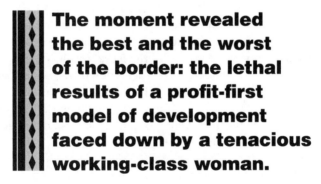

The moment revealed the best and the worst of the border: the lethal results of a profit-first model of development faced down by a tenacious working-class woman.

Carmela Castrejón, two graying but feisty, still-hopeful veterans of countless campaigns for social justice.

Mexico was to be the great success story of globalization, the showcase for the benefits of free trade, foreign investment, and development. President Bill Clinton promised in a 1993 speech that the North American Free Trade Agreement (NAFTA) would "provide an impetus for freedom and democracy in Latin America." He predicted that by embracing globalization, Mexico would "generate more jobs, they will have higher incomes, and they will buy more American products."

But in five trips to Tijuana and the U.S.–Mexico border, between February 2003 and March 2005, I've seen no evidence of these glowing predictions of freedom, democracy, and prosperity. In Mexico, as in the rest of the world, there's been no correlation between corporate investment or increased trade and social well-being. The border is a low-wage haven, a magnet for transnational corporations looking for a cheap, non-union workforce; it is also a magnet for people throughout Mexico who can no longer survive on the land or in their former jobs. It's a sprawling polluters' paradise, where toxic muck flows through neighborhoods and into streams and rivers. And it's a site for increasing numbers of deportees from the United States. But Tijuana is also home to activists and organizers, working on an array of justice issues: women's, environmental, labor, community and land rights, treatment of migrants, and many others. Hope has not been stifled by people's difficult living conditions.

My first afternoon at the border, I toured a Tyco Electronics maquiladora that produces wiring conduit for Apache helicopters and F-16 fighter planes. Minimum wage in Tijuana at the time was 43 pesos (about $4) a

SECTION 1 PHOTO: AP PHOTO/DARIO LOPEZ-MILLS
The wall between Mexico and the United States extends into the Pacific Ocean. On the U.S. side, the Border Patrol employs night vision devices, motion detectors, and other surveillance equipment as part of Operation Gatekeeper.

day, and we were told that with incentives, workers at Tyco start at $8 a day. The factory smelled poisonous. Posted on one machine I walked by was a large sign in Spanish: "Respiration equipment required to use this machine." But no one in the entire factory wore any respiration equipment. When I pointed this out to one of the Mexican managers leading our tour, he remarked, "Safety is not part of the Mexican culture."

In a factory we visited on another trip, women hovered over large tables gluing pieces of fabric or tile into sample books destined for U.S. department stores. A couple of women wore thin dust masks. When I asked about the masks, a supervisor told me that they are provided to pregnant women. In all of Tijuana, not a single worker is protected by a contract with an independent union from unhealthy conditions like these.

Maquiladoras (maquilas, for short) are concentrated in a Tijuana industrial park called Otay Mesa. Out of the Otay maquilas flows a putrid, garbage-filled stream that courses into Chilpancingo, the neighborhood below. Many Chilpancingo residents daily trudge up the hill to work in the maquilas. On one visit there, it had rained heavily and the familiar chemical smells of Chilpancingo were joined by odors of human waste. Adjacent the more established working-class Chilpancingo, hundreds of people, many of them recent arrivals from southern states like Oaxaca, Guerrero, and even Chiapas, live in the lowlands around the Río Alamar. Their homes are patched together from wooden pallets and blue plastic tarps. They have no running water, sewage connections, or garbage service.

'Rewards' of Foreign Investment

Our guide was Lourdes Lujan, whose family has lived in Chilpancingo for over 30 years. "I've known this river all my life," she told the teachers on our trip. "I've spent a lot of my life enjoying myself in this river. As a child I looked at it as something eternal. Twenty years ago the first maquilas came and the river began to be destroyed. Growing up, I always imagined that my children would be able to take part in it. Now they take part in the toxic waste. The river used to run clear, now it runs in colors." Lourdes described the high number of babies in the neighborhood born without brains or stillborn, and the young children with diseases like leukemia.

Chilpancingo provides ample evidence of the "rewards" of foreign investment that Clinton promised. Yes, many of these residents have jobs — but in unsafe conditions, at wages that cannot support decent lives. And then they return to neighborhoods poisoned by the companies they work for (see p. 97 for a reading activity on Chilpancingo).

Lourdes joined an environmental justice group to organize residents to demand that the most egregious toxic site in Otay Mesa, a defunct U.S.-owned battery recycling plant, be cleaned up. (The Mexican government says that when the plant closed, over 8,500 tons of toxic waste were simply left piled about the three-acre site.) "I never thought I could be an activist," Lourdes told our group. But she and other women doggedly went door to door in Chilpancingo alerting people about the health hazards, urging lead testing for children, and creating pressure on the state government to clean up the battery recycling site above their neighborhood. They built international support for the clean-up campaign and ended up securing an agreement that not only committed the government to clean the toxic site, but also gave Lourdes' organization, Colectivo Chilpancingo Pro-justicia Ambiental, an affiliate of Environmental Health Coalition, veto power over the clean-up plans.

During one visit to Chilpancingo, Lourdes acknowledged that she herself has been found to have exceptionally high levels of lead in her system. I wondered about the sores on her arms. On this day, fumes from the stream winding down Otay Mesa were especially awful and overpowering. I asked Lourdes if she considers leaving. "No, why should I leave?" she answered. "I was here first. I'm not leaving because I'm fighting for justice for my community."

We stood by the river. Nearby, two kids fished for crayfish in the milky water. The factories on the hill seemed to peer down on the scene below. It was a moment that revealed the worst and best of the border: the lethal results of a profit-first model of development faced down by a tenacious working-class woman who insists that her community be treated with dignity.

One night on each trip we ate dinner and talked with migrants at Casa del Migrante, a shelter in Tijuana run by the Scalabrini Order of the Catholic Church. Many of the migrants are on their way to the United States, fleeing poverty in southern Mexico. These days, however, over 60 percent of the men who show up at Casa del Migrante are deportees from the United States.

MAQUILADORA

Maquiladoras are foreign-owned assembly plants in Mexico, making everything from televisions to tractor-trailers to plastic toys. Companies import machinery and materials duty-free and export finished products.

Once touted as Mexico's salvation, the number of maquiladoras at the border began to decline after about 2001, when corporations began to seek out even lower wages in Asia, especially China.

My first visit there fell on a Valentine's Day. I met César, a small man, shy, maybe five feet one or two inches, with hair just beginning to thin, and an absolutely radiant smile. Standing in the Casa del Migrante courtyard before dinner, he told several of us in perfect English that he crossed from Mexico into the United States with his mother when he was 8 years old and went to live in Los Angeles. He said that after 17 years there, where he worked in every aspect of food service — "In a kitchen, I can do anything" — he was arrested for jay walking and sent to Tijuana. But Mexico is not "home" for César; before he arrived, he'd never been to Tijuana and knew no one here.

"What will you do now?" I asked.

"I'm sorry to tell you, sir, but I am going to go back." César said he expects to pay $1,500 to a guide — in Spanish, a *pollero*, literally a chicken-herder — to get him across the border.

While I talked with César, Rethinking Schools editor Bob Peterson spoke with Juan. He'd been pulled over by the San Jose police for driving without a license — a license he couldn't get anyway because he has no papers. So instead of going home to his two daughters, Cinthia, 9, and Karely, 8, he was turned over to *la migra*, the Immigration and Naturalization Service. They held Juan for two days, then flew him with 200 other deportees to San Diego, and bused him across the border to Tijuana, a place he hadn't been for 12 years. Juan found an abandoned car to sleep in and later made his way to Casa del Migrante. He told Bob that soon he would attempt the dangerous two-day desert crossing to return home.

Each visit to Casa del Migrante included a conversation with Gilberto Martínez, the assistant director. Gilberto is an intense and profoundly moral individual, whose anger has seemed to grow over the couple years we've come to the shelter. He talks about the situations of people like César and Juan: "They arrive here. They were working yesterday. They had family, they were renting an apartment, had a job, established lives. And suddenly, nothing. In 24 hours or less. So imagine their frustration. We try to deal with that frustration, and not let the person get lost in drugs or alcohol."

Gilberto knows that some of the people who leave Casa del Migrante to trek northward into the United States will not survive, and he acknowledged the esti-

CONNIE ARAMAKI

A woman works a sewing machine at a maquiladora in the Tijuana area. A typical wage in a Tijuana maquila is $6 a day.

mated death toll of more than 3,200 lives for the first 10 years after Operation Gatekeeper, the Border Patrol's enhanced security in the San Diego sector (see p. 31): "What is the reason that 3,200 people had to die?" he asked. "They are workers, migrants, not criminals. Why? That is the big question."

The last item on the itinerary for each tour is a meeting with representatives of the U.S. Border Patrol. It makes for an unsettling juxtaposition with the rest of our trip, and especially with the evening at Casa del Migrante. The Border Patrol's presentations are characterized by a casual dehumanization. One agent described how much better life is with the construction of multiple fences and high-powered lighting. Now, he said, after migrants climb the first fence, "it's easy pickings once they get across." People are objectified. With the advent of Operation Gatekeeper, we're told, "traffic" has moved east into the desert and mountains. "Nothing used to cross out there," an agent said.

Indeed Border Patrol agents pride themselves on not being affected by the human dramas they encounter every day. As one told us, "You cannot let your emotions get in the way of your being a professional."

The Border Patrol's world is one of clean lines that divide us from them, legal from illegal, right from wrong. "Here's how I look at it," one Border Patrol agent told us.

RICK REINHARD

Men at the Casa del Migrante shelter in Tijuana. Most of the migrants at Casa del Migrante have been recently deported from the United States.

"The United States is like our house. If someone wants to come in, then they can knock on the door and if we want to let them in, then they can come in. But they can't just break in. That's what illegal immigration is. It's breaking and entering." The metaphor has a compelling simplicity, but it ignores the reasons why one's neighbors can no longer live in their *own* house and why they are trying to break into "ours." In fact, it ignores how "we" acquired our "house" in the first place.

The spring after the first tour, my head spun with ideas and emotions. Back home, I began to piece together a curriculum on Mexico, the border and immigration for my 11th-grade global studies class at Franklin High School in Portland, Ore. My students were largely white and working-class, with a few first- and second-generation Asian and Eastern European immigrants, but none from Mexico or Latin America. For most of them, the immigration discussion has been framed in terms of "us" and "them." I struggled with how I could get students to rethink this stark dichotomy. I wanted to help them see the humanity behind the dehumanizing category "illegal alien." I wanted to help students grasp the roots of immigration in terms of policies that have benefited the wealthy (on both sides of the border) and thrown peasants off the land. I wanted to see how

what is unfolding in Mexico is part of the same processes unfolding in other parts of the world that we'd studied. And I wanted them to consider how our lives here intersect with Mexicans' lives.

The curriculum I developed took about six weeks to teach, and was divided roughly into five sections: the history of the border itself, stories of Mexican migrants today, the North American Free Trade Agreement and the economic causes of migration, life at the border, and immigration policy and its implications for students. Six weeks is not enough time to counter a lifetime of media stereotypes and simplification that have influenced most students' thinking about immigration issues. Teaching the unit turned out to be a harder undertaking than I anticipated.

This book, a snapshot of a work in progress, attempts to present the strengths and shortcomings of my curriculum on immigration and the border. It's also intended as a gesture of solidarity with the Mexican activists I've encountered on my border trips — a way to disseminate to U.S. and Canadian teachers some of these activists' insights about the world, their commitment to justice, and their hope.

TWO

Born in War

There's no denying the border's reality and its power over people's lives, but from where does it draw its legitimacy? *Where did it come from?*

As an introductory activity, I played a Jackson Browne song, "It Is One," from his *Looking East* CD. It's a beautiful melody with a gentle reggae beat that opens with an astronaut returning to reflect on an earth without borders:

He saw the sun rise seven times
And when he came back down he said:
It is one, it is one
One world spinning 'round the sun

We talked briefly about the song's insight — that a new perspective, e.g., outerspace, allows us to recognize the world's interconnectedness and lack of borders. I told students I wanted us to think about this notion of borders — that on our maps and globes we see the lines dividing different countries. But by and large people, not nature, made these borders. I pointed out that the border between our state, Oregon, and Washington to the north is much more *naturally* substantial — marked by the enormous Columbia River — than most of the border between Mexico and the United States; that there is no meaningful natural distinction between Tijuana and San Diego. One can drive unhindered up Interstate 5 over the bridge into Washington; but a drive north from Tijuana into the United States will at the very least be delayed by an inspection.

I asked students to write for a few minutes about their thoughts on borders: When are they legitimate, when illegitimate? If there is legitimacy in a border, where does it come from?

Students shared aloud some of their responses. These ran the gamut. Kyle* was at one end of the spectrum: "I don't think there should be borders. I think the world is just as equally one person's as another person's." But

* Some students' names have been changed.

BOB PETERSON

Mexican artists and activists have placed crosses on the U.S.-Mexico border wall to commemorate migrants who have died attempting to enter the United States. Migrants' ages and places of origin are written on the crosses. In many instances, the crosses are marked simply, "No identificado" — identity unknown.

this opinion was not typical. Marissa's was: "I think that borders are absolutely legit. Every country has the right and duty and obligation to protect its citizens. Borders help protect people."

Many students returned to this theme that borders protect us from "criminals and terrorists." "Without a border," wrote one student, "I think our economy would collapse due to all the poverty [in] the Mexican economy. And most of all it keeps the criminals from passing through when they want."

Another wrote, "No one can just sneak into our country and harm us ... because who knows what kind of people they are."

The fence between the United States and Mexico. The fence is rusted; through the holes, Mexicans can see the U.S. beach, with high-intensity night lights and Border Patrol vehicles on the hill above.

"Us" and "our," "them" and "they" inevitably wove through students' writing and conversation. Their language underscored that borders confer a legitimacy and concreteness to divisions between people, and for some students offered the promise of safety from evils lurking beyond — evils that "they" threaten to bring to "us." Thus, an important aim of my curriculum on Mexico, the border, and immigration was to problematize these tidy categories: to explore the origins of today's U.S.–Mexico border in an imperial war waged by the James K. Polk administration in the 1840s; and to examine the anomalous freedom with which investment and commodities flow back and forth across the border, while people — at least most Mexican people — are denied such freedom. But, as I'll return to later, I was troubled by the inability of my curriculum to penetrate some students' sense that no matter the history or illegitimacy of the border or the causes of today's Mexican immigration to the United States, "we" are entitled to lives and privileges that "they" can be denied.

I told students that we were going to begin a unit on Mexico but also on broader issues: who benefits and who is hurt by "free trade," why people migrate to the United States, and how these people are treated. Given that we were about to spend several weeks of class time on relations between the United States and Mexico, I emphasized to students that this relationship touched on just about every aspect of a global studies curriculum: race, class, gender, nationality, ethnicity, violence, war, the environment, products we buy, and the food we eat.

I gave students about five minutes to make a list of all the U.S. place names they could think of that are in Spanish. I wanted students to recognize that places that

'TEA PARTY'

The tea party is a teaching strategy that introduces students to individuals and issues that they will encounter in later study. Students receive short roles to read — based on individuals in a novel, film, or historical period, or involved with a social issue. They "become" these characters and circulate in the classroom in role, meeting one another as they seek answers to a number of written questions. (See p. 43 for the full write-up of the U.S.–Mexico War tea party; Linda Christensen's *Reading, Writing, and Rising Up*, pp. 115-120, for a fuller description of this teaching strategy; and my "Teaching Unsung Heroes," pp. 37-41 in *Rethinking Our Classrooms, Vol. 2,* for another use of tea parties.)

we consider solidly "American" were actually named by Spanish speakers and were originally part of Mexico — San Francisco, El Paso, Sacramento, Colorado, Nevada, the Sierras, Santa Fe, Las Vegas, and on and on.

We went around the classroom reading names off our lists, simply to surface the sometimes buried fact of the Spanish/Mexican origins of large tracts of the United States. I then distributed a map of Mexico prior to the U.S.–Mexico War (see p. 52), and asked them what circumstances would have made it legitimate to change this — that is, for the United States to acquire so much Mexican territory. Students suggested that the territories could have been obtained legitimately had Mexico sold or given lands to the United States.

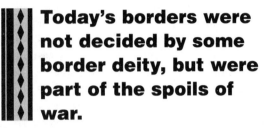

Today's borders were not decided by some border deity, but were part of the spoils of war.

I didn't want my global studies class to repeat material that students covered in their U.S. history classes. But in Oregon, high school history is supposed to begin after Reconstruction, so students rarely arrive in global studies with much if any knowledge of the 1846-48 U.S. war against Mexico. While this history of conquest was not the main focus of our study, I nonetheless wanted my students to recognize that today's borders were not decided by some border deity, but were part of the spoils of war — albeit made "legal" in the Treaty of Guadalupe Hidalgo.

I wrote a "tea party" to introduce students to some of the individuals they would meet in "We Take Nothing by Conquest, Thank God," chapter eight of Howard Zinn's *A People's History of the United States*, which I would later assign and which begins on p. 53 of this book. The tea party (sometimes called a scavenger hunt) familiarizes students with the personalities and events they'll encounter in the chapter, and works well as a pre-reading activity. (See p. 43 for a full description of the activ-

ity.) Because "We Take Nothing by Conquest, Thank God" is drawn mostly from U.S. sources, I added several Mexican characters not included in Zinn's chapter. In constructing the roles, in some instances I incorporated actual quotes from the individuals described. In most cases I've simply drawn on historical texts but tried to remain faithful to people's actual opinions. (See box on p. 14 for a typical role.)

I distributed the short tea party descriptions to students with blank name-tags for them to fill out. I told them to "become" their characters — to read their roles several times so that when they encountered other characters in the tea party they would not need to refer continually to the written role. (The book *Voices of a People's History of the United States*, edited by Howard Zinn and Anthony Arnove [available from www.teachingforchange.org], has excellent supplementary source readings, including entries from Col. Ethan Allen Hitchcock's diary, a speech and editorial by Frederick Douglass, and a handbill from deserting U.S. soldiers.)

I distributed a list of eight questions, which included, for example:

- Find someone who has an opinion on why the United States is at war with Mexico. Who is the person? What is this person's opinion about why the United States is at war?

- Find someone who was shocked by things he or she saw in the war. Who is the person? What shocked this person?

The students' assignment was to circulate in the classroom and find a different person to answer each question on the tea party/scavenger hunt sheet. I told students that it's not a race, so they should spend as long

---

THE TREATY OF GUADALUPE HIDALGO

With U.S. troops occupying Mexico City, the Treaty of Guadalupe Hidalgo was signed in 1848, ending the war between Mexico and the United States. In exchange for $15 million, Mexico agreed to the Rio Grande (called the Río Bravo by Mexicans) as the Texas border and ceded the present-day states of Arizona, New Mexico, California, Utah, Nevada, and parts of Colorado — 850,000 square miles, an area the size of France, Spain, and Italy combined. The treaty guaranteed Mexicans

living in these territories "the enjoyment of all the rights of citizens of the United States according to the principles of the Constitution; and in the meantime shall be protected in the free enjoyment of their liberty and property, and secured in the free exercise of their religion without restriction." The Mexicans wanted a provision in the treaty banning slavery in the ceded territories. The chief U.S. negotiator, Nicholas Trist, refused.

with the other person as they needed to answer the question. It was a spirited class, punctuated with lively conversations, exclamations, and some puzzled looks about the stories they were hearing from one another.

The next day, we followed the tea party with Zinn's chapter. Its thesis is probably best summed up in a diary entry by the U.S. Army's Col. Hitchcock: "It looks as if the [U.S.] government sent a small force on purpose to bring on a war, so as to have a pretext for taking California and as much of this country [Mexico] as it chooses." Zinn does a nice job of fleshing out this thesis, but also highlights anti-war material, like an excerpt from James Russell Lowell's *Biglow Papers*, written from the point of view of a New England farmer:

> They jest want this Californy
> — So's to lug new slave-states in
> To abuse ye, an' to scorn ye,
> — An' to plunder ye like sin.

Zinn also includes excerpts from Henry David Thoreau's "Civil Disobedience" and the writings of Ralph Waldo Emerson and soldiers critical of the war.

Following the tea party, I asked students to read the chapter and choose at least five quotes to write detailed reactions to — what surprised you, angered you, delighted you, confused you? — and to summarize the chapter's main points.

I opened the next day by playing "San Patricio Brigade," a song by the contemporary Irish immigrant rock group Black 47. It tells the true story of U.S. soldiers, most of them Irish immigrants, who defected to the Mexican side during the war because of the discrimination and abuse they experienced in the United States:

> Oh, they spat at my crucifix
> Laughed at my church
> They called me a papist
> And many things worse

One of the San Patricios, Sgt. John Riley, is a character in the tea party. The group Black 47 is an acquired taste, but the song tells a piece of the story hurried over, if mentioned at all, in U.S. history texts. (One exception is Milton Meltzer's fine book *Bound for the Rio Grande*,

---

COLONEL ETHAN ALLEN HITCHCOCK

I am a professional soldier, graduate of the U.S. Military Academy, commander of the 3rd Infantry Regiment. I am an aide to Gen. Zachary Taylor. Like President Polk, Taylor wanted a war with Mexico, and so he moved troops to the Rio Grande — territory claimed both by Mexico and Texas — to provoke the Mexicans. Eventually, the Mexicans did attack, as Taylor and Polk knew they would. And now U.S. leaders have their war. The United States doesn't have any right whatsoever to move into Mexico. The government is looking for war so that it can take over as much of Mexico as it wants. The United States is the aggressor. My heart is not in this war. But I am an officer in the U.S. Army and I must carry out my orders.

---

whose chapter "Traitors — or Martyrs" would be a valuable supplement to use with a high school class.)

Following the song, we read through key quotes in Zinn's chapter and discussed students' reactions. I particularly wanted them to focus on how Mexicans today might regard the war, and knowing this history, how it might influence their attitudes about the U.S.–Mexico border.

While this awareness of the U.S. war with Mexico was a crucial prologue to subsequent discussions about "illegal immigration," I was under no illusion that knowledge of this history would lead students automatically to any conclusions about these contemporary questions. But I did hope that a view of the border as the product of military might and political maneuvering would complicate the facile "us" and "them" terms of the immigration debate.

Enlisting students in a critical reflection of a mid-19th-century war was one thing. Helping them critically evaluate events today was something else. We pushed on to thornier issues.

THREE

Immigrants and Empathy

s my students and I left the relative safety of historical inquiry, I wondered how to begin to bring us forward to events today that were sure to generate more controversy and emotion. I wanted to nudge student curiosity about why people pull up roots and how they experience uprooting — or being uprooted — to move to a new country. Specifically, I wanted students to start to empathize with immigrants from Mexico.

I enlisted the help of my colleague at Franklin High School, Aníbal Rivera. Aníbal teaches a humanities class in Spanish to students who have come to the United States from other countries in Latin America, mostly Mexico. We arranged for my global studies students to interview his students about their or their parents' immigration stories.

I had students rehearse asking open-ended questions with an activity I've used over the years. I distribute interviews from writer/journalist Studs Terkel and tell the class to assume that Terkel asked a different question to elicit each paragraph in the person's response. Terkel's interviews are remarkably candid. In widely available books like *Hard Times, Working, "The Good War,"* and *Race*, Terkel removes almost all of his ques-

tions from the published interviews. So using passages from these allows students to experiment with writing open-ended questions of the type Terkel uses to generate rich story-filled responses. These sample interviews needn't be on any particular subject, and in fact, one of my favorites is the Arnold Schwarzenegger 1980 interview from Terkel's *American Dreams, Lost and Found.*

Before meeting with Aníbal's students, we brainstormed and listed questions that might trigger stories about life in the country left behind, the journey to the United States, and experiences navigating a new society. I also asked my students to think of questions that would allow their interviewees to express opinions about the border itself.

My class was about twice as large as Aníbal's, so I asked my students to pair up and to choose a main interviewer and a main note taker. I also gave them the writing assignment that would be based on the interviews so they would know to be alert to details that would help them write.

Following their interviews, each student was to choose between three writing alternatives:

1. **Personal narrative,** writing from the point of view of the person interviewed and, à la Studs Terkel, cutting out the questions to tell a story from this person's

---

READ-AROUNDS AND COLLECTIVE TEXTS

A read-around is an opportunity for students to share their writing with one another and to give each other supportive feedback on their work. These are not editing sessions, so I tell students that they may make only positive comments after hearing other students' papers. Students sit in a circle and take turns reading aloud their papers. As they listen, I also ask students to take notes on any patterns they detect as the read-around proceeds. After an individual has finished reading, I ask for comments. The student who has just

read, calls on other students and comments go student-to-student to ensure that the conversation is as much student-directed as possible. After all students have read, I ask them to write individually on what I call the "collective text" — the patterns — created by the read-around and to write about their discoveries. (See *Rethinking Our Classrooms, Vol. 1*, p. 213, and *Reading, Writing and Rising Up*, pp. 14-17, for more on the read-around.)

standpoint.

2. **Story,** taking one part of the interview and fictionalizing it. For example, if the person interviewed described his or her first day in school in the U.S., writing this up imaginatively, in either first or third person.

3. **Profile,** writing a character sketch of the person interviewed, quoting from the interview, but also adding their own observations. The assignment sheet provided examples for each of these writing choices. (See www.rethinkingschools.org/mexico for a copy of the "Immigrant Interview Write-up" assignment.)

What began as a tentative, somewhat awkward encounter between my students and Aníbal's ended as a laughter-filled session that everyone enjoyed, at least from my observations and according to students who shared their reactions.

In class the next day, my students brainstormed ways of coming at their writing and shared some of the stories that they had heard from Aníbal's students. When they returned a couple days later with their first drafts, I collected these and distributed them to other students for peer editing with a write-up checklist with stylistic questions — e.g., "Opening/introduction that grabs the reader/makes us want to read further" — as well as questions about how well the writer tackled the main issues — e.g., "Do you learn about why this person or this person's family migrated to the United States?" I also asked students to write a letter to the individual whose paper they read indicating in detail what they liked and appreciated about the piece, as well as suggestions for improvement. I provided a sample letter to show them what I was looking for. (See www.rethinkingschools.org/mexico for a copy of "Immigrant Interview Write-up: Checklist.")

Students brought in their next draft for a class read-around. As I usually do with a read-around of a personal writing assignment, I asked students to take notes on our "collective text" that they would write on after hearing the stories. I asked them to listen for:

1. Patterns that you notice about why people came to the United States or in the experiences they had in their journeys.

2. Any observations that struck you as important.

3. Ways that these stories connect with your own experiences.

Chelsea wrote about Miguel — part character portrait, part story. Miguel's parents and grandparents came from Guatemala, but crossed the Mexican border by foot. Obviously, the situations in Guatemala and Mexico are different, but this too was a border story and a tale of two cultures. Chelsea noted that Miguel "doesn't remember the journey all that well (he was 2, cut him a break)." She titled her piece "Over the ravine and through the sand, to freedom's house we go..." She opens:

> The Guatemalan sun blazed white hot upon the backs of the family. A father, mother, and baby boy strapped to her back took the risk of walking from home to a land of prosperity. Leaving culture, family, and poverty behind, Miguel and his family made the trek.

Chelsea focuses her story around a family gathering in the United States, with Miguel asking his parents and then grandparents what they left behind:

> [The question] almost brought his grandmother to tears to think about what she'd left in Guatemala.

> "I left everything I'd become accustomed to in Guatemala. My home, my family, my friends; everything I held near and dear to me. It's been hard to adapt to this fast-paced culture. Back in Guatemala, everything was slower paced; we valued time and conversations like these."

This loss of culture in exchange for greater economic security surfaced in a number of stories. Garrett summed this up in his paper's title, "More Money, Less Culture." My students had expected their immigrant interviewees to be grateful that they now live in a wealthier country. Many expressed surprise that several

---

◆◆◆◆◆◆◆◆◆◆◆◆◆◆◆◆◆◆◆◆◆◆◆

'THE DEVIL'S HIGHWAY'

As the U.S. Border Patrol has tightened security in the urban areas that straddle the U.S.–Mexico border, migrants have been pushed into the mountains and deserts. In his book *The Devil's Highway,* Luis Alberto Urrea describes a few of Arizona's desert hazards: "Much of the wildlife is nocturnal, and it creeps through the nights, poisonous and alien: the sidewinder, the rattlesnake, the scorpion, the giant centipede, the black widow, the tarantula, the brown recluse, the coral snake, the Gila monster. The kissing bug bites you and its poison makes the entire body erupt in red welts. Fungus drifts on the valley dust, and it sinks into the lungs and throbs to life. The millennium has added a further danger: All wild bees in southern Arizona, naturalists report, are now Africanized. As if the desert felt it hadn't made its point, it added killer bees." According to U.S. Customs, from Sept. 30, 2004, to Sept. 30, 2005, at least 464 migrants died attempting to cross into the United States.

DAVID BACON

A young woman in Fresno, Calif., prepares for a dance at the annual Guelaguetza festival, a celebration with roots in indigenous cultures in Oaxaca, Mexico.

of Aníbal's students said they liked life in Mexico better and would be happy to move back if the economic situation improved.

As with any assignment where students write about other people's lives, especially those from other countries or cultures, the papers contained inaccuracies, even stereotypes. These are not fatal. They offer us a chance to teach to those misunderstandings, and listening for them is part of an ongoing process to assess students' knowledge and attitudes.

'Eyes Full of Money'

The follow-up collective text assignment deepens the read-around activity because it allows us an opportunity to learn how students' own lives may intersect with what we're studying. An excellent example comes from Queenie Chau, a Chinese immigrant student who had lived in the United States only a couple of years. I quote a long passage from her collective text writing to illustrate how an assignment like this allows us to learn about our students:

> Almost all the Mexicans came to the United States seeking better lives. Many of the Mexican parents crossed the border. Even though they were illegal, they still wanted their children to become U.S. citizens. In this way, their

'It's true, nobody knows where they belong when they move to another world.' —Jasmina, student

children would be able to have more opportunities and more education than if they were in Mexico. Some of them are still upset about the society in Mexico. I can understand that because I am also an immigrant. Probably my country's society is almost the same as Mexico. The government does not treat people fairly, "justice" is not included in their dictionary, their eyes are only full of money. Money: that is all there is.

However, some Mexican kids still are kind of caught in the middle when they think deeply about what they actually are: Mexican or American? I was surprised that Mexicans were affected by racism. They are confused about whether it is wrong or right to be in the United States. They probably do not have a chance to decide to be an immigrant or not, because the only thing they have to do is follow their parents and believe things their parents do are good for them.

The thing they also have in common is they all hate borders. They are the only things stopping their moving. They all believe the United States has no right to put the borders there. I agree with that. In fact, it is wasting money. Why does the government not use the money to create jobs for their citizens, instead of building the borders that are killing innocent people? Hundreds of U.S. people lose their jobs everyday; my mom is one of those. They could change the bad things to be good.

Throughout the unit, Queenie drew on her experiences to empathize with Mexican immigrants and I could always count on her to see nuances that non-immigrants missed.

In her collective text, Jasmina, a student who had fled the war in Bosnia, quoted one of the Mexican immigrants, whose story she heard described in class: "'We have a great future in America. Life is hard in Mexico. I don't really know where I belong.'" Jasmina locked in on that last line: "It's true, nobody knows where they belong when they move to another world. ... I also know how hard it is leaving people you love, and how it feels not to belong where you have to live. I moved a lot in my life. I never had a place to call home, because to me home means where you grew up. I grew up in Yugoslavia, Bosnia, Germany, and now America. I don't know where I want to live, or where I belong, so I understand how all of them feel. Now we all share a secret."

From the sensitivity of students' papers and their reactions to one another's pieces in the read-around, it seemed to me that the interview and writing activities helped students humanize people who appeared in much of their earlier writing merely as "them." As was the case in Chelsea's piece, a number of students realized how economic opportunities in a "developed" economy are marred by the more hurried and individualistic lifestyles that can be requirements of taking advantage of those opportunities. Students genuinely tried to understand why people chose to leave their homes and risk coming to the United States. Later in the unit I came to see that, paradoxically, students' empathy could co-exist with hostility. But I'm getting ahead of myself.

Further Stories of Crossing the Border

Because the drama of border crossings played such a prominent role in students' stories — "I didn't think so many of them would have had to hire a coyote," Jonathan wrote in his collective text — I decided that we would read aloud the chapter "God of the Hearth" from Susan Straight's novel *Highwire Moon* (pp. 122-134, in the 2002 Anchor Books paperback edition). In the book, Serafina, a Mixtec Indian woman who speaks little Spanish, returns from Mexico to the United States to search for the daughter she was separated from when she was deported. She is accompanied by Florencio, a close friend of her brother's from her village. Although Straight is not herself Mexican and does not write from personal experience of crossing the border illegally, I wanted to use the chapter because it shows dramatically

— and authentically, based on first-person accounts I've read and from people I've spoken with — the gender terror that women can encounter when traveling north. Female migrants are utterly dependent on the male coyotes, or *polleros*, whom they pay to get them and sometimes their children across the border, with all the risks this dependency can entail. (Note that the excerpt is filled with swearing and violence.)

Another fine piece is Pam Muñoz Ryan's short story "First Crossing." The story depicts the attempts of Marco, a young boy, to cross the border into the United States from Mexico. He first tries to cross with a group through the desert, then is smuggled across the border in a car, wedged next to the engine. (The story is included on pp. 87-93 and Bob Peterson's account of using this story with his fifth graders begins on p. 83.)

Personal stories remind students that beneath every category — "immigrant," "migration," "border, " etc. — lies a human reality. But ultimately, students need to consider *why* things happen, not merely examine their effects, no matter how compelling or heart-rending. That was a key teaching challenge in this unit: to "story" the *causes* of migration, not migration itself. I moved on to our next section, on NAFTA and the social dislocation it has spawned.

GOD OF THE HEARTH

"Come here," [the coyote] said again.

When she was in front of him, he grabbed her by the braid and said, "This how you move *los indios*. By *la reata*." She didn't know the word, but he used her hair as a leash, pulling her head so sharply she felt her cheeks shiver like gelatin. He pushed her into the brush.

They came out in another ravine, steep walls of sand and a large cave where rushing water had scoured out a shelter. Blackened stones set in broken circles meant people had camped here, too. The sun had faded to gray shadow. The coyote's mustache was thick and black as burned rope. He jerked her around by her braid. She pulled out her roll of dollars and gave it to him.

"Kiss the money," he said, grinning. "That's all that matters here."

He shoved the dollars toward her mouth, pushed the paper between her teeth, rubbed her tongue. *I have been here before,* she thought. *I know about the money. This money.*

—From Highwire Moon, *Susan Straight*

FOUR

NAFTA and the Roots of Migration

Poverty. That was the common theme in students' stories about what led families north from Mexico. Poverty there, jobs here. But poverty is a description, not an explanation. I wanted my students not to accept Mexican poverty as some original state, but to consider its causes — to see poverty as an unfolding *process*, not as static and unchanging. I especially wanted them to interrogate the role that the United States plays in impoverishing Mexico. Sure, Mexico was poor long before NAFTA took effect in January 1994. But in the treaty's first 10 years, real wages in Mexico declined by 20 percent and the minimum wage plunged 50 percent. According to the *New York Times*, U.S. corn exports to Mexico increased 14 percent a year in the post-NAFTA decade, and corn prices in Mexico plummeted over 45 percent just between 2001 and 2004. Not surprisingly, in NAFTA's first decade an estimated one and a half million to three million farm jobs disappeared in Mexico. In 2005, Mexican agricultural production was *half* what it was before NAFTA.

NAFTA is emblematic, as well as an important component, of the neoliberal economic regime that U.S. leaders, both Republicans and Democrats, have pushed on poor countries around the globe. The idea is that these countries can grow their economies through attracting and developing export industries, and using what they have in abundance: cheap labor, land, warm weather. According to the neoliberal orthodoxy, countries should rid themselves of "inefficient" industry — like subsistence farming — by tearing down tariff and other trade barriers, welcoming competition from multinational corporations like Wal-Mart and McDonald's, and welcoming allegedly "efficiently produced" imports from abroad. In this model, trade grows enormously and everyone benefits. Of course, as the above statistics suggest, it doesn't work this way in the real world, but this is how it's promoted by its enthusiasts — a crowd as politically diverse as George W. Bush, Bill Clinton, *New York Times* columnist Thomas Friedman, and global institutions like the International Monetary Fund, the

NAFTA

The North American Free Trade Agreement (NAFTA), which took effect on Jan. 1, 1994, is an agreement between the United States, Canada, and Mexico to reduce tariff and non-tariff barriers to trade and investment. Its promoters promised that jobs would be created in all three countries and consumer prices would decrease. To sell the agreement in Mexico, President Carlos Salinas de Gortari declared that NAFTA would help make Mexico a "first world" country. For Mexico, NAFTA *has* led to a dramatic rise in exports and imports, and has linked the Mexican and U.S. economies more than ever before. U.S. investment in Mexico is up, worker productivity is up, exports are up. However, in Mexico, since NAFTA, the minimum wage is down, average manufacturing wages are down, the number of Mexicans fleeing poverty is up, prices paid to poor farmers are down, and industry-related pollution is up (see p. 77). Cheap imported corn from the United States has devastated poor farmers. Although U.S. job losses are hard to calculate, by the early 2000s, half a million workers had qualified for a special NAFTA retraining program for workers who had lost their jobs because production had moved to Mexico or Canada. As one Mexican think tank concludes, "NAFTA is an agreement that was designed by and for the transnational corporations and investors. It has been a success for the big companies and for rich people."

World Bank, and the World Trade Organization.

No one knows how many people flee Mexico for the United States every year. Estimates range from 350,000 to 750,000. I wanted students to recognize that the roots of much of this migration could be found in the impact of Mexico's neoliberal reforms — a model

WHAT IS NEOLIBERALISM?   by Arnoldo Garcia and Elizabeth Martínez

The term neoliberalism is used internationally, especially in Latin America, to describe a set of policies that have increasingly dominated political and economic developments in the last 25 years.

Neoliberalism's core policies revolve around privati-zation, deregulation, and advancement of the so-called "free market" over the public sector and the common good.

An early instance of the application of neoliberalism dates to 1973, following the U.S.-backed military coup against the socialist government of Chile's Salvador Allende.

The rise of neoliberalism as a dominant international philosophy is tied to the reign of Margaret Thatcher in Great Britain and Ronald Reagan in the United States in the 1980s. Both claimed that government support for individual and corporate interests would promote the common good — and that government had no business interfering in the "free market" and ameliorating disparities along lines of race, class, and national origin.

Neoliberalism is not confined to one particular political party. Both Democrats and Republicans, for example, embrace neoliberalism. However, the term has caused some confusion within the United States because conservatives have been the strongest promoters of neoliberal policies as they affect domestic issues such as Social Security. On international economic issues, differences between Republicans and Democrats are less evident. Prominent Democrats have supported the neoliberal policies of the World Bank and the International Monetary Fund, and NAFTA could not have passed Congress without President Clinton's aggressive backing.

Media activist and scholar Robert McChesney, writing in *Monthly Review* magazine, called neoliberalism "the defining political economic paradigm of our time — it refers to the policies and processes whereby a relative handful of private interests are permitted to control as much as possible of social life in order to maximize their personal profit."

The main points of neoliberalism include:

1. **The rule of the market.** Liberating "free" enterprise or private enterprise from any bonds imposed by the government no matter how much social damage this causes. Promoting greater international trade and investment, as in NAFTA. Reducing wages to maximize profits by undermining unions and eliminating workers' rights that had been won over many years of struggle. No more price controls. Neoliberals argue that "an unregulated market is the best way to increase economic growth, which will ultimately benefit everyone."

2. **Cutting expenditures for social services like education and health care.** Reducing the safety net for the poor and even maintenance of roads, bridges, water supply — again in the name of reducing government's role.

3. **Deregulation.** Reducing government regulation of everything that could diminish profits, including environmental protections and workplace safety.

4. **Privatization.** Selling state-owned enterprises, goods and services to private investors. This includes banks, key industries, railroads, toll highways, electricity, schools, hospitals, and even fresh water. Although usually done in the name of greater efficiency, privatization has mainly had the effect of concentrating even greater wealth in a few hands and making the public pay more for services.

5. **Eliminating the concept of "the public good" or "community" and replacing it with "individual responsibility."** Pressuring the poorest people in a society to find solutions to their lack of health care, education and social security all by themselves — then, if they fail, labeling them "lazy."

Arnoldo Garcia works with the National Network for Immigrant and Refugee Rights. Elizabeth Martínez is a longtime activist and author.

of development that was largely Made in the U.S.A., albeit embraced by Mexican rulers, especially President Carlos Salinas de Gortari (1988-1994). I thought that my students could not have an intelligent opinion about Mexican immigration without understanding the poli-cies that have been aggressively pushed by their own economic and political leaders. I hoped that in addition to lessons on the origins of the line between Mexico and the United States, this current economic context might also cast the border in a new light.

CONNIE ARAMAKI

Boys, visible through the remains of a hollowed-out television, play soccer in a dumping ground near a Tijuana maquiladora.

I wrote a role play set in 1993, early in Clinton's first term, when NAFTA was being debated and many people were making up their minds about "free trade" and neoliberalism as the economic doctrine that would guide relations between Mexico and the United States. I created the Mexico–United States Free Trade Conference, a fictional setting for a debate about real issues.

The role play structure was simple. I would play Clinton, chair the Free Trade Conference, and deliver a speech about the urgency of passing NAFTA (one Clinton actually gave). According to Clinton, NAFTA would "create the jobs of tomorrow" — a million U.S. jobs in its first five years, he promised — and, as I mentioned earlier, he promised that Mexico too would experience a jobs bonanza. All of this, he added, would be "an impetus to freedom and democracy in Latin America."

I settled on seven other roles: Mexican maquiladora workers on the U.S.-Mexico border (based on work-

The Mexico–United States Free Trade Conference is a fictional setting for a classroom debate about real issues.

ers at an assembly plant in Tijuana I've visited twice); U.S. agribusiness owners looking to expand production in Mexico; poor farmers in southern Mexico; U.S. factory workers whose jobs could be threatened by NAFTA; prosperous farmers in northern Mexico with lucrative contracts with U.S. exporters; members of a joint U.S.-Mexico environmental coalition; business leaders in the USA*NAFTA Coalition, an actual organization dedicated to getting Congress to approve NAFTA. I wanted roles that would help students recognize that "free trade" was less an issue of national interests than of *social class* interests: There were groups in Mexico that would benefit from NAFTA just as there were social groups in the United States that would be hurt. I wanted the role play to hold out possibilities for cross-border alliances that students might build as they deliberated about their response to Clinton and his promise of a land of milk and honey that NAFTA would inaugurate.

I may have been a bit too ambitious in hoping that students could tackle so many of NAFTA's complicated issues all at once. But it's hard to parse the treaty into its components and not examine them as pieces of an integrated social and economic vision being pushed by U.S. and Mexican elites. The student handout asked each group to respond to five questions, and offered additional background. The questions were:

1. President Bill Clinton has worked for a system that some people call "free trade." The idea is that countries would do away with tariffs (taxes on imports) and any laws that treat the products or industries of one country differently than the products and industries of another country. **Do you support getting rid of tariffs on all products traded between Mexico and the United States, including food crops like corn and beans, as well as the elimination of restrictions on investment? If not, what's your alternative?**

2. The Mexican Constitution grew out of the Mexican Revolution early in the 20th century. One part of the Constitution, Article 27, is especially important. It limits the amount of land that any one landholder can own. It promises poor people that they can take over and occupy unused government land and use it to farm, or they can occupy land of wealthy landholders and farm it. Article 27 establishes a system of *ejidos* [pro-

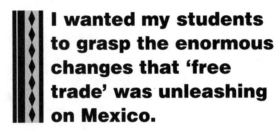

I wanted my students to grasp the enormous changes that 'free trade' was unleashing on Mexico.

nounced eh-HEE-dohs]. Ejidos are communities where people own the land in common and it can never be sold or taken. Article 27 also says that foreigners cannot own land in Mexico. **Do you approve of Mexico eliminating these parts of Article 27 from its Constitution to provide more investment freedom in Mexico and end the *ejido* form of collective ownership of land? If not, what's your alternative?**

3. NAFTA has an important provision called Chapter 11. Chapter 11 would allow a company from Mexico, the United States, or Canada to sue the government of another one of these countries if any law were passed that hurt the investment of that company. **Do you support Chapter 11 of NAFTA? If not, what's your alternative?**

4. As written, NAFTA has no significant provisions that discuss labor or environmental conditions in any of the three member countries. **What guarantees, if any, should there be that corporations do not move from country to country simply to exploit cheap labor and/or to take advantage of lower environmental standards?**

5. As it stands now, NAFTA encourages and protects the free movement of capital and goods from country to country but not the free movement of people. With NAFTA, countries can restrict immigration in any manner that they choose. **Should NAFTA be limited to the free movement of capital and goods, or should the movement of people from country to country also be included in this agreement? If so, in what way?**

Article 27 of the Mexican Constitution

The revision of Article 27 cut to the core of what neoliberalism is all about. Early in the 20th century, Mexico had enshrined collective land rights into its Constitution. Although Mexican governments have been notorious for corruption, Article 27 held out the promise that, banding together, poor farmers had a *right* to land. Indeed, in the 1930s, reform President Lázaro Cárdenas distributed 45 million acres to poor farmers in collective ejidos. He took idle land from the rich and gave it to the poor. And because ejido land was inalienable, no matter how much debt one incurred, the land could never be taken away. This provision was in absolute contradiction to the neoliberal ideal, in which collective rights may be enjoyed by corporations but individuals must enter the marketplace alone, as individual consumers or

---

CHAPTER 11

"NAFTA's Chapter 11 goes further than any other agreement in the world to extend rights and protections to international investors. The most controversial aspect of the agreement is that it allows foreign investors to sue NAFTA governments directly to demand compensation over any governmental act, including public interest laws, that diminish the value of an investment. This unprecedented power granted to corporations restricts the ability of governments to protect the environment and public welfare and to ensure that foreign investment supports social, economic, and environmental goals."

—*Sarah Anderson and John Cavanagh, Institute for Policy Studies, Washington, D.C.*

ABOLISHING THE U.S. 'EJIDOS'

Hostility to collective ownership has always been a feature of capitalism. Prior to 1887, some Native Americans on reservations held tribal land in common. But in that year, the U.S. Congress passed the Allotment Act, also known as the Dawes Act, which "allotted" 160 acres of tribal land to every male head of family — with the substantial "surplus" to be distributed to white farmers by the U.S. government under the Homestead Act. The idea was to abolish what Senator Henry Dawes called Indian "communism" in favor of individualism. In 1887, Sen. Dawes complained about the Cherokees' "defect": "[T]hey own their land in common. … There is no selfishness, which is at the bottom of civilization."

workers. Article 27 also prohibited foreign ownership of land. In limiting the rights of capital to own anything it desires to purchase in any corner of the earth, this constitutional provision was also anathema to the neoliberal worldview. In real life, Article 27 was amended in February 1992, about a year before this make-believe "Free Trade Conference," but I included this initiative in the role play because I wanted my students to grasp the enormous changes that the "free trade" project was unleashing in Mexico. As the progressive Mexican politician Cuauhtémoc Cárdenas pointed out at the time, the repeal of Article 27 would likely displace two million rural families — eight to 10 million people — about half of whom, he said, "will very likely migrate to the United States." Of course, NAFTA helped.

NAFTA was to be social engineering on a grand scale. As Mexico's Commerce Secretary, Jaime Serra Puche, later acknowledged in a Council on Foreign Relations-sponsored forum on NAFTA's 10th anniversary, it was NAFTA's framers' intention to do away with subsistence farming in Mexico and instead stimulate large-scale production for export: "And that was the whole philosophy behind the negotiation of the agricultural sector, to be shifting gradually toward those sectors that were competitive vis-a-vis the United States and Canada, and having the Americans and the Canadians producing grains and cereals."

The Role Play Game Plan

I went carefully over the Free Trade Conference issues before breaking the class into seven groups for the role play. I asked students to read and mark up their assigned role sheet and, individually, to write a short

interior monologue that might fill in details about their character's life. I urged them to incorporate information from the role sheet but to go further: "Tell something about your life story. What is your family situation? What are you worried about these days? What are you hopeful about? How could NAFTA affect you positively or negatively?" When students finished writing, I asked them to share their interior monologues with others in their group to help create a portrait of the individuals in their social group.

After students wrote and shared their interior monologues, I explained the overall game plan: First, students deliberate in their groups on the five questions before the Free Trade Conference and write out tentative answers. Second, students choose half their group as traveling negotiators who roam the classroom meeting with other groups to try to build alliances to support, amend, or defeat various pieces of NAFTA, as represented in the five questions. Third, we pull back together for our discussion/debate about NAFTA. I introduce the conference portraying President Bill Clinton and deliver Clinton's speech in praise of NAFTA, and students question me: "If you disagree with Clinton, then come at the president with sharp questions; if you agree, then use it as an opportunity to say *why* you support NAFTA."

Students went to work in their groups to decide on tentative positions and on which other social groups they might ally with. I encouraged them to think carefully about where they might be able to find points of agreement with other social groups. In the spirited "dealing" (negotiation) session, prosperous farmers in northern Mexico found common ground with U.S. agribusiness interests; and at least on some issues, like legalization of union organizing, Tijuana maquiladora workers and U.S. factory workers also agreed.

INTERIOR MONOLOGUES

An interior monologue asks students to write in first person the imagined thoughts of a character in history or literature at a particular point in time. Interior monologues are a way to promote "social imagination" — to help students nurture empathy, by attempting to put themselves in the position of individuals who may lead very different lives. See p. 64 for how to use interior monologues with the NAFTA role play. For a more general discussion about the use of interior monologues, see "Promoting Social Imagination Through Interior Monologues," pp. 126-127, in *Rethinking Our Classrooms, Vol. 1.*

HOW WE SEE THE WORLD

The Zapatistas publicly began their rebellion the day NAFTA took effect, Jan. 1, 1994. In June 2005, the Zapatistas declared a "red alert" in the regions they administer in Mexico's southernmost state of Chiapas. Its purpose was to trigger consultations with communities throughout the region to chart new political activities. One result was the Sixth Declaration of the Lacandón Forest, a portion of which is excerpted below. The translation is from Mexico Solidarity Network Weekly News and Analysis, *June 27-July 3, 2005.*

Now we are going to explain to you how we, the Zapatistas, see what is going on in the world. We see that capitalism is the strongest right now. Capitalism is a social system, a way in which a society goes about organizing things and people, and who has and who has not, and who gives orders and who obeys. In capitalism, there are some people who have money, or capital, and factories and stores and fields and many things, and there are others who have nothing but their strength and knowledge in order to work. In capitalism, those who have money and things give the orders, and those who only have their ability to work obey.

Then capitalism means that there are a few who have great wealth, but they did not win a prize, or find a treasure, or inherit from a parent. They obtained that wealth, rather, by exploiting the work of the many. So capitalism is based on the exploitation of the workers, which means they exploit the workers and take out all the profits they can. This is done unjustly, because they do not pay the worker what his work is worth. Instead they give him a salary that barely allows him to eat a little and to rest for a bit, and the next day he goes back to work in exploitation. …

And capitalism also makes its wealth from plunder, or theft, because they take what they want from others, land, for example, and natural resources. So capitalism is a system where the robbers are free and they are admired and used as examples.

And, in addition to exploiting and plundering, capitalism represses because it imprisons and kills those who rebel against injustice.

Capitalism is most interested in merchandise, because when it is bought or sold, profits are made. And then capitalism turns everything into merchandise, it makes merchandise of people, of nature, of culture, of history, of conscience. According to capitalism, everything must be able to be bought and sold. And it hides everything behind the merchandise, so we don't see the exploitation that exists. And then the merchandise is bought and sold in a market. And the market, in addition to being used for buying and selling, is also used to hide the exploitation of the workers. In the

market, for example, we see coffee in its little package or its pretty little jar, but we do not see the *campesino* who suffered in order to harvest the coffee, and we do not see the *coyote* who paid him so cheaply for his work, and we do not see the workers in the large company working their hearts out to package the coffee. Or we see an appliance for listening to music like *cumbias*, *rancheras* or *corridos*, or whatever, and we see that it is very good because it has a good sound, but we do not see the worker in the maquiladora who struggled for many hours, putting the cables and the parts of the appliance together, and they barely paid her a pittance of money, and she lives far away from work and spends a lot on the trip, and, in addition, she runs the risk of being kidnapped, raped and killed as happens in Ciudad Juárez in Mexico.

So we see merchandise in the market, but we do not see the exploitation with which it was made. And then capitalism needs many markets … or a very large market, a world market.

And so the capitalism of today is not the same as before, when the rich were content with exploiting the workers in their own countries, but now they are on a path which is called Neoliberal Globalization. This globalization means that they no longer control the workers in one or several countries, but the capitalists are trying to dominate everything all over the world. And the world, or planet Earth, is also called the "globe," and that is why they say "globalization," or the entire world.

And neoliberalism is the idea that capitalism is free to dominate the entire world, and so tough, you have to resign yourself and conform and not make a fuss, in other words, not rebel. So neoliberalism is like the theory, the plan, of capitalist globalization. And neoliberalism has its economic, political, military, and cultural plans. All of those plans have to do with dominating everyone, and they repress or separate anyone who doesn't obey so that his rebellious ideas aren't passed on to others.

Then, in neoliberal globalization, the great capitalists who live in the powerful countries, like the United

As President Clinton, I stood behind the podium and welcomed the groups to the Mexico–United States Free Trade Conference. I distributed Clinton's (my) speech. It's tough to imitate Clinton's aw-shucks charm, but I did my best. In the speech (p. 69) Clinton dismisses U.S. workers' concern that free trade would lead to corporations relocating plants to Mexico and destroying family-wage jobs, saying jobs are always lost "when you open up the mix to new competition." But he claims more jobs will be created. He's like a football coach giving a pep talk, asking his audience rhetorically, "[A]re we going to compete and win, or are we going to withdraw?"

I invited students to challenge the president's posi- tions, or anything they heard someone from another group express that they wanted to respond to, and we moved on to a discussion of the first question. See p. 63 for a fuller description of how I conduct the role play.

I think the role play succeeded in teaching students lots about important aspects of NAFTA and how these issues touched people in both countries. As students who portrayed poor farmers and environmentalists described the dire conditions NAFTA would unleash throughout Mexico, the groundwork was being laid for students to recognize that "illegal immigration," and what was

---

HOW WE SEE THE WORLD, continued

States, want the entire world to be made into a big business where merchandise is produced like a great market. A world market for buying and selling the entire world and for hiding all the exploitation from the world. Then the global capitalists insert themselves every- where, in all the countries, in order to do their big business, their great exploitation. Then they respect nothing, and they meddle wherever they wish. As if they were conquering other countries. That is why we Zapatistas say that neoliberal globalization is a war of conquest of the entire world, a world war, a war being waged by capitalism for global domination. Sometimes that conquest is by armies who invade a country and conquer it by force. But sometimes it is with the economy, in other words, the big capitalists put their money into another country or they lend it money, but on the condition that they obey what they tell them to do. And they also insert their ideas, with the capitalist culture, which is the culture of merchandise, of profits, of the market.

Then the one which wages the conquest, capitalism, does as it wants, it destroys and changes what it does not like and eliminates what gets in its way. For example, those who do not produce nor buy nor sell modern merchandise get in their way, or those who rebel against that order. And they despise those who are of no use to them. That is why the indigenous get in the way of neoliberal capitalism, and that is why they despise them and want to eliminate them. And neolib- eral capitalism also gets rid of laws that do not allow them to exploit and to have a lot of profit. They demand that everything can be bought and sold, and, since capitalism has all the money, it buys everything. Capitalism destroys the countries it conquers with neoliberal globalization, but it also wants to adapt

everything, to make it over again, but in its own way, a way that benefits capitalism and that doesn't allow anything to get in its way. Then neoliberal globalization, capitalism, destroys what exists in these countries, it destroys their culture, their language, their economic system, their political system, and it also destroys the ways in which those who live in that country relate to each other. So everything that makes a country a country is left destroyed.

Then neoliberal globalization wants to destroy the nations of the world so that only one Nation or country remains, the country of money, of capital. And capital- ism wants everything to be as it wants, in its own way, and it doesn't like what is different, and it persecutes it and attacks it, or puts it off in a corner and acts as if it doesn't exist.

Then, in short, the capitalism of global neoliberalism is based on exploitation, plunder, contempt and repression of those who refuse. The same as before, but now globalized, worldwide.

But it is not so easy for neoliberal globalization, because the exploited of each country become discon- tented, and they will not say well, too bad, instead they rebel. And those who remain and who are in the way resist, and they don't allow themselves to be eliminated. And that is why we see, all over the world, those who are being screwed over making resistances, not putting up with it, in other words, they rebel, and not just in one country but wherever they abound. And so, as there is a neoliberal globalization, there is a globaliza- tion of rebellion.

—Clandestine Revolutionary Indigenous Committee, General Command of the Zapatista Army of National Liberation

BENJAMÍN PRADO—AFSC—U.S. MEXICO BORDER PROGRAM

A family picnics on both sides of the border at Border Field State Park, formerly Friendship Park, in San Diego County, Calif.

occurring at the border, was not exclusively a Mexican problem. I hoped that through the role play, students would begin to see that not all Mexicans shared the same opinions about NAFTA and not all U.S. groups did either. However, in retrospect I wish I had done more with the multiple ways that the NAFTA development model threatened groups in the United States. As I discovered later in the unit, my students' grasp on how they were also affected by these political and economic choices was shakier than I had thought. More discussion would have helped, especially on issues such as workers' rights and the environment, where U.S. and Mexican groups might have been able to build alliances.

Instead of a "here's what happened in real life" lecture, I gave students packets of articles — some required and others to choose from. Excerpts from "Hemisphere for Sale," a report by the independent grassroots group Witness for Peace, were especially helpful (www. witnessforpeace.org/publications). Adapting an assignment that Sandra Childs had created, one of my questions was: "Based on the articles that you read, explain who the main winners of NAFTA are and who the main losers are. Cite your sources."

Katrina's answer was typical. She draws on the role play and readings to describe NAFTA's impact on particular social groups, but doesn't sustain this analysis. By the end, her answer reverts back to an us/them nationalism. As a "winner" Katrina listed "wealthy farmers,"

presumably both U.S. and Mexican, who were able to acquire even more land thanks to NAFTA, and who, because poor farmers were losing their land, were able to hire the landless as cheap labor. As a "loser" she cited poor farmers hurt by the elimination of provisions in Article 27. But then she listed another loser: "U.S.A. *lost* because we now have Mexicans here in the U.S. *taking our jobs* and also the big companies went to Mexico so our jobs are gone." [emphasis in original]

I found this an interesting yet contradictory observation. Katrina analyzes NAFTA's effects from the standpoint of U.S. workers — and it's true that hundreds of thousands in the United States have lost jobs thanks to NAFTA. But Katrina conflates the "U.S.A." with those U.S. workers who lost jobs. She neglects to note that some of the "U.S.A." benefited, especially large corporations. For example, one article the students read describes a study by Kate Bronfenbrenner, director of Labor Education Research at Cornell University, which shows that during a two-year period, over half the corporations facing union organizing drives took advantage of NAFTA by threatening their workers with closure of all or part of their U.S. plants. It's free trade extortion: Stop unionizing or we'll head to Mexico. Ultimately, Katrina returns to a nationalized us/them opposition where Mexicans are "taking our jobs." This passage recalls familiar patterns from U.S. history: working-class anger at the rich and at employers, but an oftentimes racialized and even sharper hostility toward the immigrants who are "taking our jobs." This is an attitude I would confront even more pointedly later in the unit.

'Trading Democracy'

Following the role play activities, we watched Bill Moyers' excellent video, *Trading Democracy*, on the effects of NAFTA's Chapter 11. Moyers looks at several instances where democracy in Canada, the United States, and Mexico was trumped by the Chapter 11 provision that promises corporations that they will never be threatened by expropriation of their assets or by government measures that might be "tantamount to expropriation."

One egregious example cited by Moyers is a toxic waste dump in the state of San Luis Potosí that had been shut down. Nearby residents believed the dump was responsible for the cancer epidemic in the region. No one — not the local community of Guadalcazar, nor the state government — wanted this poisonous landfill reopened. No one, that is, except the U.S. corporation, Metalclad, that had purchased the site. Metalclad had received a permit to reopen the dump from Mexico's National Ecological Institute (INE), but received no permission from the people affected by the site's operation. Ultimately, the state governor shut down the project, declaring the region a protected ecological zone. Under Chapter 11, Metalclad claimed that it was the victim of an act that was tantamount to expropriation, as the value of its investment was harmed and the company was denied future profits. Under NAFTA rules, Chapter 11 complaints are heard in secret by a panel of arbitrators, aptly called "private justice" by one international trade official. No witnesses and no third party testimony are allowed. The NAFTA arbitration tribunal agreed with the substance of Metalclad's complaint and ordered the Mexican government to pay Metalclad over $16.7 million.

> ## Nothing in the role play had prepared students for the shocking stories of corporate malfeasance in *Trading Democracy*.

Nothing in the role play had prepared students for the shocking stories of corporate malfeasance included in *Trading Democracy*, with secret trade tribunals used to challenge U.S. legislation. However, I wondered if students' outrage was especially acute in this instance because "we" also had been hurt — U.S. citizens, not just Mexicans, were the victims. For example, Moyers reports on a $970 million suit filed against the U.S. government by Methanex, a Canadian corporation, alleging that because the California state legislature voted to phase out the cancer-causing gas additive MTBE that was turning up in people's water, Methanex was deprived of future profits. A NAFTA panel finally ruled against Methanex in August 2005, but, as Moyers points out in *Trading Democracy*, the very fact that such a suit could be filed has had a chilling effect on legislation to protect public health.

The NAFTA role play, the follow-up readings and video engaged students in a big picture look at social dynamics and helped point out who benefits and who suffers from various policies. As they attempted to build alliances in the role play, students recognized the common interests of seemingly disparate groups. Through exploring issues from multiple perspectives, they analyzed the justice or injustice of various measures. But this kind of role play doesn't lend itself to students seeing how social policy reaches into the most intimate aspects of people's lives. Nor does it help students see how people make and remake their lives every day through the choices they exercise — albeit in circumstances not of their choosing. This kind of understanding-of-the-heart would require a different kind of teaching strategy. I moved on to the next phase of the curriculum, one focused on people, not just policy.

FIVE

Free Trade's Intimate Impact

Throughout our Rethinking Schools–Global Exchange trips to the U.S.-Mexico border, I've listened for stories that reveal the difficult choices that people regularly confront. I've especially listened for stories that I could turn into improvisation situations for my students — situations that they could perform in class. Improvisation is the kind of "small picture" role play that is particularly effective at humanizing the societies we study. In the case of the border, I hoped the improvs could breathe life into grandiose expressions such as neoliberalism and free trade. Improvs drawn from real people's lives also effectively counter the image of the helpless Third World victim that is so common in the discourse about global inequality, and that characterizes many otherwise helpful teaching resources.

> **Given the abusive, painful circumstances that students would write about in their interior monologues, I wanted them to reflect on hopeful aspects and instances of resistance.**

I divided the class into seven groups of about four students each and distributed the 14 situations I'd written (a couple contributed by my colleague Sandra Childs, who also went on a Rethinking Schools–Global Exchange trip to the border). Each group was responsible for reading and deciding how to perform brief improvs of two different situations. Here are typical ones, the first based on a meeting I attended at a women's organization, Grupo de la Mujer - Factor X, in Tijuana. The second grew out of the story a man told us during dinner at the migrant shelter Casa del Migrante. (See p. 113 for detailed teaching instructions and all the improvisation situations.)

- A Mexican family has moved to Tijuana from southern Mexico. In the community where they were living previously, both parents worked very hard, but they did different kinds of work. The man did most of the farming on their small plot of land and sometimes hired himself out to larger land owners in order to make a little extra money. The woman did all the cooking, made clothes, took care of the children, kept up their small house, and at times worked in their herb garden. In order to survive in Tijuana, both need to work. However, most of the jobs in the maquiladoras in Tijuana are for women. She found a job in a box factory but he has not been able to find a job. It seems that he takes his frustrations out on his wife. She comes home from work and he starts bossing her around: "Go make me coffee." "When will dinner be ready?" One day the woman comes home and is especially exhausted. He starts ordering her around and she responds. (As an alternative, you might have a number of women in similar situations meet in a Tijuana women's center, Factor X, and discuss how to respond to their husbands.)

- Three undocumented Mexican workers are living in southern California. Only one of them speaks English. They have been hired by a man who is a U.S. citizen to help him move furniture and boxes out of a house. They were promised $10 an hour for their labor and they worked a little over eight hours during the day. At the end of the day the man gave each of them $50. He apologized and said it was all he had. "Besides," he chuckled, "that's a lot more than you'd ever make in a day in Mexico." How do the men respond?

As students discussed how to perform their improvs, I wandered from group to group answering questions and, when it seemed appropriate, suggesting possible approaches. But mostly I listened to students' conversations. I also volunteered to be an "extra" in any improv — and a couple of groups took me up on the offer. I made sure that students knew that they needn't script out the full improv — they weren't writing a play — but that they should know exactly who would perform which part and how their characters would approach the problem they were confronted with. Some students went out in the hallway to rehearse.

We reconvened in a large circle, students sitting with their respective groups. I told them that after they'd performed the improvs, we would write interior monologues from the point of view of one of the characters; they could write from any character in any of the improvs, not

DAVID BACON

A family at work taking the husks off tomatillos in Cañon Buenavista, a community of mostly indigenous farmworkers in Baja California created by land invasions.

necessarily one they performed, so they should listen carefully for lines to "steal."

Introducing an improv activity is always a bit touchy. On the one hand, if students don't take these seriously, the improvs can have the opposite effect of what I intend, and students can miss the import of the dilemmas that migrants and border residents face. In years past, I've called a halt to improvs when students acted so silly that it felt contemptuous of the lives they were portraying. I've sent students back to their groups, told them to get serious, and then we'd start over. On the other hand, the improvs are not a funeral; students will inevitably laugh during the performances and I don't want kids to feel ashamed. Sometimes I begin by saying that when we occasionally laugh it's not because we think the situations are funny, but that we're not accustomed to seeing our peers in the roles of other people. Sometimes the improvisational situations are so wrenching or uncomfortable that laughter can ease the pain.

With this class, students performed the first improv with absolute realism. Chelsea played a Mexican mother living in a squatter village in Tijuana's Río Alamar riverbed; Blake played her son. The mother works in a maquiladora and wants to stay living in the shantytown so she can save money for the trek to the United States. The son is tired of living in such squalor and has friends nearby in

the still-poor but much more livable *colonia* (neighborhood) of Chilpancingo. Chelsea and Blake's conversation exhibited the affection of mother and son, but also captured the tension in their different visions of the future.

After each improv, I encouraged students to applaud their peers' efforts. I asked the performers to stay in character and to answer questions from the class and from me about the considerations underlying the choices they made. I also encouraged people to offer positive feedback. Obviously, there is no correct answer in any of these and the aim is not to figure out what "really happened," but to give a human face to the abstractions of free trade, NAFTA, neoliberalism, economic growth, corporate investment, and U.S. immigration policy.

ollowing the improvs, which took a couple class periods, I asked students to choose an individual in one of the situations that we had performed and to write his or her inner thoughts, an interior monologue. I gave them a few minutes to decide on the situation they wanted to write about. I turned out the lights and asked students to put their heads on their desks and to close their eyes — a ritual they're familiar with when we begin to write an imaginative or personal piece. I urged them to play the performance over in their minds as they remembered it from class. I paused 20 seconds or so between prompts: "Get an image in your mind's eye of the person whose point of view you're going to write from. ... Where are you? Outside, inside? ... Who's there with you? ... Bring yourself into the situation: What are you feeling? Anger, fear, frustration, hope, worry? ... What are the voices in your head telling you?"

I told them that I was going to turn the lights back on and did not want to hear any talking, but only wanted to see people writing. I wrote too, and this silent period — even if only 15 minutes or so — ensured that students left class with at least a substantial beginning to their pieces. I asked them to finish these for homework.

A number of students wrote movingly about an improv situation where maquiladora women workers debated what to do about a supervisor who is sexually harassing them — "a wolf hunting his meat," as one student wrote.

Blake Weber wrote from the character he portrayed, who disagreed with his mother over her determination to save money to cross into the United States:

DAVID BACON

Isabel Zaragoza and her infant daughter, Lagoberta, live in a labor camp in Vicente Guerrero, a town in the San Quintin Valley in Baja California. Isabel and her husband arrived recently from Oaxaca in southern Mexico. They work as migrant farmworkers.

> Since I can remember, my parents spoke of a place called the U.S. They said that it held a better future for me and the family. And that when we got there we'd no longer be forced to scavenge for food and take horribly inhumane jobs. Throughout my entire childhood we moved from town to town. The longest I remember staying at a specific place was a year. I'm sick of moving. I'm sick of eating rice for lunch nearly every day. I'm sick of this ramshackle hut of used metal slabs and wooden boxing. My parents say that one day it'll all be better, but I'm beginning to doubt that. Everywhere I look poverty is present. My parents try to put a better face on things, but it's all a mirage. Their smiling faces are a mask of despair. I want a better life for my family. I want to smile and really mean it. The U.S. is a fairy tale that my parents tell me everyday I go to sleep. It's nothing but a hope that will never come true. But a house ... a house is real. It's not something you hear about from others, it's something you can see with your own two eyes. Yet my mom said no. No!? How could she say no? She insists that we should save up money for the trip to the U.S. That getting a house would slow down our savings. Know what I have to say to that? Screw it. Screw the U.S. Screw the foggy future. I want to settle down now. I want to have long-term friendships. Yet my mom says it's for our future. So I give in. Maybe one day I'll see this fabled U.S., or maybe we'll finally settle down. Our future is uncertain, there's no doubt to that.

As part of our read-around of students' writing, I shared my interior monologue as well (based on Lourdes Lujan, the environmental justice organizer I mentioned at the outset, who continues to live, work, and hope in a neighborhood badly polluted by nearby maquiladoras on Otay Mesa in Tijuana) and a poem that Rethinking Schools editor Bob Peterson wrote after we visited Casa del Migrante, "Valentine's Day at Casa del Migrante" (see www.rethinkingschools.org/mexico for both of these).

The Collective Text

The students' writing was as intense and heartfelt as anything they'd produced all year. As students read their pieces aloud I asked them to take notes on four questions that I would ask them to write about in our collective text:

1. Which of the situations/circumstances that people wrote about did you find most affecting, moving, poignant?

2. What kind of resistance did you notice?

3. Where can we find hope?

4. What parts of these writings remind you of anything we've studied this year or anything in your own life?

OPERATION GATEKEEPER

Operation Gatekeeper began in October 1994 as an attempt to seal the San Diego sector of the U.S.–Mexico border, traditionally one of the most popular places for undocumented migrants to cross. Gatekeeper was "the forward deployment of our resources and manpower in the San Diego sector," one Border Patrol agent told our Rethinking Schools–Global Exchange tour group in a meeting thick with military jargon. The Border Patrol stationed many more officers than previously in the 66-mile-long San Diego sector, and began the construction of three fences between Mexico and the United States, with stadium lighting illuminating the arid zone between fences. Gatekeeper also gave the Border Patrol night vision devices and hundreds of motion detectors buried along the border.

This "forward deployment" of resources — developed with the help of the U.S. Department of Defense's Center for Low Intensity Conflicts — has left the San Diego sector the most heavily fortified part of the U.S.–Mexico border. In a sense, Operation Gatekeeper has "worked," insofar as it has pushed migrants out of urban San Diego and into remote areas, where people are more likely to be caught. "If they're out in the desert, we've got hours to catch them, if not days," one Border Patrol agent told us. But people are also more likely to die. As the U.S. Justice Department Inspector General's office admits, the Otay Mountains, east of San Diego, are "extremely rugged, and include steep, often precipitous, canyon walls and hills reaching 4,000 feet." And Gatekeeper has pushed migrants farther east, where conditions are even harsher, with peaks rising over 6,000 feet in the Tecate Mountains. The Border Patrol has launched similar security initiatives in other urban areas along the U.S.–Mexico border, including Operation Hold the Line in El Paso-Ciudad Juárez, and Operation Safeguard in the Nogales region. In the first 10 years of Operation Gatekeeper, more than 3,200 people died trying to enter the United States from Mexico. Given that the acknowledged aim of increased Border Patrol security measures is to push migrants into more hostile terrain, increased death is a predictable byproduct of this policy.

Given the painful conundrums and abusive circumstances that students would write about in their interior monologues, I wanted them also to reflect on hopeful aspects and instances where people stood up for themselves or for one another. In his collective text reflection, Jonathan wrote that he was impressed by people's efforts to gain "independence. I saw people stand up for what they thought was right." Kristina appreciated the interior monologue about a woman artist who refuses to be pushed around by a Tijuana cop (based on a true story about Carmela Castrejón, one of our guides on the border trips). "The artist stood her ground and called him on the irrational shots he made," Kristina wrote. She also commented that resistance was not necessarily always visible. She noted that in one interior monologue read in class, a woman continues to work in a maquiladora where a supervisor sexually harasses women, but nonetheless maintains her dignity — "the resistance was internal." Not surprisingly, students saw the United States as the chief source of hope in people's interior monologues. Abe wrote, "The stars and stripes

> **One student noted that resistance isn't always visible — sometimes resistance is internal.**

of the American flag personify hope. 'America the land of the free' was declared over and over and over again in our writing, the hope for a better tomorrow and better life and better quality of life. … The beginning of those dreams start with the word America, but unfortunately many times they end with the word border."

Abe's and other students' observation about the United States as a beacon of hope highlights a problem in a curriculum like mine. On the one hand, I want to emphasize the tremendously difficult circumstances of people who decide to leave their homes and make the increasingly treacherous journey north. For them, the pull of U.S. economic opportunity is real and urgent. On the other hand, I don't want the curriculum to make students feel complacent, that the rest of the world is wretchedly poor and our country is a prosperous utopia. In fact, I want them to recognize that the forces tearing at Mexico are also creating insecurity and inequality here, although in different ways. If there is to be any resolution to this tension, it lies in an ongoing effort to ground the curriculum in the nature of our own society

Franklin High School student Abe Figueroa titled his metaphorical drawing "For Every Action, There Is an Opposite and Equal Reaction." In his commentary on the drawing, Abe wrote, "Operation Gatekeeper will inevitably increase the number of deaths on the border."

and in the lives of our students.

My fourth question encouraged students to connect their lives to the lives of Mexicans on the border. My student Jerome, with his football lineman's physique, a baseball hat perpetually cocked on his head, and a regular seat amid other "jocks" in class, would be easy to stereotype as someone who might not be taking this unit to heart. But on question #4, Jerome wrote:

> Some of these writings are letters to family who are far away, and you can't see them. I remember when I was younger and I wrote a letter to someone that I had loved dearly, but I didn't know if I would ever see them again, because he had gone to prison. Why I did not know. When would I see him again? I did not know. I was about 12 and wrote him a letter, but when he got out he said I was the only one who cared what would happen to him, but I don't see him much anymore. But not

knowing what is gonna happen next is what I think all of these people feel.

Mexico in Metaphor

Following the improvs and a read-around of their interior monologues, I showed a succinct and effective video, *Death on a Friendly Border*, produced by Rachel Antell (available from www.teachingforchange.org). The documentary looks at Operation Gatekeeper, an initiative of the Clinton administration in October 1994, 10 months after NAFTA took effect, to further seal the border for migrants. The video describes the U.S. government's new security measures, with migrants driven into the deserts and mountains looking for a route to cross into the United States. As a result, many more are dying, including Yolanda Gonzalez-Martínez, whose story is chronicled in the video. Although it doesn't discuss NAFTA or any of the economic reforms in Mexico that have made survival more difficult, the video provides a poignant visual overview of the increasingly militarized border and its human effects. In addition to the improvisations and the interior monologues, the video was another attempt to inject humanity and individuality into our study of the border.

It was time to wrap up. What I had anticipated would be about a four-week unit had stretched into six weeks and, still, I knew I'd left out lots. But I wanted to give my students the opportunity to collect their thoughts in a final essay. To launch the essay, I assigned students a metaphorical drawing on any aspect of what we'd studied about Mexico, the border, and immigration issues. A metaphorical drawing asks students to take an insight about an issue and turn it into a picture. It's a helpful pre-writing activity because it encourages students to distill their knowledge to essential points, and thus helps students generate thesis statements for their essays. Over the years, I've appreciated how metaphorical drawings allow students who may be less verbal or less skilled writers to nonetheless express profound understanding of topics we study (see, for example, "Thinking in Pictures," www.rethinkingschools.org/archive/17_02/Rg172.shtml).

Some student drawings were graphically simple. Abe's was titled, "For Every Action, There Is an Opposite and Equal Reaction." The image was of a cross in front of a wall. The cross cast a large shadow on the ground and up the wall (see drawing, opposite page). His explanation of the drawing: "This is a commentary on how the increased 'security' in the form of Operation Gatekeeper will inevitably increase the number of deaths on the border."

Kyle's metaphorical drawing was more complicated. His portrayed a box hanging from a long chain, hovering just above water with shark fins visible. The box is labeled "Mexico" and has what appears to be a steel grate in front; a large ball inside reads "U.S." His written commentary explains:

> The cage represents Mexico, and the ball inside represents the U.S. The space that the U.S. is taking up in

The metaphorical drawing encourages students to distill their knowledge to essential points.

Mexico. The U.S. is taking jobs from small farmers, which are being pushed out of Mexico because of this. Mexico is a cage because even though the farmers are being pushed out they still can't get out because the borders are blocked. They are basically being crushed in between Mexico and the U.S., which results in an unending state of poverty. The shark represents cops and immigration because if the Mexicans do make it out of Mexico, there's always a chance that they could be caught outside.

We went around the classroom and students shared their drawings and written explanations with each other.

Afterwards I assigned the final essay, which asked students to write on any aspect of what we'd studied about the relationship between the United States and Mexico — the U.S. war with Mexico, NAFTA, border issues, Operation Gatekeeper, immigration, and the like. I gave students a number of specific topic possibilities — e.g., how the immigration issue might appear to many Mexicans, the effects of NAFTA's Chapter 11, a long-term solution to "illegal immigration," etc. (See www.rethinkingschools.org/mexico for a copy of the essay assignment.) To get students started, we brainstormed thesis statements growing out of their metaphorical drawings.

Students were off to a good start on their essays, with thesis statements like: "We as a people need to understand that there is no such thing as an illegal human, only people who are not officially documented," and "NAFTA has been taking lives; here are the facts."

But this was not a class that ever spoke with one voice. At the other end of the spectrum were statements such as: "Increasingly, illegal immigrants are coming into the United States each year. They are taking our jobs, our benefits from taxes, and our security away from us."

As I was soon to find out, this fearful thesis spoke for more students in class than I'd realized.

SIX

'They're Taking Our Jobs'

Despite my declaration that we were at the end of the unit, it felt incomplete, as if I hadn't engaged students in grappling with what this study meant in terms of U.S. policy toward Mexico. As students did research for their essays I decided to use class time to pose a number of policy options. Because this was a class that could be somewhat subdued when I led discussions, but sprang to life when I sat back and let them take command, I constructed this lesson to be "a 'role play' in which you play yourselves," as I wrote on their assignment sheet. I gave them four policy proposals to discuss as a class, emphasizing that they could modify any of them:

1. **The Proposition 187 option.** This would prohibit public schools from admitting students who are not legal residents of the United States. It would also prohibit individuals who are not living here legally from getting access to publicly provided medical or other services. Should this be adopted in all states?

2. **Extend the wall between Mexico and the United States to cover the entire border.**

3. **End Operation Gatekeeper. Legalize immigration from Mexico.**

4. **Abolish NAFTA. Aid the poor in Mexico.**

Each policy choice was accompanied by a summary of arguments on both sides. For example, arguments for the Proposition 187 option included:

Supporters argue that this is just common sense. If you are not here legally, then why should you be able to use public services that are meant for legal residents? They also argue that any services provided to illegal immigrants simply encourage more illegals to come. The point is to *discourage* immigration, not *encourage* it. Supporters of this measure argue that immigrants harm legal citizens, draining needed funds, and, they claim, turn to crime more frequently. Proposition 187 might not be the entire solution, they argue, but it is part of it.

Opponents say that this measure especially penalizes children who had no say-so about whether or not to be in the United States. Education is a human right, and it does no one any good to deny education to innocent children — nor to deny them or anyone else medical care. Even from a practical standpoint, they argue, if someone has a communicable disease, what good does it do "legal" citizens to deny medical care to "illegal" ones? They also argue that this measure ignores the roots of the problem: Economic policies pushed by rich people in both the United States and Mexico keep Mexicans in poverty and force them off their land, lead-

PROPOSITION 187

Proposition 187 was a measure passed by 59 percent of California voters in 1994 to deny public education, social services, and non-emergency health care to undocumented immigrants. U.S. District Judge Mariana Pfaelzer ruled the following year that key portions of 187 were unconstitutional, writing in her decision that immigration is "unquestionably, exclusively a federal power." Pfaelzer said that the state cannot deny social services, education, and other federally funded programs, and cannot make independent determinations of immigration status. However, the ruling indicated that the state could refuse to spend its own money on undocumented immigrants. The judge also did not strike down provisions that denied higher education benefits to undocumented students. Proposition 187 was opposed by the American Civil Liberties Union, the Mexican-American Legal Defense/Education Fund, the League of United Latin American Citizens, and many other immigrant rights and social justice organizations. See p. 137 for a description of *Fear and Learning at Hoover Elementary,* an excellent video about the effects of the Proposition 187 campaign at a large Los Angeles elementary school.

ing them to migrate to the United States simply for survival.

In this student-run activity, I sat outside the circle, took verbatim notes on their discussion, and promised not to participate unless they asked for clarification or additional information. Students called on each other and decided when they had reached a decision on each issue.

Frankly, I'm not sure what I expected the class to come up with. I suppose that I'd included the hateful (and, as it turned out, mostly unconstitutional) Proposition 187 option to provide "balance" — making sure that the choices I offered wouldn't prejudice the outcome. But I didn't expect students to support it. After all of our study and students' heartfelt expressions of empathy, I was unprepared for the blizzard of narrowly nationalistic comments this first proposal generated. Chelsea began on a note of reason and care, as I had come to expect from her, but the discussion quickly took a harsh turn. Here's a sampling of the discussion taken word for word from my notes:

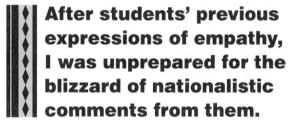

After students' previous expressions of empathy, I was unprepared for the blizzard of nationalistic comments from them.

> Chelsea: Let's remember that we're talking about human lives. They're not coming to steal our jobs. They want to improve their lives. They want better lives for their kids.

> Rhonda: Someone mentioned people coming from Mexico and bringing poor children. Maybe people would be discouraged from coming here if something like this passed.

> Marissa: They're not legal. Our benefits aren't to benefit their country. It's our children who we should educate, not theirs.

> James: I agree with what Rhonda said. If we treat them good, then there will be more of them who'll want to come.

> Kyle: These people are here illegally and they shouldn't be getting benefits. They're using benefits and not paying taxes. If this keeps up, we'll rocket down.

> Katy: The United States needs to focus on the United States. We need to make sure that we're all accounted for and OK. We need to worry about us.

> Sara: The illegal immigrants are taking our jobs and using our resources. Oregon is the hungriest state. People here are dying of starvation. Why should we support people who don't belong here?

> Marissa: It's screwing our economy when they come here. Maybe it's not nice, but it's true. They're taking our jobs and it sucks.

Of those voting, students approved the Proposition 187 proposal, 14 to 7. I was stunned. Where did all this we/they stuff come from? How could students express such contradictory sentiments just a few days apart? Recall Kyle's Mexican cage metaphorical drawing, and his comment at the beginning of the unit: "I don't think there should be borders. I think the world is just as equally one person's as another person's." Marissa

---

MEXICO'S MASK

"The government has tried to portray Mexico as a First World country. They want to show the World Trade Center, the big malls, the Zona Rosa, the big, modern cities — Acapulco, Cancun, Mexico City, Monterrey, Guadalajara. They want to show the tourists the lovely Mexican culture — the mariachis, the folkloric dancing, the beautiful clothing and crafts of the indigenous people. But behind this picture is the real Mexico, the Mexico of the millions of Indians who live in extreme poverty.

"We have helped to peel off the mask to reveal the real Mexico. We've shown that in Chiapas, the Mexican government and a handful of businesses extract all the wealth — the oil, electric energy, tropical trees, cattle, coffee, corn, cacao, bananas. And what do they leave behind? Death and disease — death from curable diseases like respiratory infections, enteritis, parasites, amoebas, malaria, tuberculosis, cholera, and measles. Our uprising was the only way to draw attention to the poverty and injustices that the indigenous people have been suffering for over 500 years."

—Subcomandante Marcos, from an interview with Medea Benjamin in First World, Ha, Ha, Ha! The Zapatista Challenge, *ed. Elaine Katzenberger (San Francisco: CityLights Books, 1995).*

had drawn not one but three metaphorical drawings, each attacking the exploitative U.S. relationship with Mexico. One of these, "The Corporate A-Bomb," pictured an enormous exploding building in Mexico. In her written explanation, she summed up the relationship: "That's what NAFTA is doing, bringing a part of corporate America that isn't good at all to Mexico, so that people in America can get rich while other people in Mexico work until they die and get nothing."

And now, just days later, she told the class with certainty: "It's our country. We need to keep them out."

The vote was a tie on whether or not the United States should extend the Operation Gatekeeper wall the full length of the border. When at one point Chelsea said in frustration, "We exiled and killed so many Mexican people we can't count them. What makes it 'ours'?" Will shot back: "Great. We stole it, but now it's ours. If we don't keep people out then we will lose our way of life."

Still, a number of Proposition 187 supporters balked at the money that an expanded wall would cost. Patrick said, "It doesn't work to throw money at the problem. We have to figure out why people are coming here for it to work."

When it came to abolishing Operation Gatekeeper,

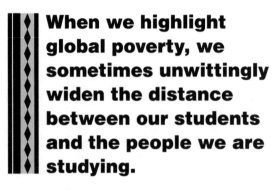

When we highlight global poverty, we sometimes unwittingly widen the distance between our students and the people we are studying.

only two students favored this route. As Sara said, "OK. The wall comes down. So all the poor of Mexico come here. If we let Mexicans in, then we're not going to have two countries. We'll be one. We'll all look like Tijuana, with houses on top of each other." Sara's remark highlighted a paradoxical dimension of this unit: Attempting to kindle students' empathy by exposing them to the poverty of migrant life at the border could instead simply heighten their own insecurities about the future.

Students voted unanimously not to abolish NAFTA, reasoning that so many people had already been thrown off the land that to end NAFTA could hurt Mexicans' employment possibilities in maquiladoras along the border. Many students, however, were eager to change parts of NAFTA: scrapping Chapter 11 and allowing Mexico to reinstitute tariffs on food were a couple of important examples. In the conversation, Kyle offered a remark that made me aware of a fundamental problem in how I'd framed the discussion. He said, "I don't think we can help Mexicans even if we wanted to. Look at how the U.S. improved: with strikes and labor struggles. That's what Mexico needs to do." (Note to myself: Congratulate Kyle's U.S. history teacher.)

I think that by framing these choices as *policy* deci-

THE ZAPATISTAS

The Zapatista uprising in Mexico began on New Year's Day 1994, the day that NAFTA, the North American Free Trade Agreement, took effect. The rebels of the Zapatista National Liberation Army (EZLN) came out of the Lacandón Forest, in the southeastern state of Chiapas, demanding an end to the exploitation and repression of the largely indigenous peasantry of the region.

Chiapas is home to about four million people, of whom at least a million are Indians — Tzotzil, Tzeltal, Ch'ol, Tojolobal, and others. At the time the rebellion began, according to government statistics, 35 percent of the region's dwellings had no electricity, 51 percent had dirt floors, and most had no easy access to clean water. Four out of every 10 workers made less than the minimum wage of about $3 a day. And conditions for most

indigenous people of Chiapas and Mexico were worse.

The region itself is not poor. For example, more than half of all of Mexico's hydroelectricity comes from dams in Chiapas. But, as Zapatista leader Subcomandante Marcos wrote in 1992, before the rebellion began: "Chiapas is bled through thousands of veins: through oil ducts and gas ducts, over electric wires, by railroad cars, through bank accounts, by trucks and vans, by ships and planes, over clandestine paths, third-rate roads, and mountain passes."

For a classroom-friendly reading, see "Prayers for a Dignified Life: A Letter to Schoolchildren About the Zapatista Uprising," by Subcomandante Marcos, included in *Rethinking Globalization: Teaching for Justice in an Unjust World* (pp. 321-322, from which the above is excerpted).

sions, I unwittingly implied that the state — i.e., the U.S. government — would be the instrument of justice. I hadn't offered students other ways to consider effecting change. In fact, Mexicans *do* have strikes and labor struggles — and women's struggles and environmental struggles and indigenous struggles and land struggles. I had begun planning but never finished some activities on the Zapatista movement (see box, p. 36). Kyle's comment indicates that clearly I could have done a better job featuring Mexican activism in the unit. Perhaps had we focused more on these organizing efforts and on some of the cross-border alliances between Mexicans and people in the United States, students would not have become so stifled by their own fears. (A fine film that could be excerpted or possibly used in full is *Granito de Arena*, about Mexican teachers' struggles for quality education and against neoliberal reforms; see p. 140.)

No doubt, my students have good reason to be afraid. Unemployment and hunger rates in Oregon are among the highest in the nation, as Sara alluded to during the students' discussion. Every year sees new cuts here in government services. When my students were sophomores, for example, the district

CONNIE ARAMAKI

A young boy is caged in his Tijuana home by sheet metal and bed springs so that he cannot leave while his parents are at work in the maquiladoras.

almost shut schools five weeks early because of a budget shortfall, and trimming the school year still remains a threat. Tuition fees for public colleges and universities continue to leap higher with every incoming class. This is how I understand the source of their comments in this final activity: For my largely white working-class students, immigration is zero-sum — anything awarded to Mexicans is subtracted from them. When it's strictly in people-to-people terms, as in the improvisations we performed, students display huge hearts. But their hearts shrink up when they think with their fear.

An Injury to One …

Before the second day of deliberation in this final role play, I read my students highlights of the previous day's discussion that I had transcribed. Hearing their own words taken seriously in this way delighted them, and

a number of students commented on this in evaluations at the end of the year. I hoped that listening to key arguments raised in the debates would allow them to stand back from some of the positions they'd espoused and reconsider. I stayed true to my promise not to intervene in their conversations, but reflecting now on this final activity, I think that hearing student after student revive "they're gonna get us" fears took me aback and left me conceptually tongue-tied at the end of the unit.

It appears that most of my students never recognized that pursuing their own self-interests did not necessarily preclude acting on their empathy for others. There were times I could have initiated this kind of reflection better — perhaps by debriefing and building off the NAFTA role play more thoughtfully; perhaps by exploring in greater depth the effects of today's global capitalism and the neoliberal model of development on

Portland and my students' own lives, explicitly searching for patterns between "our" circumstances and "theirs"; and perhaps by bringing in people doing cross-border organizing to have them speak directly to the issue of why working-class U.S. kids should care what happens to Mexicans.

 don't mean to over-generalize based on my students' reactions to this unit. Would students from other backgrounds have responded in different ways to this curriculum? Undoubtedly. I've led workshops for prospective teachers and new teachers in the I-Teach program at Chapman University in Orange, Calif. Participants were overwhelmingly Latino, most of whose families came from Mexico. Some of them were still undergraduates, recently out of high school. We did the "Transnational Capital Auction" (see p. 105), which simulates poor countries' race to the bottom as they compete to create "friendlier" investment climates, and followed this activity with the Mexico border improvisations. For these young people, the lessons were not about "them," but about "us."

"This is not *my* story, but it *is* my father's story," one

IMMIGRATION JUSTICE ALLIANCE

The year after I taught this curriculum at Franklin High School, I went on leave. Teachers Tim Swinehart and Sandra Childs taught many of these lessons again, but wisely reworked the activity on immigration policy that had generated such narrow us-against-them responses in my class. Their first modification was to turn the activity into a role play, with all students portraying members of the Immigration Justice Alliance (IJA), a made-up U.S.-based organization advocating policy changes and dedicated to "promoting the human rights of immigrants." The role play was structured as an IJA strategy-building forum, and would allow students to "try on" the personas of immigrant rights activists.

IJA members were confronted with tough choices. According to the IJA meeting ground rules, they could concentrate their organization's resources in only two areas, and the role play handout presented them with six: preventing the expansion of Operation Gatekeeper and the building of new border walls; advocating a Guestworker program granting Mexicans temporary work visas; promoting the DREAM Act (that, if passed, would make it easier for undocumented students to receive financial aid and in-state tuition); working to secure lawful permanent residency for undocumented immigrants; revising or ending free trade agreements — NAFTA and its offspring, CAFTA, which similarly would pry open markets and grant corporations enhanced powers in Central America and the Dominican Republic; and advocating an "Open Door" policy for Mexican immigrants, along the lines of the European Union. (The student handout is at our website, www.rethinkingschools.org/mexico.)

The handout presented numerous arguments on all sides of these choices; this was not a correct-answer activity, with a fixed objective in mind. Instead, the aim was for students to grapple with immigration issues, using knowledge gleaned from the larger unit. I sat on the perimeter of the circle and watched the debates; the students ran the discussion themselves. One student, Julia, dismissed working for the Guestworker plan with the comment, "I don't think this is a good idea. It's putting a band-aid on something that needs plastic surgery." Nick agreed: "It turns immigrants into demons, like they're a sub-class." Much of the discussion focused on whether to work to reform or abolish NAFTA and CAFTA. Will argued: "What would be the point of changing them? They are still free trade agreements and will cost a lot in terms of grief." Eron favored putting their resources and energy into making conditions concretely better for immigrants through the DREAM Act, acknowledging that it was only a limited measure, but "You gotta start somewhere." Others chafed at being presented only six choices; "Are these it?" complained one student. In the end, the Immigration Justice Alliance voted to expend their energies opposing NAFTA and CAFTA, but also to support work toward the DREAM Act — a choice likely influenced by the real-world organizing of Latino students in the Portland area.

At times chaotic, at times off-track, students' conversation mostly seemed sincere and intelligent. The lesson was a clear improvement on the immigration policy activity that had produced so many fearful expressions in my class. Or was this role play just that, play? Were students submerging the same attitudes that my students expressed in order to be faithful to the assignment? Perhaps. But from where I sat, the lesson allowed class members an opportunity to imagine themselves as social justice activists. It allowed them to blend analysis and heart.

"Yo Fui Bracero" — I was a Bracero. Former migrant worker Marcelino Guzman takes part in a 2002 demonstration in Mexico City, as one of a group of elderly men demanding repayment of millions of dollars in withheld wages for work they did in the United States decades earlier as part of the Bracero program. This program provided temporary visas for Mexicans to do farm-work in the United States. Between 1942 and 1964, 4.6 million Mexican workers entered the United States under the Bracero program. The poster reads, "They made us strip and then fumigated us."

woman on the verge of tears said in describing her reaction to the improv she performed. With seemingly every discussion after an improvisation, participants had personal examples that illustrated the tension in the improv situation. The conversation had an immediacy and intimacy lacking in my Franklin High School class.

Still, I believe my students' contradictory responses to this unit highlight a basic issue in a critical global education. Yes, we need to feature situations around the world that acknowledge the yawning gaps between the haves and the have-nots and explore the roots of this inequality. The wretched of the earth are growing and becoming more wretched. Our students need to learn about that — and learn about the roots of this process.

However, when we highlight global poverty, sometimes we do it in a way that unwittingly widens the distance between our students and the people we're studying. In emphasizing the dire consequences of neo-liberalism in Mexico, I may have heightened my students' fears about economic refugees coming to take their jobs and further erode their security. We need to find ways to acknowledge in our curriculum the great inequalities throughout the world, but also explore how all of our lives — at least those of us who are not members of the very elite — are shaped and harmed by the same social forces. My students' fears and hopes need to be connected to the fears and hopes of people at the Mexican border and around the world, not placed in opposition.

As the Industrial Workers of the World insisted over 100 years ago on their founding: An injury to one is an injury to all. Today, we need to nurture a curriculum that brings that truth to life in our classrooms. ■

Historical Roots of the Border

The U.S.-Mexico War Tea Party
'We Take Nothing by Conquest, Thank God'

Today's border with Mexico is the product of invasion and war. Grasping some of the motives for that war and some of its immediate effects begins to provide students the kind of historical context that is crucial for thinking intelligently about the line that separates the United States and Mexico. The tea party activity introduces students to a number of the individuals and themes they will encounter in Howard Zinn's "We Take Nothing by Conquest, Thank God." (See p. 11 for more on how this activity might fit into the broader curriculum.)

Materials Needed

- Tea party roles, cut up. One for every student in the class.
- Blank nametags. Enough for every student in the class.
- Copies of "The U.S.–Mexico War: Questions" for every student.
- Copies of "We Take Nothing by Conquest, Thank God" for every student.
- Copies of the U.S.–Mexico maps on page 52.

Time Required

- One class period for the tea party. Time for follow-up discussion.
- A portion of one class period to assign "We Take Nothing by Conquest, Thank God," and a portion of another to discuss.

Suggested Procedure

1. Explain to students that they are going to do an activity about the U.S. war with Mexico, 1846–1848. Distribute one tea party role to each student in the class. There are only 21, so in most classes, some students will be assigned the same historical character. (Most but not all of the roles are based on individuals included in Zinn's "We Take Nothing by Conquest, Thank God," as the tea party is intended as a pre-reading activity. A couple are drawn from the chapter "Foreigners in Their Own Land: Manifest Destiny in the Southwest," in Ronald Takaki's *A Different Mirror;* others are based on material in Milton Meltzer's *Bound for the Rio Grande,* Matt S. Meier and Feliciano Rivera's *The Chicanos: A History of Mexican Americans,* Elizabeth Martínez's *500 Años del Pueblo Chicano/500 Years of Chicano History in Pictures,* and Deena J. González's "The Widowed Women of Santa Fe: Assessments on the Lives of an Unmarried Population, 1850–1880" in *Unequal Sisters: A Multicultural Reader in U.S. Women's History,* Ellen Carol DuBois and Vicki L. Ruiz, eds.)

2. Have students fill out their nametags, using the name of the individual they are assigned. Tell students that in this activity you would like each of them to attempt to become these people from history. Ask students to read their roles several times and to memorize as much of the information as possible. Encourage them to underline key points.

SECTION 2 PHOTO: DAVID BACON

3. Distribute a copy of "The U.S.–Mexico War: Questions" to every student. Explain their assignment: Students should circulate through the classroom, meeting other individuals from the U.S–Mexico War. They should use the questions on the sheet as a guide to talk with others about the war and complete the questions as fully as possible. They must use a different individual to answer each of the eight questions. (This is not *The Twilight Zone*, so students who have been assigned the same person may not meet themselves.) Tell them that it's not a race; the aim is for students to spend time hearing each other's stories, not just hurriedly scribbling down answers to the different questions. I like to begin this activity by asking for a student volunteer to demonstrate with me an encounter between two of the individuals, so that the rest of the class can sense the kind of interaction I'm looking for.

4. Afterwards ask students to share some of their findings with the whole class. This needn't be exhaustive, as students will learn a lot more about these issues when they read the excerpt from Howard Zinn's *A People's History of the United States*. Possible questions:

    ⇒ What surprised you about this activity?
    ⇒ Who found someone with an opinion very different than your character's opinion?
    ⇒ What were some of the different opinions you encountered on why the United States and Mexico went to war?
    ⇒ Why do you think the United States and Mexico went to war?
    ⇒ What were the results of the war?
    ⇒ What questions does this activity leave you with?

'We Take Nothing by Conquest, Thank God'

5. As follow-up, assign the U.S.–Mexico maps and Howard Zinn's "We Take Nothing by Conquest, Thank God" (see pp. 52 and 53). Another reading to consider using is Milton Meltzer's chapter focusing on the U.S. soldiers from Ireland who went over to the Mexican side as the San Patricio Battalion, "Traitors — or Martyrs," from his book *Bound for the Rio Grande*. Similarly, I've used the song "San Patricio Brigade" from *New York Town*, a CD by the Irish-American rock group Black 47, to talk with students about the Irish resistance to the war. Black 47 can at first-listen sound odd, but my students seemed to enjoy hearing this raucous song about a "boy from the green fields of Galway."

6. Ask students to complete a "talk-back" journal with the Zinn reading. They should locate at least five passages from the reading that they found amusing, important, startling, moving, confusing, outrageous, or odd. They should write out each quote and their detailed reaction to it. You might ask students to find material that they can relate to information they learned in the tea party, to their own lives, or to things going on today. Also encourage students to raise at least two questions that they would like to discuss with the rest of the class.

7. In addition to students' own questions, here are some questions for further discussion or writing:

    ⇒ Why did the U.S. government want to obtain California?
    ⇒ What is meant by the term "manifest destiny"?
    ⇒ What were the pressures on the U.S. government to push for expansion?
    ⇒ What if you believed the war with Mexico was immoral, but both major parties, Democratic and Whig, supported it? What would you do to try to bring an end to the war?
    ⇒ Reread Abraham Lincoln's quote on page 54. Lincoln believes that even though Whigs opposed the war before it began, once the war began they should allocate money to support it. Explain why you agree or disagree.
    ⇒ Comment on this belief of some Americans: The Mexican War was a good thing, because it gave the blessings of liberty and democracy to more people.
    ⇒ In what ways could it be said that the Mexican War was a racist war? Give examples.
    ⇒ Describe the resistance to the war. How effective was the opposition?

- From a Mexican standpoint, given the origins and nature of the U.S.-Mexico War, how might people today respond to the efforts to exclude Mexicans from U.S. territory, and to treat them as criminals once they are here?

- In his essay "Civil Disobedience," Henry David Thoreau writes that what is legal is not necessarily what is right. Do you agree? Can you think of any examples from history or current events?

- The Rev. Theodore Parker said that Mexicans must eventually give way, as did the Indians. What similarities do you see between the Mexican War and the wars against the Indians?

- Why might ordinary citizens — workers or farmers, with no slaves and no plans to move onto Mexican territory — support the U.S. war against Mexico? Does war itself hold attraction for people, or was it the Mexican War in particular that excited some Americans?

- As was the case with the organized opposition to Indian Removal in the 1820s and 1830s, racism infected the movement against the war with Mexico. Give some examples. Why do you think this racism existed?

- If the U.S. Army was supposed to bring liberty and civilization to Mexico, why do you think rape and mistreatment of Mexicans was so widespread?

- Who benefited from the Mexican War?

Some Additional Activities and Projects

- Design a monument or memorial exhibit to commemorate the U.S. war with Mexico. Consider what symbols might best represent this war. Given that your audience is likely to know little about the war, what essential points should you teach? Perhaps design the commemoration from a Mexican standpoint.

- Read Henry David Thoreau's "Civil Disobedience" and write a response.

- Write a diary entry or letter explaining why you are volunteering to fight in Mexico. Or write a diary or letter explaining why you oppose the war and will refuse to fight.

- Write an interior monologue from the point of view of an individual mentioned in the reading or tea party — for example, a California Indian listening to Navy officer Revere, a Mexican woman in Santa Fe as Gen. Kearny's troops enter, a volunteer U.S. soldier experiencing the horrors of war for the first time, one of Gen. Cushing's men as he speaks to them at their reception dinner in Massachusetts.

The U.S.-Mexico War: Roles

Cut out the 21 tea party roles found on this and the following four pages. Give one role to each student in the class. In larger classes, some of the characters will be assigned to more than one student. See page 43 for complete instructions.

Colonel Ethan Allen Hitchcock

I am a professional soldier, graduate of the U.S. Military Academy, commander of the 3rd Infantry Regiment. I am an aide to Gen. Zachary Taylor. Like President Polk, Taylor wanted a war with Mexico, and so he moved troops to the Rio Grande — territory claimed both by Mexico and Texas — to provoke the Mexicans. Eventually, the Mexicans did attack, as Taylor and Polk knew they would. And now U.S. leaders have their war. The United States has no right whatsoever to move into Mexico. The government is looking for war so that it can take over as much of Mexico as it wants. The United States is the aggressor. My heart is not in this war. But I am an officer in the U.S. Army and I must carry out my orders.

Congressman Abraham Lincoln, Whig Party, Illinois

The Whigs were accused of being opposed to the war against Mexico. Well, that's true or false, depending on how you look at it. It's true that we spoke out in Congress against the war. In a speech, I challenged President Polk to name the exact spot where Mexicans supposedly shed American blood. I was against Polk pushing this war with Mexico. But once the war started, we consistently voted to supply funds to wage the war and support the troops. In fact, I even gave a speech in Congress supporting the candidacy of Gen. Zachary Taylor for president. And Taylor was the first general in charge of waging the war.

President James K. Polk

I won the presidency by a close vote in 1844 and now I am President of the United States of America. I am a Democrat, and a believer in manifest destiny. It is God's plan that the United States should spread from the Atlantic to the Pacific. In 1846, I ordered U.S. troops into an area that was claimed both by Texas and Mexico, historically occupied by Mexicans. I knew that it was a provocation. As I confided to my Secretary of the Navy: I want California to be part of the United States. It's part of Mexico and the only way to get it away from them is war. As I'd expected, the Mexicans attacked and I convinced Congress to declare war against Mexico. Some of my opponents say that I want this war only because I own slaves and this is a war to extend slavery to Mexico. Nonsense. There is much more at stake than slavery. This is about defending America's honor and our national interest.

William Lloyd Garrison, founder, American Anti-Slavery Society

I oppose the Mexican War, as do all true opponents of slavery. President Polk is a slave owner and like all slave owners, he wants to expand slavery everywhere. That's why this war is being fought: to steal more territory from Mexico so that Mexico can be carved up into new slave states. Mexico abolished slavery in 1829, and the Texans left Mexico and established their own "country" so that they could keep their slaves. Now Texas is entering the United States as a slave state. My organization and I will speak out, organize protest meetings, write articles, publish pamphlets, and do everything legal we can do to oppose this immoral war. In our newspaper, *The Liberator,* we have written that we hope the Mexicans will win this war. It's not a popular statement these days, but when it comes to justice, we cannot compromise.

Reverend Theodore Parker

I am a Unitarian minister in Boston with a congregation of 7,000. I oppose this war with Mexico because this is a war to expand slavery. Slavery should be ended not expanded. I am not opposed to the war because I like the Mexicans. As I have written, they are "a wretched people; wretched in their origin, history and character." We Americans are vastly superior, but we must not take them over by force. We should resist this war. I urge young men not to enlist, bankers should refuse to lend money for the war, ship owners should refuse to let their ships be used for the war; manufacturers should refuse to produce cannons, swords, and gun-powder for the war. Let the government prosecute me as a traitor. I answer only to God.

General Stephen Kearny

I command the U.S. Army in the West. I had the honor of winning New Mexico for the United States during the war with Mexico. The high point for me was taking the city of Santa Fe. I wanted to conquer but not to kill. I sent word that if the people didn't fight us we wouldn't fight them. We marched into Santa Fe with our bayonets and knives out, hoping that we would frighten the residents so they would not fight us. And they didn't. We raised the American flag and fired our cannon in a glorious salute to the United States of America. Apparently this had a strong effect on the town's women because many of them let loose a "wail of grief," as one of my officers described it. The sound of their crying rose above the noise of our horses as we rode along.

Henry David Thoreau

I live in Concord, Mass., where I work as a writer. In order to support this war with Mexico, Massachusetts passed a poll tax. I won't pay it. Simple as that. The government wants to force people into this unjust war to go kill Mexicans or be killed. I won't support that. For my "crime," they put me in jail for a night. My friend, the famous writer Ralph Waldo Emerson, came to visit me in jail. He said, "What are you doing in there?" I replied, "What are you doing out there?" Against my wishes, friends of mine paid my tax and I was released. But I have come to believe that the way to stop injustice is not merely to speak out against it, but also to refuse to obey unjust laws.

Frederick Douglass

I was born a slave. When I was about 20 years old, I ran away from my so-called master and came to live in the North, where I have become famous speaking and writing against slavery. I publish an anti-slavery journal called the *North Star*. This war with Mexico is dis-graceful and cruel. Mexico is a victim of those white people of America who love to push around people who aren't white. Unfortunately, even many abolitionists (people who are working to end slavery) have continued to pay their taxes and do not resist this war with enough passion. It's time that we risk every-thing for peace.

U.S. Navy officer

I'm a lucky man. I got to sail into California to seize that territory for the United States of America. It's ours now, not the Mexicans'. Here's what I wrote in my diary when I sailed up from South America and landed in Monterey, Calif.: "Asia will be brought to our very doors. Population will flow into the fertile regions of California. The resources of the entire country will be developed. The public lands lying along the route of railroads will be changed from deserts into gardens, and a large population will be settled." This is where I'm going to settle after we defeat the Mexicans once and for all.

U.S. Army officer

I thought the war was going to be a lot of fun. How could the Mexicans put up much of a fight when they were up against the powerful United States? But soon enough the reality of war set in. As we moved up the Rio Grande, it was incredibly hot, hotter than I'd ever experienced. The water was bad and many of my men got diarrhea, dysentery and other diseases. It was awful. We lost a thousand men just from sickness. I watched some men do horrible things. As I wrote in my diary: "We reached Burrita about 5 p.m., many of the Louisiana volunteers were there, a lawless drunken rabble. They had driven away the inhabitants, taken possession of their houses, and were emulating [copying] each other in making beasts of themselves." They raped many women there.

Lieutenant, U.S. Army infantry

In a place called Huamantla, the Mexicans killed one of our officers, a man by the name of Walker. He was a friend of Gen. Lane. The general told us to "avenge the death of the gallant Walker, to take all we could lay hands on." And we did. We broke open liquor stores and got drunk. Then we went after the women and girls. They were stripped of their clothing and terrible outrages were committed against them. We shot dozens of men and ransacked their churches, stores, and houses. We even killed the Mexicans' horses. Drunken U.S. soldiers were everywhere, yelling, screeching, breaking open houses or chasing Mexicans, who ran for their lives. As I wrote my parents, "Such a scene I never hope to see again. It made me for the first time ashamed of my country."

Francisco Márquez, Mexican cadet

I am a cadet, studying at a military school in Mexico City. The school is in a castle high up on a hill in the beautiful Chapultepec region of the city. I love my country and I want to defend it from the invading U.S. Army. Why are they attacking my country? Because they want to bring back slavery to Mexico? Because they want to steal California and other territories of Mexico? Why? They have done brutal things to my people. I will fight to the death. We have been ordered by our officers to leave the military school because we are too young to fight as soldiers. But I will stay and fight. I will fight until I am the last one alive, and then I will wrap myself in the Mexican flag and jump to my death before allowing myself to be captured by the Americans.

General Mariano Vallejo

I live in California, a part of Mexico. I am a wealthy man. I own 175,000 acres. This is where my 16 children were born. I have always been very kind to visitors who come from the United States, and some even say that I am famous for the hospitality I show my guests. In the 1840s, more and more people from the United States began arriving. Unbelievably, most of them looked down on Mexicans and called us "greasers" and an inferior race — we who were born here and built wealthy *ranchos*. Now that war has broken out, it is clear what the North Americans are looking for: They want to steal California away from Mexico and make it a part of the United States. Before the war, they wanted to buy California from Mexico, but Mexico wouldn't sell. So now they are making war on us so that they can take it away. I fear that I will lose everything I've worked so hard for.

Oregon Trail wagon train member

In 1844, I took a wagon train from Missouri to the Oregon territory, but someone said there was better farmland in California, and warmer weather. So I headed south to the San Joaquin Valley. It's a part of Mexico, but there are more and more people arriving all the time from the United States. And now war has broken out. Soon this won't be Mexico any more. It will be the United States of America. Manifest destiny is what they call it, and from sea to shining sea, soon it will be filled with free, white, English-speaking farmers and ranchers. Too bad it's going to take a war to make it happen, but the Mexicans wouldn't sell California, and then they attacked us. So fair's fair.

Jefferson Davis, Mississippi

I'm one of the largest plantation owners in the United States. Every year, it seems that the people against slavery just get louder and louder. They're trying to keep slavery out of the Western territories like Kansas and Nebraska. And now, like a gift from God, along comes this war against Mexico. Think of all the new territory we can conquer for freedom — the freedom to take our slaves wherever we like. First Mexico, then Cuba, and then Nicaragua. I can see the day when the United States could rule all of Mexico and Central America, and all that territory will be added to our country — new states, new slave states. This is a great war. Thank heavens the Mexicans attacked us first. Justice is on our side.

María Josefa Martínez, Santa Fe, New Mexico

Two years ago, in 1846, the United States invaded Mexico. That summer, Gen. Stephen W. Kearny of the U.S. Army marched into Santa Fe to take control. Up until that moment, I was a Mexican woman. Since then, I have been a conquered Mexican woman. There are about 25,000 to 30,000 women in New Mexico. The white male conquerors treat us badly. They have contempt for all Mexicans, especially women. As a woman, under Mexican law I was allowed to own property in my maiden name, and sell or give it away without my husband's signature. I could even farm my own land apart from my husband's land or land that we owned together. U.S. women don't have these rights. Unlike the invaders, I speak Spanish not English. But English is the language used by lawyers, judges, and tax assessors. I worry that the U.S. authorities will use my lack of English to take away my rights and property.

Doña Francesca Vallejo

I live in California, a part of Mexico. I am a wealthy woman, a wealthy Mexican woman. With my husband, I own 175,000 acres. I have numerous servants. I have two for my own personal service. Four or five servants grind corn for tortillas, for we entertain so many guests that three servants could not feed them all. About six or seven work in the kitchen. Five or six are continually occupied washing the clothes of my 16 children and the rest are employed in the house; and finally, nearly a dozen attend to the sewing and spinning. This is where my children were born. I have always been very friendly to visitors who come from the United States, and some even say that I am famous for the hospitality I show my guests. And now there is a war. The United States will try to take California away from Mexico, but they have no right, and we won't let them.

Sergeant John Riley, San Patricio Battalion, formerly U.S. Army

Originally, I'm from a small town in Ireland. I joined the U.S. Army and became a drillmaster at West Point, training men to be soldiers. Now the Army considers me a deserter and a traitor. That's not how I see it. I was sent to invade Mexico with the Army. The U.S. had no right to be there. It was like the British occupying Ireland. Mexicans were treated cruelly. The Mexicans appealed to me to leave the U.S. Army and to join theirs. And I did. I became a lieutenant and about 260 U.S. soldiers joined me fighting on the Mexican side. In Boston and Philadelphia, the Protestants had burned our Catholic churches. The Mexicans are Catholic too. But now, we are captured. Most of us have been sentenced to death by hanging. The "lucky" ones are to be given 50 lashes with a whip, forced to dig the graves for our friends who will be executed, and then branded on our cheeks with the letter "D" for deserter.

Padre Antonio José Martínez

In the struggle between the rich and the poor, I stand with the poor. In fact, I am called the Padre (Father) of the Poor. I founded the first school for boys and girls in the entire Southwest and also began one of the first newspapers in the region. And I opposed the U.S. invaders when recently they came to take over our territory in New Mexico. Even though I am a priest, many believe that I was a leader of the Revolt of Taos in 1847. On Jan. 19, 1847, 2,000 Indians and Mexicanos together rose up and killed the U.S.-installed governor in his mansion as well as other U.S. officials who were stealing our land. The rebels marched through the snow and took refuge in a Catholic church in the Taos pueblo, thinking they would be safe. They weren't. The U.S. Army destroyed the church with cannon fire. The U.S. authorities put six leaders on trial and found them guilty in 15 minutes. The six men were hanged, holding hands as they died.

Wotoki, Miwok Indian, California

I live in northern California, in Sonoma. No matter who wins this war between Mexico and the United States, nothing changes the fact that this is Miwok land, our land, that they are fighting over. First, the Spaniards took over, then the Mexicans. Now the Americans are taking over. But they all mistreated the Miwok people. Our land is now owned by one of the richest men in California, the Mexican General Mariano Vallejo. They say he and his wife, Doña Francesca, are kind to visitors. But he is not kind to his Indian workers. I work on his land. Vallejo treats us almost like slaves. And the Americans here are no better. An American named Captain Sutter orders "his" Indians to eat out of four-feet-long troughs, as if Indians are pigs. Sutter whips them when they disobey. I have no idea what this war between Mexico and the United States is about. To me, it looks like Americans and Mexicans killing each other so that they can steal our land.

Cochise, Chiricahua Apache leader

Some of the whites think that my land belongs to the United States. Some think it belongs to Mexico. They are all wrong. My land belongs to my people, the Apaches. We roam the lands that Mexico calls Sonora and that the United States considers New Mexico and Arizona. First, Spain claimed this land, then the Mexicans, now the Americans. Over the years, we've fought them all — the European invaders — and we will continue to fight. Before this latest war, the Mexicans paid Americans to help track us down. In fact, a group of them killed my father. When I was young I walked all over this country, east and west, and saw no other people than the Apaches. Now the invaders are everywhere. Mexicans, Americans: I want them all gone from my land.

The War with Mexico: Questions

1. Find someone who was affected by the war. Who is the person?

   How was this person affected?

2. Find someone who supports the U.S. war with Mexico. Who is the person?

   Why does this person support the war?

3. Find someone who opposes the U.S. war with Mexico. Who is the person?

   Why does this person oppose the war?

4. Find someone who has an opinion on why the United States is at war with Mexico. Who is the person?

   What is this person's opinion about why the United States is at war?

5. Find someone who saw things in the war that he or she found shocking. Who is the person?

   What shocked this person?

6. Find someone who does not support either the United States or Mexico in this war. Who is the person?

   What is this person's perspective on the war?

7. Find someone who stands to gain from the war. Who is this person?

   How might this person benefit?

8. Find someone who stands to lose from the war. Who is the person?

   How might this person suffer?

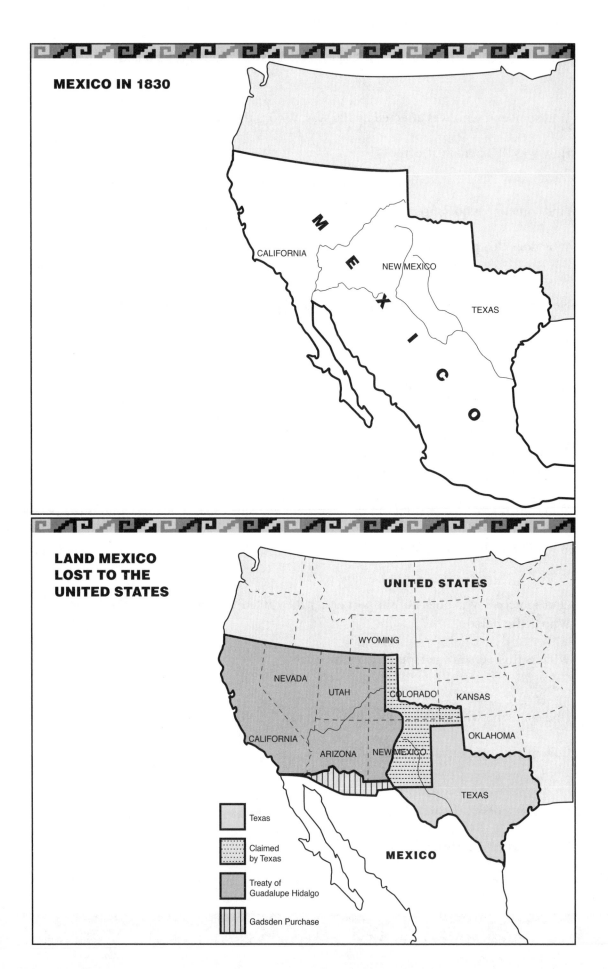

MEXICO IN 1830

CALIFORNIA

NEW MEXICO

TEXAS

M
E
X
I
C
O

LAND MEXICO LOST TO THE UNITED STATES

UNITED STATES

WYOMING

NEVADA

UTAH

COLORADO

KANSAS

CALIFORNIA

ARIZONA

NEW MEXICO

OKLAHOMA

TEXAS

MEXICO

Texas

Claimed by Texas

Treaty of Guadalupe Hidalgo

Gadsden Purchase

BY HOWARD ZINN

We Take Nothing by Conquest, Thank God

This chapter is excerpted from Howard Zinn's classic book, A People's History of the United States. *Between 1846 and 1848, the United States fought a war with Mexico. Zinn explores the war's main causes and examines its effects on people's lives.*

Col. Ethan Allen Hitchcock, a professional soldier, graduate of the Military Academy, commander of the Third Infantry Regiment, a reader of Shakespeare, Chaucer, Hegel, Spinoza, wrote in his diary:

Fort Jesup, La., June 30, 1845. Orders came last evening by express from Washington City directing Gen. Taylor to move without any delay to … take up a position on the banks of or near the Rio Grande, and he is to expel any armed force of Mexicans who may cross that river. Bliss read the orders to me last evening hastily at tattoo. I have scarcely slept a wink, thinking of the needful preparations. … Violence leads to violence, and if this movement of ours does not lead to others and to bloodshed, I am much mistaken.

Hitchcock was not mistaken. Jefferson's Louisiana Purchase had doubled the territory of the United States, extending it to the Rocky Mountains. To the southwest was Mexico, which had won its independence in a revolutionary war against Spain in 1821. Mexico was then an even larger country than it is now, since it included what are now Texas, New Mexico, Utah, Nevada, Arizona, California, and part of Colorado. After agitation, and aid from the United States, Texas broke off from Mexico in 1836 and declared itself the "Lone Star Republic." In 1845, the U.S. Congress brought it into the Union as a state.

In the White House now was James Polk, a Democrat, an expansionist, who, on the night of his inauguration, confided to his Secretary of the Navy that one of his main objectives was the acquisition of California. His order to Gen. Zachary Taylor to move troops to the Rio Grande was a challenge to the Mexicans. It was not at all clear that the Rio Grande was the southern boundary of Texas, although Texas had forced the defeated Mexican general Santa Anna to say so when he was a prisoner. The traditional border between Texas and Mexico had been the Nueces River, about 150 miles to the north, and both Mexico and the United States had recognized that as the border. However, Polk, encouraging the Texans to accept annexation, had assured them he would uphold their claims to the Rio Grande.

Ordering troops to the Rio Grande, into territory inhabited by Mexicans, was clearly a provocation. Taylor's army marched in parallel columns across the open prairie, scouts far ahead and on the flanks, a train of supplies following. Then, along a narrow road, through a belt of thick chaparral, they arrived, March 28, 1846, in cultivated fields and thatched-roof huts hurriedly abandoned by the Mexican occupants, who had fled across the river to the city of Matamoros. Taylor set up camp, began construction of a fort, and implanted his cannons facing the white houses of Matamoros, whose inhabitants stared curiously at the sight of an army on the banks of a quiet river.

'Our Manifest Destiny'

The *Washington Union,* a newspaper expressing the position of President Polk and the Democratic party, had spoken early in 1845 on the meaning of Texas annexation: "Let the great measure of annexation be accomplished, and with it the questions of boundary and claims. For who can arrest the torrent that will pour onward to the West? The road to California will be open to us. Who will stay the march of our western people?"

It was shortly after that, in the summer of 1845, that John O'Sullivan, editor of the *Democratic Review,* used the phrase that became famous, saying it was "our manifest destiny to overspread the continent allotted by Providence for the free development of our yearly multiplying millions." Yes, manifest destiny.

All that was needed in the spring of 1846 was a military incident to begin the war that Polk wanted. It came in April, when Gen. Taylor's quartermaster, Col. Cross, while riding up the Rio Grande, disappeared. His body was found 11 days later, his skull smashed by a heavy blow. It was assumed he had been killed by Mexican guerrillas crossing the river.

The next day (April 25), a patrol of Taylor's soldiers was surrounded and attacked by Mexicans, and wiped out: 16 dead, others wounded, the rest captured. Taylor sent a dispatch to Polk: "Hostilities may now be considered as commenced."

 **The Mexicans had fired the first shot. But they had done what the American government wanted.**

The Mexicans had fired the first shot. But they had done what the American government wanted, according to Col. Hitchcock, who wrote in his diary, even before those first incidents:

> I have said from the first that the United States are the aggressors. ... We have not one particle of right to be here. ... It looks as if the government sent a small force on purpose to bring on a war, so as to have a pretext for taking California and as much of this country as it chooses. ... My heart is not in this business ... but, as a military man, I am bound to execute orders.

On May 9, before news of any battles, Polk was suggesting to his cabinet a declaration of war. Polk recorded in his diary what he said to the cabinet meeting:

> I stated ... that up to this time, as we knew, we had heard of no open act of aggression by the Mexican army, but that the danger was imminent that such acts would be committed. I said that in my opinion we had ample cause of war, and that it was impossible ... that I could remain silent much longer ... that the country was excited and impatient on the subject.

The country was not "excited and impatient." But the president was. When the dispatches arrived from Gen. Taylor telling of casualties from the Mexican attack, Polk summoned the cabinet to hear the news, and they unanimously agreed he should ask for a declaration of war. Polk's message to Congress was indignant: "Mexico has passed the boundary of the United States, has invaded our territory and shed American blood upon the American soil."

Congress then rushed to approve the war message. The bundles of official documents accompanying the war message, supposed to be evidence for Polk's statement, were not examined, but were tabled immediately by the House. Debate on the bill providing volunteers and money for the war was limited to two hours, and most of this was used up reading selected portions of the tabled documents, so that barely half an hour was left for discussion of the issues.

The Whig party also wanted California, but preferred to do it without war. Nevertheless, they would not deny men and money for the operation and so joined Democrats in voting overwhelmingly for the war resolution, 174 to 14. In the Senate there was debate, but it was limited to one day, and the war measure passed, 40 to 2, Whigs joining Democrats. John Quincy Adams of Massachusetts, who originally voted with "the stubborn 14," later voted for war appropriations.

Abraham Lincoln of Illinois was not yet in Congress when the war began, but after his election in 1846 he had occasion to vote and speak on the war. His "spot resolutions" became famous — he challenged Polk to specify the exact spot where American blood was shed "on the American soil." But he would not try to end the war by stopping funds for men and supplies. Speaking in the House on July 27, 1848, he said:

> If to say "the war was unnecessarily and unconstitutionally commenced by the president" be opposing the war, then the Whigs have very generally opposed it. ... The marching an army into the midst of a peaceful Mexican settlement, frightening the inhabitants away, leaving their growing crops and other property to destruction, to you may appear a perfectly amiable, peaceful, unprovoking procedure; but it does not appear so to us. ... But if, when the war had begun, and had become the cause of the country, the giving of our money and our blood, in common with yours, was support of the war, then it is not true that we have always opposed the war. With few individual exceptions, you have constantly had our votes here for all the necessary supplies.

A handful of antislavery Congressmen voted against all war measures, seeing the Mexican campaign as a means of extending the southern slave territory. One of these was Joshua Giddings of Ohio, a fiery speaker, physically powerful, who called it "an aggressive, unholy, and unjust war."

After Congress acted in May 1846, there were rallies and demonstrations for the war in New York, Baltimore, Indianapolis, Philadelphia, and many other places. Thousands rushed to volunteer for the army. The poet

Presidential candidate Gen. Zachary Taylor sits atop a mound of skulls in this 1848 cartoon criticizing his role in the U.S. war against Mexico.

Walt Whitman wrote in the *Brooklyn Eagle* in the early days of the war: "Yes: Mexico must be thoroughly chastised! … Let our arms now be carried with a spirit which shall teach the world that, while we are not forward for a quarrel, America knows how to crush, as well as how to expand!"

Accompanying all this aggressiveness was the idea that the United States would be giving the blessings of liberty and democracy to more people. This was intermingled with ideas of racial superiority, longings for the beautiful lands of New Mexico and California, and thoughts of commercial enterprise across the Pacific. The *New York Herald* said, in 1847: "The universal Yankee nation can regenerate and disenthrall the people of Mexico in a few years; and we believe it is part of our destiny to civilize that beautiful country."

The *Congressional Globe* of Feb. 11, 1847, reported:

Mr. Giles, of Maryland — I take it for granted, that we shall gain territory, and must gain territory, before we shut the gates of the temple of Janus. … We must march from ocean to ocean. … We must march from Texas straight to the Pacific ocean, and be bounded only by its roaring wave. … It is the destiny of the white race, it is the destiny of the Anglo-Saxon race.

Anti-War Sentiment

The American Anti-Slavery Society, on the other hand, said the war was "waged solely for the detestable and horrible purpose of extending and perpetuating American slavery throughout the vast territory of

Mexico." A 27-year-old Boston poet and abolitionist, James Russell Lowell, began writing satirical poems in the *Boston Courier* (they were later collected as the *Biglow Papers*). In them, a New England farmer, Hosea Biglow, spoke, in his own dialect, on the war:

> Ez fer war, I call it murder —
> — There you hev it plain an' flat;
> I don't want to go no furder
> — Than my Testyment fer that. ...
>
> They jest want this Californy
> — So's to lug new slave-states in
> To abuse ye, an' to scorn ye,
> ⸺ An' to plunder ye like sin.

The war had barely begun the summer of 1846, when a writer, Henry David Thoreau, who lived in Concord, Mass., refused to pay his Massachusetts poll tax, denouncing the Mexican war. He was put in jail and spent one night there. His friends, without his consent, paid his tax, and he was released. Two years later, he gave a lecture, "Resistance to Civil Government," which was then printed as an essay, "Civil Disobedience."

> It is not desirable to cultivate a respect for the law so much as for the right. ... Law never made men a whit more just; and, by means of their respect for it, even the well-disposed are daily made the agents of injustice. A common and natural result of an undue respect for law is, that you may see a file of soldiers ... marching in admirable order over hill and dale to the wars, against their wills, ay, against their common sense and consciences, which makes it very steep marching indeed, and produces a palpitation of the heart.

His friend and fellow writer Ralph Waldo Emerson agreed, but thought it futile to protest. When Emerson visited Thoreau in jail and asked, "What are you doing in there?" it was reported that Thoreau replied, "What are you doing out there?"

The churches, for the most part, were either outspokenly for the war or timidly silent. The Rev. Theodore Parker, a Unitarian minister in Boston, combined eloquent criticism of the war with contempt for the Mexican people, whom he called "a wretched people; wretched in their origin, history and character," who must eventually give way as the Indians did. Yes, the United States should expand, he said, but not by war, rather by the power of her ideas, the pressure of her commerce, by "the steady advance of a superior race, with superior ideas and a better civilization."

The racism of Parker was widespread. Congressman Delano of Ohio, an antislavery Whig, opposed the war because he was afraid of Americans mingling with an inferior people who "embrace all shades of color ... a sad compound of Spanish, English, Indian, and negro bloods ... and resulting, it is said, in the production of a slothful, ignorant race of beings."

 s the war went on, opposition grew. The American Peace Society printed a newspaper, the *Advocate of Peace,* which published poems, speeches, petitions, sermons against the war, and eyewitness accounts of the degradation of army life and the horrors of battle. Considering the strenuous efforts of the nation's leaders to build patriotic support, the amount of open dissent and criticism was remarkable. Antiwar meetings took place in spite of attacks by patriotic mobs.

As the army moved closer to Mexico City, the antislavery newspaper *The Liberator* daringly declared its wishes for the defeat of the American forces: "Every lover of Freedom and humanity, throughout the world, must wish them [the Mexicans] the most triumphant success."

Frederick Douglass, a former slave and an extraordinary speaker and writer, wrote in his Rochester newspaper, the *North Star,* Jan. 21, 1848, of "the present disgraceful, cruel, and iniquitous war with our sister republic. Mexico seems a doomed victim to Anglo Saxon cupidity and love of dominion." Douglass was scornful of the unwillingness of opponents of the war to take real action (even the abolitionists kept paying their taxes):

> No politician of any considerable distinction or eminence seems willing to hazard his popularity with his party ... by an open and unqualified disapprobation of the war. None seem willing to take their stand for peace at all risks; and all seem willing that the war should be carried on, in some form or other.

Where was popular opinion? It is hard to say. After the first rush, enlistments began to dwindle. Historians of the Mexican war have talked easily about "the people" and "public opinion." Their evidence, however, is not from "the people" but from the newspapers, claiming to be the voice of the people. The *New York Herald* wrote in August 1845: "The multitude cry aloud for war." The *New York Morning News* said "young and ardent spirits that throng the cities ... want but a direction to their restless energies, and their attention is already fixed on Mexico."

It is impossible to know the extent of popular support of the war. But there is evidence that many organized workingmen opposed the war. There were demonstrations of Irish workers in New York, Boston, and Lowell against the annexation of Texas. In May, when the war against Mexico began, New York workingmen called a meeting to oppose the war, and many Irish workers came. The meeting called the war a plot by slave owners and asked for the withdrawal of American troops from disputed territory. That year, a convention of the New England Workingmen's Association condemned the war and announced they would "not take up arms to sustain the Southern slaveholder in robbing one fifth of our countrymen of their labor."

Some newspapers, at the very start of the war, protested. Horace Greeley wrote in the *New York Tribune,* May 12, 1846:

> We can easily defeat the armies of Mexico, slaughter them by thousands. ... Who believes that a score of victories over Mexico, the "annexation" of half her provinces, will give us more Liberty, a purer Morality, a more prosperous Industry, than we now have? ... Is not Life miserable enough, comes not Death soon enough, without resort to the hideous enginery of War?

The Recruits

What of those who fought the war — the soldiers who marched, sweated, got sick, died? The Mexican soldiers. The American soldiers. We know little of the reactions of Mexican soldiers. We know much more about the American army — volunteers, not conscripts, lured by money and opportunity for social advancement via promotion in the armed forces. Half of Gen. Taylor's army were recent immigrants — Irish and German mostly. Their patriotism was not very strong. Indeed, many of them deserted to the Mexican side, enticed by money. Some enlisted in the Mexican army and formed their own battalion, the San Patricio (St. Patrick's) Battalion.

At first there seemed to be enthusiasm in the army, fired by pay and patriotism. Martial spirit was high in New York, where the legislature authorized the governor to call 50,000 volunteers. Placards read "Mexico or Death." There was a mass meeting of 20,000 people in Philadelphia. Three thousand volunteered in Ohio.

This initial spirit soon wore off. One young man wrote anonymously to the *Cambridge Chronicle:*

> Neither have I the least idea of "joining" you, or in any way assisting the unjust war waging against Mexico. I have no wish to participate in such "glorious" butcheries of women and children as were displayed in the capture of Monterey, etc. Neither have I any desire to place myself under the dictation of a petty military tyrant, to every caprice of whose will I must yield implicit obedience. No sir-ee! ... Human butchery has had its day. ... And the time is rapidly approaching when the professional soldier will be placed on the same level as a bandit, the Bedouin, and the Thug.

There were extravagant promises and outright lies to build up the volunteer units. A man who wrote a history of the New York Volunteers declared: "Many enlisted for the sake of their families, having no employment, and having been offered 'three months' advance,' and were promised that they could leave part of their pay for their families to draw in their absence. ... I boldly pronounce, that the whole Regiment was got up by fraud."

By late 1846, recruitment was falling off, so physical requirements were lowered, and anyone bringing in acceptable recruits would get $2 a head. Even this didn't work. Congress in early 1847 authorized 10 new regiments of regulars, to serve for the duration of the war, promising them 100 acres of public land upon honorable discharge. But dissatisfaction continued.

The romance of the recruiting posters was quickly forgotten.

The Reality of Battle

And soon, the reality of battle came in upon the glory and the promises. On the Rio Grande before Matamoros, as a Mexican army of 5,000 under Gen. Arista faced Taylor's army of 3,000, the shells began to fly, and artilleryman Samuel French saw his first death in battle. John Weems describes it: "He happened to be staring at a man on horseback nearby when he saw a shot rip off the pommel of the saddle, tear through the man's body, and burst out with a crimson gush on the other side."

When the battle was over, 500 Mexicans were dead or wounded. There were perhaps 50 American casualties. Weems describes the aftermath: "Night blanketed weary men who fell asleep where they dropped on the trampled prairie grass, while around them other prostrate men from both armies screamed and groaned in agony from wounds. By the eerie light of torches the surgeon's saw was going the livelong night."

Away from the battlefield, in army camps, the romance of the recruiting posters was quickly forgotten. The Second Regiment of Mississippi Rifles, moving into New Orleans, was stricken by cold and sickness. The regimental surgeon reported: "Six months after our regiment had entered the service we had sustained a loss of 167 by death, and 134 by discharges." The regiment was packed into the holds of transports, 800 men into three ships. The surgeon continued:

> The dark cloud of disease still hovered over us. The holds of the ships ... were soon crowded with the sick. The effluvia was intolerable. ... The sea became rough. ... Through the long dark night the rolling ship would dash the sick man from side to side bruising his flesh upon the rough corners of his berth. The wild screams of the delirious, the lamentations of the sick, and the melancholy groans of the dying, kept up one continual

scene of confusion. ... Four weeks we were confined to the loathsome ships and before we had landed at the Brasos, we consigned 28 of our men to the dark waves.

Meanwhile, by land and by sea, Anglo-American forces were moving into California. A young naval officer, after the long voyage around the southern cape of South America, and up the coast to Monterey in California, wrote in his diary:

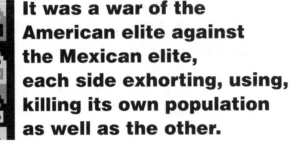

It was a war of the American elite against the Mexican elite, each side exhorting, using, killing its own population as well as the other.

Asia ... will be brought to our very doors. Population will flow into the fertile regions of California. The resources of the entire country ... will be developed. ... The public lands lying along the route [of railroads] will be changed from deserts into gardens, and a large population will be settled.

It was a separate war that went on in California, where Anglo-Americans raided Spanish settlements, stole horses, and declared California separated from Mexico — the "Bear Flag Republic." Indians lived there, and naval officer Revere gathered the Indian chiefs and spoke to them (as he later recalled):

I have called you together to have a talk with you. The country you inhabit no longer belongs to Mexico, but to a mighty nation whose territory extends from the great ocean you have all seen or heard of, to another great ocean thousands of miles toward the rising sun. ... Our armies are now in Mexico, and will soon conquer the whole country. But you have nothing to fear from us, if you do what is right ... if you are faithful to your new rulers. ... I hope you will alter your habits, and be industrious and frugal, and give up all the low vices which you practice. ... We shall watch over you, and give you true liberty; but beware of sedition, lawlessness, and all other crimes, for the army which shields can assuredly punish, and it will reach you in your most retired hiding places.

Gen. Stephen Kearny moved easily into New Mexico, and Santa Fe was taken without battle. An American staff officer described the reaction of the Mexican population to the U.S. army's entrance into the capital city:

Our march into the city ... was extremely warlike, with drawn sabers, and daggers in every look. ... As the American flag was raised, and the cannon boomed its glorious national salute from the hill, the pent-up emotion of many of the women could be suppressed no longer ... as the wail of grief arose above the din of our horses' tread, and reached our ears from the depth of the gloomy-looking buildings on every hand.

That was in August. In December, Mexicans in Taos, New Mexico, rebelled against American rule. The revolt was put down and arrests were made. But many of the rebels fled and carried on sporadic attacks, killing a number of Americans, then hiding in the mountains. The American army pursued, and in a final desperate battle, in which 600 to 700 rebels were engaged, 150 were killed, and it seemed the rebellion was now over.

In Los Angeles, too, there was a revolt. Mexicans forced the American garrison there to surrender in September 1846. The United States did not retake Los Angeles until January, after a bloody battle.

Gen. Taylor had moved across the Rio Grande, occupied Matamoros, and now moved southward through Mexico. But his volunteers became more unruly on Mexican territory. Mexican villages were pillaged by drunken troops. Cases of rape began to multiply.

As the soldiers moved up the Rio Grande to Camargo, the heat became unbearable, the water impure, and sickness grew — diarrhea, dysentery, and other maladies — until a thousand were dead. At first the dead were buried to the sounds of the "Dead March" played by a military band. Then the number of dead was too great, and formal military funerals ceased. Southward to Monterey and another battle, where men and horses died in agony, and one officer described the ground as "slippery with ... foam and blood."

The U.S. Navy bombarded Vera Cruz in an indiscriminate killing of civilians. One of the Navy's shells hit the post office, another a surgical hospital. In two days, 1,300 shells were fired into the city, until it surrendered. A reporter for the *New Orleans Delta* wrote: "The Mexicans variously estimate their loss at from 500 to 1000 killed and wounded, but all agree that the loss among the soldiery is comparatively small and the destruction among the women and children is very great."

Col. Hitchcock, coming into the city, wrote: "I shall never forget the horrible fire of our mortars ... going with dreadful certainty ... often in the centre of private dwellings — it was awful. I shudder to think of it." Still, Hitchcock, the dutiful soldier, wrote for Gen. Scott "a sort of address to the Mexican people" which was then printed in English and Spanish by the tens of thousands saying "we have not a particle of ill-will towards you ...

we are here for no earthly purpose except the hope of obtaining a peace."

It was a war of the American elite against the Mexican elite, each side exhorting, using, killing its own population as well as the other. The Mexican commander Santa Anna had crushed rebellion after rebellion, his troops also raping and plundering after victory. When Col. Hitchcock and Gen. Winfield Scott moved into Santa Anna's estate, they found its walls full of ornate paintings. But half his army was dead or wounded.

The Battle for Mexico City

Gen. Scott moved toward the last battle — for Mexico City — with 10,000 soldiers. They were not anxious for battle. Three days' march from Mexico City, at Jalapa, seven of his 11 regiments evaporated, their enlistment times up, the reality of battle and disease too much for them.

On the outskirts of Mexico City, at Churubusco, Mexican and American armies clashed for three hours and thousands died on both sides. Among the Mexicans taken prisoner were 69 U.S. Army deserters.

As often in war, battles were fought without point. After one such engagement near Mexico City, with terrible casualties, a marine lieutenant blamed Gen. Scott: "He had originated it in error and caused it to be fought, with inadequate forces, for an object that had no existence."

In the final battle for Mexico City, Anglo-American troops took the height of Chapultepec and entered the city of 200,000 people, Gen. Santa Anna having moved northward. This was September 1847. A Mexican merchant wrote to a friend about the bombardment of the city: "In some cases whole blocks were destroyed and a great number of men, women and children killed and wounded."

Gen. Santa Anna fled to Huamantla, where another battle was fought, and he had to flee again. An American infantry lieutenant wrote to his parents what happened after an officer named Walker was killed in battle:

> Gen. Lane … told us to "avenge the death of the gallant Walker" … Grog shops were broken open first, and then, maddened with liquor, every species of outrage was committed. Old women and girls were stripped of their clothing — and many suffered still greater outrages. Men were shot by dozens … their property, churches, stores, and dwelling houses ransacked. … It made me for the first time ashamed of my country.

One Pennsylvania volunteer, stationed at Matamoros late in the war, wrote:

> We are under very strict discipline here. Some of our officers are very good men but the balance of them are very tyrannical and brutal toward the men. … [T]onight on drill an officer laid a soldier's skull open with his sword. … But the time may come and that soon when officers and men will stand on equal footing. … A soldier's life is very disgusting.

On the night of Aug. 15, 1847, volunteer regiments from Virginia, Mississippi, and North Carolina rebelled in northern Mexico against Col. Robert Treat Paine. Paine killed a mutineer, but two of his lieutenants refused to help him quell the mutiny. The rebels were ultimately exonerated in an attempt to keep the peace.

Desertion grew. In March 1847 the army reported over a thousand deserters. The total number of deserters during the war was 9,207 (5,331 regulars and 3,876 volunteers). Those who did not desert became harder and harder to manage. Gen. Cushing referred to 65 such men in the First Regiment of Massachusetts Infantry as "incorrigibly mutinous and insubordinate."

The glory of victory was for the president and the generals, not the deserters, the dead, the wounded. The Massachusetts Volunteers had started with 630 men. They came home with 300 dead, mostly from disease, and at the reception dinner on their return their commander, Gen. Cushing, was hissed by his men.

As the veterans returned home, speculators immediately showed up to buy the land warrants given by the government. Many of the soldiers, desperate for money, sold their 160 acres for less than $50.

Mexico surrendered. There were calls among Americans to take all of Mexico. The Treaty of Guadalupe Hidalgo, signed February 1848, just took half. The Texas boundary was set at the Rio Grande; New Mexico and California were ceded. The United States paid Mexico $15 million, which led the *Whig Intelligencer* to conclude that "we take nothing by conquest. … Thank God." ∎

Used by permission of Howard Zinn. This reading is excerpted from *A People's History of the United States* (teaching edition), by Howard Zinn (New York: The New Press, 1997).

BY MARTÍN ESPADA

Heart of Hunger

SMUGGLED IN BOXCARS through fields of dark morning,
tied to bundles at railroad crossings,
the brown grain of faces dissolved in bus station dim,
immigrants: mexicano, dominicano,
guatemalteco, puertorriqueño, orphans and travelers,
refused permission to use gas station toilets,
beaten for a beer in unseen towns with white porches,
or evaporated without a tombstone in the peaceful grass,
a centipede of hands moving,
hands clutching infants that grieve,
fingers to the crucifix,
hands that labor.

Long past backroads paved with solitude,
hands in the thousands reach for the crop-ground together,
the countless roots of a tree lightning-torn,
capillaries running to a heart of hunger,
tobaccopicker, grapepicker, lettucepicker.

Obscured in the towering white clouds of cities in winter,
thousands are bowing to assembly lines,
frenzied in kitchens and sweatshops,
mopping the vomit of others' children,
leaning into the iron's steam
and the steel mill glowing.

Yet there is a pilgrimage,
a history straining its arms and legs,
an inexorable striving,
shouting in Spanish
at the police of city jails
and border checkpoints,
mexicano, dominicano,
guatemalteco, puertorriqueño,
fishermen wading into the North American gloom
to pull a fierce gasping life
from the polluted current.

Martín Espada is an award-winning poet who teaches at the University of Massachusetts. This poem is from *Cantos al Sexto Sol: An Anthology of Aztlanahuac Writing,* edited by Cecilio García-Camarillo, Roberto Rodríguez, and Patrisia Gonzales (San Antonio: Wings Press, 2002).

NAFTA's Impact

The NAFTA Role Play
'Mexico-United States Free Trade Conference'

Every year, the U.S. government spends huge sums building and policing barriers between the United States and Mexico. But the intent of the North American Free Trade Agreement (NAFTA) is to pull down barriers between the United States and Mexico. The question is: Which barriers and for whom?

My students generally come into class thinking about the world in terms of nation-states. This activity asks students to consider trade issues in terms of social class, which is a more helpful way of thinking about the "free trade" debate. The role play helps students understand why NAFTA has been so popular with some groups and has been so devastating for others — and that these lines do not slice cleanly between Mexico and the United States (see pp. 21-27 for more context about the use of this role play). These activities also help students begin to see some of the economic roots of Mexican migration.

Preparation

- On the board or overhead, write: Mexico-United States Free Trade Conference, Fall 1993
- Also write the names of the seven groups in the role play, and President Bill Clinton. Note that Green Garden Corporation, Martin's jeans, and the U.S.-Mexico Environmental Justice Coalition are composite, fictionalized roles.
  - Maquiladora workers, Tijuana, Mexico
  - Green Garden Corporation executives, United States
  - Poor farmers, Chiapas, Mexico
  - Martin's jeans workers, United States
  - Prosperous farmers, northern Mexico
  - U.S.-Mexico Environmental Justice Coalition
  - USA*NAFTA Coalition, United States
  - President Bill Clinton (played by the teacher)

Materials Needed

- Copies for everyone of the student handout "Mexico-United States Free Trade Conference."
- Copies for every student of "Support the North American Free Trade Agreement," by President Bill Clinton. [Note: The handout is excerpted from a speech that President Clinton delivered at the White House on Sept. 14, 1993, when he signed NAFTA and side agreements, but before Congressional ratification. The portions in italics are added to tailor Clinton's remarks to the role play's Free Trade Conference. The other portions of the speech are his exact words. For ease of reading, I eliminated ellipses from the speech. The full speech can be found at www.multied.com/Documents/Clinton/SigningNAFTA.html.]
- Copies of roles for each of the seven groups (one role per student in each group.)
- Placards for each group in the role play, and colored markers.
- Copies of "Rethinking the NAFTA Record" for each student.

A farmer holds a handful of cedar seeds for planting and sale in Petatlán in the southwestern state of Guerrero. The Peasant Ecologists of the Petatlán Sierra struggle against deforestation — a greater threat because of the provisions of NAFTA.

Time Required

Approximately four (50-minute) class periods, with additional follow-up on NAFTA's results.

Suggested Procedure

1. Explain to the class that they'll be doing a role play about one of the most important international agreements in recent years, the North American Free Trade Agreement. Distribute copies of "Mexico–United States Free Trade Conference."

    Read aloud and discuss with students the issues that they'll be dealing with in the role play. See pp. 22-23 for more information on NAFTA's Chapter 11 provision and Article 27. (Note that Article 27 was actually amended about a year prior to the NAFTA debate, but its change was part of the Mexican government's embrace of "free trade" and is seen in Mexico as part of the NAFTA process. Thus I folded this issue into the role play.)

2. After students seem to grasp the gist of the issues they'll be dealing with in the role play, count the class off into seven groups and distribute roles to each group. Students will learn more about these issues from reading information in their roles, so they needn't master these before moving into their groups. (Note that everyone in a group receives the same role.) Ask students to read their roles carefully and to highlight parts that they think are important and give clues to how they might feel about the various issues in the Free Trade Conference.

3. Once students have finished reading their roles, ask them each to write an interior monologue from the point of view of a member of their group. An interior monologue is simply the inner thoughts of an individual at a particular point in time, so they should be sure to write in the first person. Encourage students to invent a persona — they might give themselves a name, a family, a history — and to explore some events or experiences that have shaped them. Ask them to think about their hopes or fears, especially related to the changes proposed in the Free Trade Conference. To help prompt students' imaginations, you might read to them excerpts from Franklin High School student Molly McCullough's interior monologue from the point of view of a Green Garden executive:

    > I grew up in a well-to-do family in Albany, Ore., and attended Oregon State University, where I earned a master's degree in agricultural science. Immediately after graduating, I was offered an internship at Green Garden Foods in the Tacoma/Seattle area, and began to work my way up the corporate ladder. The rest is history. I am proud to be a member of the Green Garden team, where "we're passionate about making vegetables an inspiration on your plate and in your life."

    > … Sometimes, though, late at night when I can't sleep, a sickening feeling of guilt creeps over me. I wonder how the Mexican farmworkers (many with large families) can possibly survive on $4 a day. That amount wouldn't even cover my morning Starbucks habit. But they have to provide food and clothes and shelter for their whole family for the price of my daily Caramel Macchiato. But at least they have jobs.

    Allow students about 10 to 15 minutes to write. Note that students should write these individually, not as a group.

4. After students have completed writing their interior monologues, have them read these aloud to other students in their group.

5. Ask students to work in their small groups to come up with tentative answers to the five questions posed on the "Mexico–United States Free Trade Conference" handout. Reassure them that they will be more familiar with some issues than with others, and that they will have a chance to meet with and hear from other groups later on in the role play. You should circulate and help students think through their tentative positions on various issues.

6. Ask students to choose half their group to be "traveling negotiators," and to decide which other groups would be likely to be most receptive to building alliances around any of the issues before the Free Trade Conference. So, for example, the prosperous farmers might want to get together with Green Garden executives and see what they have in common. Encourage students to be open to alternatives and also to remember that each group has information in

their role that no one else has. The "dealing" session is an opportunity to share that information with other groups that don't have it.

7. Begin the negotiation session. Be sure to tell travelers that they may meet only with other seated groups and not with other travelers. (This prevents travelers from clumping up and leaving other students out of the role play.) Travelers may circulate separately or together. If you are pressed for time, one way to speed things up a bit is to ask students in each group to concentrate their negotiating on the one issue that they feel most strongly about. The dealing session should provide students with enough time to talk with other groups about key issues, but not exhaust them and undercut enthusiasm for the large-group conference to come.

8. After students have completed meeting other groups and building alliances on the five issues, they should return to their own group and prepare arguments for the whole-class Free Trade Conference. These needn't be formal presentations, but each student should have written notes on the group's stance on every issue and the reasons for those positions.

9. Convene the class into a large circle (if possible) with students seated with their group. Their name placards should be visible.

10. Distribute Clinton's speech, "Support the North American Free Trade Agreement." As President Clinton, welcome everyone to the Free Trade Conference. Indicate that you'd like to share with them some opening remarks, and that they can follow along as you read. At the speech's conclusion, ask if anyone has any questions or comments. For some groups, Clinton's glib embrace of the "new world economy" may generate disagreement, but keep Clinton's Q & A session brief, because you don't want to drain energy from the Free Trade Conference.

11. There is no "right way" to proceed with the conference and I've handled it differently with different classes. Generally, I prefer a relatively informal process, where we move issue by issue with students offering comments in support or opposition and proposing alternatives, but not in the form of actual resolutions. Because students have such different information in the roles, I encourage them to ground their opinions about the five issues in details about their lives, and how a particular change might affect them. This makes for richer, more concrete exchanges in class. I always ask for a show of hands on various issues but I tell students that these votes are merely advisory, and that I (President Clinton) will make the final determination on the nature of the North American Free Trade Agreement before submitting it to Congress for approval.

Role Play Follow-Up

12. It's important that students have an opportunity to pull away from their roles at the conclusion of the role play. You might ask students to write on what they think will happen to each of the various groups in the role play if NAFTA passes. Ask them to share these with a partner, and then list responses on the board or overhead. Some questions that could be discussed or written about include:

   - How is NAFTA likely to affect the poor in Mexico?
   - How is NAFTA likely to affect the environment?
   - Which groups are likely to benefit from NAFTA?
   - Will NAFTA tend to create jobs in the United States or eliminate them?
   - How is NAFTA likely to affect the number of Mexicans immigrating to the United States?
   - How would you respond if someone asked you whether Mexico (or the United States) benefited from NAFTA?
   - How do you think NAFTA has affected or might affect you personally?
   - On the day that NAFTA took effect, Jan. 1, 1994, the Zapatistas, an armed group made up largely of poor and indigenous farmers in the Mexican state of Chiapas, launched a rebellion against the Mexican government. Why might they have chosen that date to begin their uprising?
   - Make a list of what you think would be likely to increase or grow as a result of NAFTA.

13. After students have completed the list, distribute copies of "Rethinking the NAFTA Record"

adapted from Sarah Anderson and John Cavanagh (see p. 77). Have students look at the first page of this handout but ask them not to look at the second page yet. Compare students' predictions with the post-NAFTA results. Note that according to the handout, total trade between NAFTA partners more than doubled between 1993 and 2002. Direct investment in Mexico increased almost five times, from $4.4 billion in 1993 to $21 billion in 2001. Exports from Mexico more than doubled, from $49.4 billion in 1994 to $138.1 billion in 2003. And even though it peaked in 2000 and then declined, overall maquiladora employment increased from 550,000 in 1994 to 1.07 million in 2004. Ask students which other increases they predicted.

Some additional increases were suggested by NAFTA supporters in a Council on Foreign Relations-sponsored forum on NAFTA's 10th anniversary: NAFTA has led to increased "efficiencies," predictability, mobility, and freedom for corporations; exports and imports account for a larger share of the Mexican gross national product than before NAFTA; Mexico now exports more to the United States than all of the rest of Latin America combined; agricultural exports have gone up 100 percent since NAFTA; and NAFTA has enhanced "global efficiency," according to former U.S. trade representative and chief NAFTA negotiator Carla Hills, who bluntly explained, "Mexico has a labor surplus, and it does repetitive work at an efficient rate."

14. After discussing the indicators on the first page of "Rethinking the NAFTA Record" ask students: What are some other measurements we might use to determine how NAFTA has affected people's lives here and in Mexico? Encourage them to think about the different social groups in the role play and ways NAFTA might affect them. Based on the role play, students might suggest categories like wages, poverty, pollution, inequality, land ownership, farm employment, immigration, insecurity, and unionization. List student suggestions on the board or overhead and then continue to review "Rethinking the NAFTA Record." Some questions you might raise based on information included in the student handouts:

- Why would real wages in Mexico drop by 9 percent between 1994 and 2003 if investment and employment both increased?
- By 2004, the U.S. Department of Labor had certified that over 524,000 U.S. workers lost their jobs as a result of NAFTA. The Washington-based Economic Policy Institute estimated the figure to be closer to 880,000. Why would NAFTA negatively affect at least some U.S. workers?
- In addition to job losses, how else might NAFTA affect U.S. workers? (As mentioned in one of the Free Trade Conference roles, even the awareness that a plant might move to Mexico can discourage organizing and make people more fearful.)
- Since NAFTA took effect in 1994, poverty in Mexican rural areas has increased. What role might NAFTA have played in creating more rural poverty in Mexico?
- A 2000 Tufts University study ("Trade Liberalization and Industrial Pollution in Mexico") found that air pollution from manufacturing in Mexico increased since NAFTA. Why? Promoters of NAFTA and globalization say that as a poor country attracts more foreign investment it will spend more on environmental protection. Why might this not be true?

Obviously, there are other factors at work besides NAFTA in explaining economic and social changes. As one report from the International Relations Center put it, "NAFTA is a moment in a wider policy process in which the Mexican government has increasingly prioritized the needs of some of its citizens over others." Thus, to make NAFTA the sole cause of any particular social or economic change would be misleading. Still, NAFTA is important, and is also emblematic of broader changes going on in both Mexico and the United States.

15. You may want to follow the role play with additional articles on NAFTA's effects, such as "After NAFTA: Mexico, a Ship on Fire," p. 79. Other articles and the research handout that Sandra Childs and I used to help students debrief the role play can be found at www. rethinkingschools.org/mexico. Also, I recommend showing at least part of the Bill Moyers documentary *Trading Democracy,* about NAFTA's Chapter 11 provisions that allow corporations to sue governments in NAFTA tribunals. The segment on the Metalclad corporation's toxic waste dump in San Luis Potosí, Mexico, is an especially effective portrait of Chapter 11 in action. The documentary is described in Resources (see p. 140).

Mexico-United States Free Trade Conference

Spring 1993: You have been invited to a gathering of individuals and organizations to discuss the proposed North American Free Trade Agreement (NAFTA) and related issues. Here are the issues about which each group will need to make at least one specific proposal:

1. President Bill Clinton has worked for a system that some people call "free trade." The idea is that countries would do away with tariffs (taxes on imports) and any laws that treat the products or industries of one country differently than the products and industries of another country. **Do you support getting rid of tariffs on all products traded between Mexico and the United States, including food crops like corn and beans, as well as the elimination of restrictions on investment? If not, what's your alternative?**

2. The Mexican Constitution grew out of the Mexican Revolution, early in the 20th century. One part of the Constitution, Article 27, is especially important. It limits the amount of land that any one landholder can own. It promises poor people that they can take over and occupy unused government land and use it to farm, or they can occupy land of wealthy landholders and farm it. Article 27 establishes a system of *ejidos* [pronounced eh-HEE-dohs]. Ejidos are communities where people own the land in common and it can never be sold or taken. Article 27 also says that foreigners cannot own land in Mexico. **Do you approve of Mexico eliminating these parts of Article 27 from its Constitution to provide more investment freedom in Mexico and end the ejido form of collective ownership of land? If not, what's your alternative?**

3. NAFTA has an important provision called Chapter 11. Chapter 11 would allow a company from Mexico, the United States, or Canada to sue the government of another one of these countries if any law were passed that hurt the investment of that company. **Do you support Chapter 11 of NAFTA? If not, what's your alternative?**

4. As written, NAFTA says very little about labor or environmental conditions in any of the three member countries. **What guarantees, if any, should there be that corporations do not move from country to country simply to exploit cheap labor and/or to take advantage of lower environmental standards?**

5. As it stands now, NAFTA encourages and protects the free movement of capital and goods from country to country but not the free movement of people. With NAFTA, countries can restrict immigration in any manner that they choose. **Should NAFTA be limited to the free movement of capital and goods, or should the movement of people from country to country also be included in this agreement? If so, in what way?**

 **President Bill Clinton**

Support the North American Free Trade Agreement

I'*m here to ask all of you to support the North American Free Trade Agreement — NAFTA. Free trade will make us all more prosperous.* NAFTA means jobs, American jobs and good-paying American jobs. *But NAFTA doesn't mean jobs and prosperity for just Americans, it means it for Mexicans and Canadians, too.*

NAFTA will expand trade, and when trade grows, jobs are created. Look at the history. Global trade grew from $200 billion in 1950 to $800 billion in 1980. As a result, jobs were created and opportunity thrived all across the world.

I want to say to my fellow Americans here, when you live in a time of change the only way to recover your security and to broaden your horizons is to adapt to the change, to embrace it, to move forward. *Today* factories or information can flash across the world, and people can move money around in the blink of an eye.

This debate about NAFTA is a debate about whether we will embrace these changes and create the jobs of tomorrow, or try to resist these changes, hoping we can preserve the economic structures of yesterday.

NAFTA will create 200,000 American jobs in the first two years of its effect. NAFTA will create a million jobs in the first five years of its impact. I believe that that is many more jobs than will be lost, as inevitably some will be, as always happens when you open up the mix to new competition.

NAFTA will generate jobs by fostering an export boom to Mexico, by tearing down tariff walls. *Why focus on Mexico?* The average Mexican citizen is now spending $450 per year per person to buy American goods. That is more than the average Japanese, the average German, or the average Canadian buys; more than the average German, Swiss, and Italian citizens put together.

In 1987, Mexico exported $5.7 billion more of products to the United States than they purchased from us. We had a trade deficit. *But with the new free trade policies of the Mexican government, supported by my friend, President Carlos Salinas,* that $5.7 billion trade deficit has been turned into a $5.4 billion trade surplus for the United States. It has created hundreds of thousands of jobs.

When Mexico boosts its consumption of *U.S. products, it means more American jobs — whether in Louisiana or Illinois. But when there is more trade between Mexico and the United States, it also means more jobs in Chiapas and Guanajuato.*

Many Americans are still worried that this agreement will move jobs south of the border because they've seen jobs move south of the border and because they know that there are still great differences in the wage rates *between the United States and Mexico. But* businesses do not choose to locate based solely on wages. If they did, Haiti and Bangladesh would have the largest number of manufacturing jobs in the world. Businesses choose to locate based on the skills and productivity of the work force, the attitude of the government, the roads and railroads, a market close enough to make the transportation costs meaningful, the communications networks. That is our strength, and it will continue to be our strength. As it becomes Mexico's strength and they generate more jobs, they will have higher incomes, and they will buy more American products. *We all benefit from free trade.*

My friends, are we going to compete and win, or are we going to withdraw and give in to our fears *and insecurities that NAFTA will hurt our jobs or our environment?*

We have to create a new world economy. If we walk away from this, we have no right to say to other countries in the world, "You're not fulfilling your world leadership; you're not being fair with us." This is our opportunity to provide an impetus to freedom and democracy in Latin America and create new jobs for America as well. It's a good deal, and we ought to take it.

Thank you.

Maquiladora worker, Tijuana, Mexico

You live in an area of Tijuana called Chilpancingo [CHEEL-pahn-SING-go]. You work in a small U.S.-owned factory, or maquiladora, that manufactures big books of fabric, tile, or flooring samples that are used in department stores in the United States. In some ways, it's not a bad job. You get to do a lot of different things, from cutting materials to gluing — and compared to some places that you've worked, it's pretty relaxed. Still, the pay is very low. If for some reason you don't make your production quota in a week, or you have to take a day off because your child is sick, you can end up making as little as the minimum wage: about $4.50 a day. Some weeks, you'll make more than that, but in the whole time you've worked at this maquiladora, you've never made more than $9 in a day. Someone once told you that this company used to be located in Costa Mesa, Calif., and that most of the workers there made $13 an hour.

Some people may think that money goes far in Mexico, but in Tijuana, prices are pretty high. In fact, people who can get permission to cross into the United States do their shopping in San Ysidro, Calif., because most prices are lower than in Mexico and quality is better. Rents in your neighborhood are also not cheap.

The talk these days is about a new treaty between the United States and Mexico: the North American Free Trade Agreement (NAFTA). From what you've heard, this would mean many more maquiladoras in Tijuana. Mexico's President Carlos Salinas and U.S. President Bill Clinton say that this would mean more jobs for everyone, and higher wages and better lives. If that were true, it would be great. Yes, more factories in Tijuana would mean more jobs and more choices of places to work. But would these be better jobs? Would they be higher-paying jobs? Would NAFTA mean that you could join an independent union, one that's not government-controlled? Or do companies want to come to Tijuana just to take advantage of low wages? Will NAFTA mean that you can travel more freely? Will NAFTA mean that you can go to the United States to look for an even higher-paying job? That's what you'd really like. You've heard that in the United States you make as much in an *hour* as you can make in a *day* in Tijuana. Now, if Mexicans want to go to the United States, they have to sneak in. It's dangerous and they're treated like criminals.

Something that really bothers you is that the maquiladoras have made Chilpancingo a very dangerous place to live. The factories often dump poisons into the streams that run through your community. These poisons end up in the river, the Río Alamar, which used to be clean and have fish in it, but is now filled with garbage and chemicals. For example, there is a company that makes fire extinguishers for export to the United States, and when the company paints these they just dump the red paint into the streams. What will NAFTA do to clean up Chilpancingo and to stop companies from polluting your neighborhood? Will more factories mean more pollution?

You're not necessarily opposed to NAFTA, but you have a lot of questions about this new treaty.

◆ Green Garden Corporation executive, United States ◆

You are executives with Green Garden, a major United States-based frozen food company. This is an exciting time in the frozen food business. Once upon a time, if people in the United States wanted broccoli or cauliflower or carrots, they had to wait until these were in season. Now, thanks to you, they can get them all year round. That is, thanks to you *and* farmers in Mexico — and, of course, free trade.

Years ago, the Mexican government had so many restrictions that you couldn't invest freely, and you couldn't import produce freely back into the United States. But with the coming of free trade pushed by the U.S. and Mexican governments, you can now invest wherever you want, whenever you want. It's true, there are still some annoying and needless restrictions, like Article 27 of the Mexican Constitution, which limits how much land a farmer can own and restricts ownership of land by foreigners like you. But now that the Mexican government is pushing the North American Free Trade Agreement (NAFTA), it's also working to get rid of most of Article 27.

Here's how your business works these days. You go to Mexico and set up agricultural processing centers. You contract with big Mexican growers to supply you with vegetables. You supply them the seeds, fertilizer, and pesticides (which they pay for) and then you wait for them to bring you the fresh vegetables for processing. You pay them based on the quality of what they bring you. If these don't meet your standards, you don't pay them anything. You don't actually *own* any farms yourself, so the Mexican farmers are the ones taking all the risk. If a hailstorm destroys the crops, or a blight hits, it's the farmers who are out the money, not you. But it's a great deal for them too because they're making more per acre of land than ever before. Free trade is win-win.

A lot of the smaller Mexican farmers who don't own much land complain that you don't deal with them, only with the big farmers. Well, they're right, you do only want to deal with the big farmers. But it's not that you have anything against the small farmers. It just makes life easier for you if you contract with only a few farmers who own lots and lots of land, rather than with hundreds of farmers who may farm only a few acres each. It's simply more efficient. This is another reason why you hope Article 27 will be changed, because it means that more of the land will be in the hands of larger farmers, which makes your life simpler. Sure, the small farmers lose out, but that's one of the costs of free trade. Only the strong survive. But in the long run, everyone benefits. And besides, it's not like the smaller farmers are going to starve. They can always go to work for the larger Mexican farmers, weeding, spraying pesticides, and picking crops. And you'll hire some of them, too, to work in your packing plants, or as truck drivers or security guards.

One more thing. It may sound hard-hearted, but NAFTA is about freedom for corporations to move their capital and products across borders, not for individuals to move across borders. There are a bunch of reasons that it would not be smart to just open the borders for Mexican immigrants to flood into the United States. But you have one reason that is admittedly self-interested: If anyone who wanted to come to the United States could simply leave Mexico, then that would lead to a shortage of labor in Mexico. The minimum wage in Mexico is about $4 a day. Who wants to work for that when they could make maybe 10 times that in a day in the United States? One of the main reasons you benefit from the arrangement with Mexico is that labor there is very cheap; low farmworker wages keep the big farmers' costs down, which keeps your costs down, which keeps your profits high. But, again, this is a good thing for everyone: Lots of food gets produced; there are cheap prices for food and jobs for Mexicans and Americans alike.

Finally, NAFTA has a very important provision: Chapter 11. This provision protects companies like yours. For the first time ever, it gives companies the right to sue governments if they pass laws or take any steps that could unfairly limit your ability to make a profit. Suppose, for example, that you invested in land where you planned to put a pesticide factory for farmers you contract with, and then the Mexican government passed a regulation claiming that the factory would hurt the environment and people's health. If you thought this was unfair, instead of suing in a Mexican court, you could sue the Mexican government before a special NAFTA court.

 **Poor farmer, Chiapas, Mexico**

Life is incredibly hard for poor farmers like you in southern Mexico. And if this North American Free Trade Agreement (NAFTA) thing passes, life will only get harder.

Just a few words about where you live. The state of Chiapas is the southernmost state in the country, right next to Guatemala. In many respects, Chiapas is a rich area. Chiapas's powerful rivers provide Mexico with a majority of the country's hydroelectric power. The state has timber, cattle, oil, sugar, and coffee. Chiapas has only 3 percent of the Mexican people, but grows 13 percent of Mexico's corn. But its people are the poorest in Mexico. Fewer than half of all the people of Chiapas have running water. One of every three people has no electricity. Four of every 10 people make less than the minimum wage in southern Mexico of $3 a day. And most people in Chiapas still have dirt floors.

But at least poor farmers in Chiapas always had hope. The Mexican Constitution, under Article 27, promised poor farmers land. In the 1930s, President Lázaro Cárdenas distributed thousands of acres to poor farmers in Chiapas — a total of 45 million acres throughout Mexico in just five years. Cárdenas took idle land from the rich and gave it to the poor. As called for by the Constitution, the land was distributed collectively, which meant that it could not be bought or sold, but could be passed on to future generations to continue farming. To you, this was what Emiliano Zapata and the Mexican Revolution was all about: land to the poor.

In the years since President Cárdenas, Mexican governments often dragged their feet on land reform and supported the rich against the poor. But still, governments always at least *claimed* that they wanted to live up to the promises of the Mexican Revolution. But no more. Now the government says that NAFTA and "free trade" are the way for Mexico to climb out of poverty. Here is their plan. The Mexican government decided that the corn and beans that you produced didn't help Mexico. They wanted your land for large growers, who would produce cash crops like carrots and broccoli for the global market. The government thought that whatever money was spent on poor farmers like you was wasted — money down the drain. So they now want to eliminate most of Article 27 and end land reform. Changes in Article 27 would allow collectively held land to be divided into individual parcels where

it could be bought or sold, opening the way for land to once again to fall into the hands of large land owners. For poor farmers throughout Mexico, this would be the end of hope.

Another horrible part of "free trade" is the plan to end just about all tariffs on food, even corn. This will be a disaster. Someone told you recently that in Iowa, in the United States, corn marketed by big corporations now sells for $110 a ton. In Mexico, corn sells for $240 a ton. Those big farms produce three times the amount of corn per acre as you produce. You grow some of your corn for your family, but most of it you sell on the market. Cheap corn imports from the United States will destroy your ability to survive as a farmer. This will be a disaster. What will you do? What's supposed to become of you? The government's idea is that you would go to work as farmworkers for rich farmers or migrate to the cities to work in factories. Right. Maybe you can move to Mexico City with the other 25 million people, so that you can live in a cardboard shack and starve. Even if NAFTA passes, it should not apply to basic foods like corn. Corn is sacred in Mexico. Mexicans should be self-sufficient in corn, not depend on U.S. corporations and the ups and downs of the world market.

There is still another way in which NAFTA could badly hurt you. NAFTA and "free trade" will allow global logging corporations like Boise Cascade to log, even clearcut, the forests of southern Mexico, including Chiapas. Forests bring rain to the farms, and with no forests there will be no rains, and then no farms. Also, the most skilled Chiapas farmers know how to use the shade of the forests to grow many different kinds of crops. The government will take land meant for poor farmers like you and give it to rich logging corporations from the United States.

Finally, even though NAFTA is supposed to be about free trade, there is no freedom for Mexicans to move to the other NAFTA countries: the United States and Canada. U.S. companies will bring their cheap products to Mexico and destroy your ability to make a living. Companies will be able to move freely and products will be able to move freely — but not people. If you're thrown off the land, where will you go? The only place to make a decent living will be the United States.

Martin's jeans worker, United States

For the last 20 years, you have worked at a plant making Martin's jeans. Your job pays $13 an hour with decent health, vacation, and retirement benefits. Not bad for someone who didn't finish high school. You're never going to get rich in this job, but you aren't going to starve either.

Over the last 10 years or so, lots of U.S. companies have moved to Mexico to take advantage of the cheaper labor there. Now comes this new treaty, pushed by President Bill Clinton and Mexican President Carlos Salinas: the North American Free Trade Agreement (NAFTA). If this passes the U.S. Congress, it will mean an end to almost all tariffs (taxes on imports) between the United States, Mexico, and Canada. And it will eliminate other restrictions on U.S. investment in Mexico. Then it will only be a matter of time before Martin's takes all its production to Mexico, like so many other U.S. corporations. And why? Are the Mexican workers better or faster than the U.S. workers? No. They just work for less money. Recently, you read an article about a place called Buena Vista, Mexico, where workers make $3.90 a *day*. A day. You did the math: 6,000 workers at all Martin's U.S. plants, make, say, $13 an hour for an eight-hour day. That's a daily wage bill for Martin's of $624,000. Paying 6,000 workers in Buena Vista $3.90 a day would cost Martin's $23,400 — a savings of more than $600,000 a day. And even if Martin's wanted to stay in the United States, once Levi Strauss, DKNY, Old Navy, or any of their competitors took off for Mexico, it would force them all to do it.

"Free trade" means that Martin's and other companies have the freedom to take jobs wherever they like. But what kind of freedom is that for you?

Of course, Martin's will say "sorry," but to you, "sorry" will not be good enough. There is no other job where you can make $13 an hour. The best you could do would be possibly $8 an hour as a clerk at a department store, but more likely you'd only be able to find work at a Burger King or 7-Eleven for minimum wage. It would take two full-time jobs to equal the money you were making at Martin's.

One last irony: At the same time that some young woman in Buena Vista, Mexico, may be stitching the same jeans that you used to stitch, you will be here in the United States competing with other Mexican immigrants who seem more than happy to make minimum wage at McDonald's or some place. You're not sure who is to blame, but that just doesn't feel right. Will "free trade" mean that Mexican workers are free to cross the border whenever they want?

There ought to be some way to stop U.S. companies from throwing their workers out on the street, and from running all around the world looking for cheap labor. Somebody ought to stand up for ordinary working people. What can be done to protect people like you?

Prosperous farmer, northern Mexico

It's true that some farmers probably will lose out when the North American Free Trade Agreement (NAFTA) takes effect and when most of Article 27 of the Mexican Constitution is eliminated. But not you — at least you hope not. Even before NAFTA has been approved and cuts almost all tariffs (taxes on imports), you are benefiting from the arrival of U.S. agribusiness companies.

You live in a very productive part of Mexico, where the land is excellent. You have 1,500 acres planted in crops that will be exported to the United States: lettuce, broccoli, cauliflower, squash, celery, carrots, peas, beans, spinach, cucumbers, and sweet corn. Technically, because of Article 27, you are not allowed to own more than about 250 acres of irrigated land, so you have to pretend that most of this land actually belongs to other farmers. With Article 27 still in effect, you worry that poor peasants could invade your land and demand that your "excess" land be given to the poor. That's what the law allows, and even encourages. This is a ridiculous and annoying holdover from the Mexican Revolution. But soon Article 27 will be abolished or changed, and you won't have to be secretive about how much land you own. Finally, you'll be free to buy as much land as you can afford. And a bigger farm is a much more efficient approach to growing food for the world. Of course, when you're able to own more land, you'll be free to become even more prosperous.

Right now, some of your fields are planted in basic grains like corn, wheat and sorghum. Prices for these staples don't vary that much. On the other hand, prices for export crops can go up or down pretty dramatically. But, if you play your cards right, the export crops are where the big money is. It is a gamble, because with NAFTA, Canadian wheat and U.S. corn will be sold in Mexico at prices that will very likely be lower than what you can afford to sell yours for. But in Canada and the United States, they can't grow vegetables all year long, and you can. Plus, your labor costs are much lower than in the United States or Canada.

So when NAFTA eliminates all tariffs, this is when you can start really making money.

You can export some of your crops directly to the United States. And you're experimenting all the time, with crops like parsley and coriander. But what is great about free trade between Mexico and the United States is that you have lots of different arrangements. You freeze some of your vegetables and sell them to big corporations like Green Garden or Birds Eye for export to the United States. Some crops you grow directly for U.S. corporations, which pay high prices for vegetables that they will sell in the United States for even higher prices. The bottom line is that you benefit from free trade.

You've even expanded into other agricultural areas with the cooperation of foreign corporations. Your family has its own agricultural implement factories, making tractors, plows, reapers, and fumigators, for sale to other Mexican farmers. You also produce pesticides in cooperation with U.S. chemical companies. Because of your ties to foreign corporations, NAFTA will only help you: You'll be able to import and export freely and own as much land as you can buy. The sky is the limit. Some Mexicans complain about this new "foreign invasion," but for Mexicans who are creative and innovative, this so-called invasion will be for the best. NAFTA rewards creativity and hard work.

One more thing: On the one hand, you are offended that people from the United States can come freely into Mexico, but Mexicans cannot go freely into the United States. It's a double standard. However, you actually benefit from immigration restrictions. If poor Mexicans were free to pick up and leave Mexico then it would lead to a shortage of workers who pick your crops and who work in your factories. You'd have to pay much more to attract labor and that could seriously damage your profits. Besides, wealthy Mexicans like you will be able to travel to the United States whenever you feel like it.

◆ U.S.-Mexican Environmental Justice Coalition ◆

Your group is made up of people who live on both sides of the U.S.–Mexico border who are concerned about the environment. You are especially worried about the potential impact that the North American Free Trade Agreement (NAFTA) could have on the environment in Mexico, but also indirectly in the United States. The idea of NAFTA is deceptively simple: End trade barriers between Canada, the United States, and Mexico, which will increase trade and investment between companies, produce more profits, and produce more jobs.

Sounds simple. However, from the standpoint of the environment, this could be a disaster. For example, what's to stop U.S. companies from leaving the United States to take advantage of Mexico's weaker enforcement of environmental regulations? This happens already. U.S. companies in places like Reynosa, Ciudad Juárez, and Tijuana, Mexico, set up factories where they dump poisonous wastes into the rivers or pump pollution into the skies. As NAFTA begins to eliminate barriers to investment, this will happen more and more. You're familiar with one U.S.-owned company located in Tijuana, Metales y Derivados, which until recently extracted lead from used batteries. But the company just dumped all its waste products right on the site. It could never do this in the United States, but in Mexico, the company got away with it. When the rains come, the wastes drain into streams that flow down into a neighborhood, Chilpancingo, below. Many children in the neighborhood are being born with severe birth defects, and it's suspected that children have high contents of lead in their bodies. Ultimately, the wastes flow into the Río Alamar, which flows into the Tijuana River, which flows back into the United States — a kind of toxic boomerang. Free trade means that companies are freer to pollute.

With the repeal of most of Article 27 of the Mexican Constitution, it will mean that U.S. logging companies can start buying up Mexican forests and clearcutting them. On paper, it looks great: Mexico's growth rate goes up, its gross national product increases. But just like in the United States, clearcutting will have disastrous environmental effects, destroying the main habitat for the monarch butterfly, polluting rivers, eliminating entire species of life. Free trade means the freedom to destroy.

And NAFTA will speed up the arrival of U.S. agribusiness companies in northern Mexico, like Green Giant, Campbell's, Birds Eye, and others. Already, these companies are moving in and contracting with Mexican farmers for them to grow vegetables and fruits for the U.S. market. At first glance, this may seem like a good idea. But these U.S. companies require Mexican farmers to use huge quantities of chemical fertilizers and pesticides. Again, this has horrible effects on Mexico, leading to more air and water pollution, but it also gives Americans food tainted with poisons.

In fact, the whole system of free trade hurts the environment. U.S. companies relocate their factories to Mexico — to produce blue jeans, cars, shirts, toys, plastic bags, Jostens graduation gowns — everything. Then all these products have to be transported back to the United States. Some come by truck, some by boat, some by air — but all of this transport requires the use of fossil fuels that pollute the air, and leads to the production of greenhouse gases and global warming.

One final problem with NAFTA is Chapter 11. This provision would allow companies from one country to sue another government if it passes any laws to protect their own people or environment. For example, suppose that a U.S. corporation bought land in Mexico to dump toxic waste, but then a Mexican community passed a law banning toxic waste dumps in their area. The company could actually sue and take Mexico to a special, secret NAFTA court. Again, free trade means lots of freedom for corporations, but not much freedom for people or the environment.

USA*NAFTA Coalition

You are a member of a coalition of U.S. businesses that strongly supports the North American Free Trade Agreement (NAFTA). Some members of your coalition include Xerox, General Electric, Alcoa, Zenith, and other major American corporations.

Once upon a time, Mexico was not a very friendly place to do business. There were many restrictions on U.S. companies operating there, limiting their right to own land in Mexico, specifying what percentage of a particular export product had to be made in Mexico, discriminating against U.S. companies that were in competition with Mexican companies, and the like. NAFTA will greatly increase your freedom. Basically, when tariffs are eliminated, operating in Mexico will be the same as operating in the United States — but with some important differences:

Labor costs a lot less in Mexico. Right now, companies in the USA*NAFTA Coalition pay high wages to employees — $10 an hour, $15 an hour, or even more. In northern Mexico, where most of the maquiladora assembly plants are located, the minimum wage is around $4 a day. Obviously, it's not like you're going to suddenly move all your factories to Mexico, but U.S. companies will move some of them. And you'll save a lot of money. Some of your critics claim that you're just out to take advantage of "cheap labor," but in a global economy, you have to respond to what your competitors do. For example, Japan is moving more of its production to Southeast Asia and China. If they pay just a few dollars a day for their workers, you can't really afford to pay a few dollars an hour for yours. And here's something else about possibly moving your factories to Mexico: It scares workers and their unions in the United States. This is not a bad thing, it's a good thing, and simply good business. Unions already have too much power. If workers in the United States realize that you have more freedom to pick up and move to Mexico, then they'll be less likely to make demands for higher wages or unreasonable working conditions.

Labor will be easier to work with in Mexico. Not only will workers in Mexico be less costly than in the United States, they'll also be less likely to complain. Why? Because they don't have any independent unions there. In Mexico, almost all the unions are government-controlled or connected with political parties that are pro-U.S. investment. For example, in the entire Tijuana area, with hundreds of foreign-owned factories, there is not one single contract with an independent union.

Environmental regulations are not as strict in Mexico. A lot of NAFTA critics say that NAFTA will make the environment worse. You have no intention of going to Mexico to pollute their air and water. But it is true that there is less strict enforcement of environmental regulations in Mexico. So this will give you more freedom to operate. In the United States, environmentalists have too much power, and they seem to care more about the spotted owl than about people's jobs.

Mexico has enormous markets to sell to. Mexico has over 100 million people. When there are no more tariffs on U.S. exports to Mexico, many of your products will easily out-compete Mexican products. For example, right now Iowa corn sells for $110 a ton and Mexican corn sells for $240 a ton. U.S. farms produce over three times the amount of corn per acre as Mexican farms. After NAFTA phases out tariffs, Mexicans will obviously want to buy cheap U.S. corn rather than expensive Mexican corn. Finally, all the poor of Mexico will be able to afford tortillas.

Another good thing about NAFTA is Chapter 11. Under NAFTA's Chapter 11, a company could sue the Mexican government if it passed any laws that would hurt investments there. Suppose that one of your companies bought a factory in a particular area where they intended to recycle the lead from batteries, but then the town passed a law banning this kind of factory. Under NAFTA's Chapter 11, that company could sue the Mexican government if it didn't force the town to get rid of its law.

Last point: Some people may say that "free trade" ought to apply to Mexicans immigrating to the United States to look for higher paying jobs. There are lots of reasons why this would be a bad idea. Perhaps the most important one, from your standpoint, is that it would defeat the purpose of NAFTA. If workers in Mexico could just pick up and leave any time they felt like it, this would lead to Mexican migrants flooding into the United States. It would upset both the Mexican and U.S. economies, and of course, deprive companies operating in Mexico of workers. No, "free trade" refers to investment and products, not to people.

Rethinking the NAFTA Record

TOTAL TRADE INCREASE

NAFTA supporters emphasize that total trade among the NAFTA countries has more than doubled since the deal went into effect on Jan. 1, 1994.

Total Trade Among NAFTA Partners

in billions of dollars

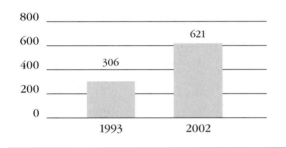

Source: U.S. Trade Representative.

EXPORT SURGE TO THE UNITED STATES

Mexican exports to the United States increased from $49.4 billion in 1994 to $138.1 billion in 2003.

Mexican Exports to the United States

in billions of dollars

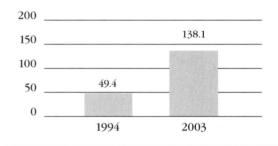

Source: U.S. Census Bureau, "U.S. Trade Balance with Mexico."

FOREIGN INVESTMENT BOOM

NAFTA made Mexico more appealing to foreign investors in two ways:

■ By requiring Mexico to allow free entry and exit of investment in all sectors.
■ By lifting trade barriers (making production there for export to the United States more profitable).

As a result, U.S. companies have increased long-term investment in Mexican factories and other businesses.

Net Foreign Direct Investment in Mexico

in billions of dollars

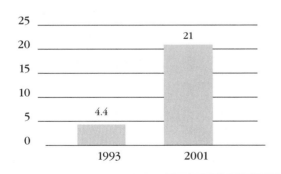

Source: World Bank, *Global Development Finance 2002.*

RISE AND FALL IN MAQUILADORA EMPLOYMENT

The number of Mexicans employed in factories that produce goods for export more than doubled during the first six years of NAFTA. But since then the country has lost more than 230,000 export assembly jobs.

Maquiladora Employment

in millions of people

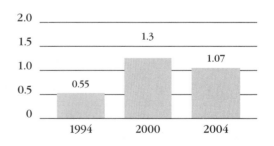

Source: Instituto Nacional de Estadística Geografía e Informática (INEGI).

WAGE DROP

Despite the flood of foreign investment in Mexican manufacturing, average workers have seen few of the benefits. The real value of the average manufacturing wage dropped 9 percent between 1994 and 2003.

Mexican Manufacturing Wages and Productivity

index: 1994 = 100

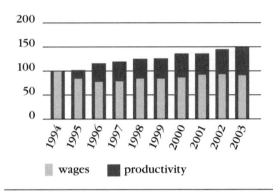

Source: Instituto Nacional de Estadística Geografía e Informática (INEGI).

INCREASE IN POVERTY

Since Mexico's neoliberal reforms and NAFTA, prices for farm produce in Mexico, especially corn, have fallen dramatically. Of working Mexicans, 25 percent are still farmers, compared to less than 2 percent of working people in the United States.

Rural Mexicans Living in Poverty

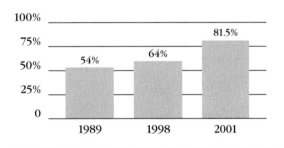

Source: Mexican Agricultural Ministry, SAGARPA, in "Corn, and Mexico's Agricultural Trade Liberalization," by Gisele Henriques and Raj Patel, International Relations Center, 2004.

INDUSTRY-RELATED POLLUTION

Air pollution from Mexican manufacturing has increased since NAFTA went into effect. Despite promises by NAFTA promoters, the increase in pollution from both industry and the growing population has not coincided with sufficient investment in environmental infrastructure.

Air Emissions in Mexican Manufacturing

in thousands of tons

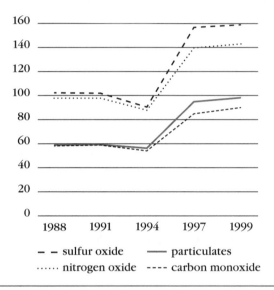

Source: Kevin Gallagher, "Trade Liberalization and Industrial Pollution in Mexico: Lessons for the FTAA," Tufts University, October 2000.

IMMIGRATION TO THE UNITED STATES

Immigration from Mexico increased dramatically after the passage of NAFTA. It declined after the 9/11 attacks, but began to rise again in 2004.

Immigrants from Mexico to the United States

in thousands

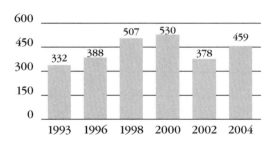

Source: Jeffrey S. Passel and Roberto Suro, "Rise, Peak, and Decline: Trends in U.S. Immigration, 1992–2004," Pew Hispanic Center, 2005.

Adapted from "Rethinking the NAFTA Record," by Sarah Anderson and John Cavanagh, Institute for Policy Studies, 2004.

After NAFTA: Mexico, a Ship on Fire

Poorer Than His Parents Ever Were

[In the late 1980s], Javier Pérez could provide for his family. He grew enough corn and beans on his small plot of land in southern Mexico to feed his wife and five children, and sold his extra harvest for money to buy shoes, schoolbooks, and other necessities. Over the years, Javier earned enough to send his five children to primary school and fix up his modest, dirt-floor house.

Then Javier lost his market for corn and beans. Upon Mexico's entry into the North American Free Trade Agreement (NAFTA) with Canada and the United States in 1994, imported U.S. corn and other basic foods flooded the Mexican market, leaving Javier with nowhere to sell his crops. At the same time, cuts in government support to small farmers raised his cost of production.

In recent years, Javier has planted papaya, cantaloupe, tomatoes and watermelon in turn. But without resources, technology, or a secure market, he ended up with a barn full of rotting fruit and a growing debt with the bank. Like the majority of Mexicans, Javier is now poorer than his parents ever were. In order to keep the family afloat financially, his eldest son has already left for the United States, where he found work as a migrant farmworker and sends money home periodically. Another son and daughter are considering emigrating. The results of a trade agreement between a developing country and the world's largest economy are as anyone would predict. [Y]ears after NAFTA's implementation, U.S. corporate profits are skyrocketing. In fact, the economic elite on both sides of the border reap huge benefits, while the majority of Mexicans watch their buying power drop and wages stagnate.

From "A Hemisphere for Sale: The Epidemic of Unfair Trade in the Americas," by Witness for Peace, 2001, www.witnessforpeace.org/downloads/hemisphere_1.pdf.

Small Farmers Can't Compete

The river of cheap American corn began flooding into Mexico after NAFTA took effect in 1994. Since then, the price of corn in Mexico has fallen by half. A 2003 report by the Carnegie Endowment says this flood has washed away 1.3 million small farmers. Unable to compete, they have left their land to join the swelling pools of Mexico's urban unemployed. Others migrate to the United States to pick our crops — former farmers become day laborers.

The cheap U.S. corn has also wreaked havoc on Mexico's land, according to the Carnegie report. The small farmers forced off their land often sell out to larger farmers who grow for export, farmers who must adopt far more industrial (and especially chemical- and water-intensive) practices to compete in the international marketplace. Fertilizer runoff into the Sea of Cortez starves its marine life of oxygen, and Mexico's scarce water resources are leaching north, one tomato at a time.

Mexico's industrial farmers now produce fruits and vegetables for American tables year-round. It's ridiculous for a country like Mexico whose people are often hungry to use its best land to grow produce for a country where food is so abundant that its people are obese — but under free trade, it makes economic sense.

Meanwhile, the small farmers struggling to hold on in Mexico are forced to grow their corn on increasingly marginal lands, contributing to deforestation and soil erosion.

From "A Flood of U.S. Corn Rips at Mexico," by Michael Pollan, *Los Angeles Times,* April 23, 2004, www.commondreams.org/views04/0423-02.htm.

Economic Devastation

Predictions of U.S. job losses [after NAFTA passed] were, if anything, underestimated. By November 2002, the U.S. Department of Labor had certified 507,000 workers for extensions of unemployment benefits under the treaty because their employers had moved their jobs south of the border. Most observers believe that is actually a significant undercount, partly because many workers losing jobs don't know they qualify for trade-related benefits. According to the Economic Policy Institute in Washington, NAFTA eliminated 879,000 U.S. jobs because of the rapid growth in the net U.S. export deficit with Mexico and Canada.

While the job picture for U.S. workers was grim, NAFTA's impact on Mexican jobs was devastating. Before leaving office (and Mexico itself, pursued by charges of corruption), President Carlos Salinas de Gortari promised Mexicans they would gain the jobs Americans lost. In the United States, he promised that this job gain would halt the northward flow of Mexican job-seekers.

NAFTA's first year saw instead the loss of more than a million jobs across Mexico. To attract investment, NAFTA-related reforms required the privatization of factories, railroads, airlines and other large enterprises. This led to huge waves of layoffs. Mexican enterprises and farmers, who couldn't compete with U.S. imports, also shed workers, and the subsequent peso devaluation cost even more jobs. Because unemployment and economic desperation in Mexico increased, immigration to the United States has been the only hope for survival for millions of Mexicans.

For a while, however, it seemed that the growth of maquiladora factories along the border would make up for at least part of the job loss. By 2001, more than 1.3 million workers were employed in some 2,000 border plants, according to the Maquiladora Industry Association. But tying the jobs of so many Mexicans to the U.S. market, for which the plants were producing, proved a disaster as well. When U.S. consumers stopped buying as the recession hit in 2001, maquiladoras also began shedding workers. The Mexican government estimates that more than 400,000 jobs disappeared in the process — as the saying goes on the border, when the U.S. economy catches cold, Mexico gets pneumonia.

From "NAFTA's Legacy — Profits and Poverty," by David Bacon, *San Francisco Chronicle,* Jan. 14, 2004, www.organicconsumers.org/corp/nafta011904.cfm.

Trade Brings Riches — to the Rich

While the percentage of poor Mexicans is about the same now as it was in the early 1980s — a little more than 50 percent — the population has grown over the same period, from 70 million to 100 million. That means about 19 million more Mexicans are living in poverty than 20 years ago, according to the Mexican government and international organizations. About 24 million — nearly one in every four Mexicans — are classified as extremely poor and unable to afford adequate food.

… Studies show that the richest 10 percent now control about half of the country's financial and real estate assets. Most of those who are extremely poor live in rural areas. Government figures show that more than 40 percent of Mexicans in rural areas earn less than $1.40 a day, unable even to feed themselves decently. As a result, people are bailing out of the countryside as if it were a ship on fire.

Mexico's rural population is less than half the size it was in the 1950s. Government surveys show that between 400 and 600 people a day are packing up, fleeing to cities or to the United States.

Alberto Gomez, an influential farmers' leader who recently organized a march on the capital by tens of thousands of farmers, said the situation was desperate. "We don't want to come to the city and we don't want to immigrate to the United States. But people have no money," said Gomez, head of the 180,000-member National Union of Agriculture Organizations.

Gomez and many politicians blame much of their problem on NAFTA, which they say bankrupted Mexican farmers who cannot compete with their heavily subsidized, more technologically advanced U.S. counterparts. While a boon to the maquiladoras and a blessing to certain bigger farmers, NAFTA has inflicted more pain on already ailing small farmers, most economists and analysts here agree.

Beginning in the 1980s, the government began systematically withdrawing subsidies and aid to the countryside, partly because a severe financial crisis strangled the budget, and partly because it believed that free market reforms would ultimately strengthen the sector.

Money for irrigation, crop storage facilities, government agricultural research and fertilizer was virtually zeroed out. Price supports were reduced. According to José Luis Calva, an economist who specializes in rural Mexico, government aid to the countryside has dropped 95 percent since 1982. At the same time, the value of some of the most important Mexican crops, including corn, beans, and coffee, has fallen as worldwide production has risen.

From "Trade Brings Riches, but Not to Mexico's Poor," by Mary Jordan and Kevin Sullivan, *Washington Post,* March 22, 2003, www. globalpolicy.org/component/content/article/213/45611.html

First Crossing

BY BOB PETERSON

Crossing Borders, Building Empathy

Reading about NAFTA and economic policy can feel distant and academic. But these policies enter the world as explosions in people's lives. What begins as desperation in the Mexican countryside ultimately winds its way to the Mexico–U.S. border. Here, fifth-grade teacher Bob Peterson describes how he uses Pam Muñoz Ryan's short story "First Crossing" to promote empathy for Mexicans entering the United States without documents. The NAFTA role play, described earlier, helps students consider some of the root causes of Mexican migration. "First Crossing" puts a human face on this migration.

As we shared a meal of beans and rice at the Casa del Migrante, a migrant shelter in Tijuana, Juan Torres told me how badly he missed his two daughters — third and fourth graders who were born in the United States and are U.S. citizens. In a soft voice he spoke of being arrested in California a few days earlier for driving without a license, a license he can't legally obtain because he is undocumented. He explained that he made his first crossing to the United States years ago as a teenager; after 12 years of not being able to visit Mexico, he had few friends or family back in his homeland.

Juan's eyes moistened as he told me of his recent phone call to his daughters, who pleaded for him to return and said, "We miss you, Papi." My mind raced, thinking of my own two daughters and how horrific a forced separation would be. I also thought of my fifth-grade students in Milwaukee, some of them separated for various reasons from their parents. I realized that when I taught about immigration in the future, I would try to help students look beyond the statistics and see the human realities.

Later, back in Milwaukee, I reflected on my trip to

DAVID BACON

An indigenous Mixtec boy, from the state of Oaxaca, working in a field of cilantro near Maneandero, in Baja California. Wages are so low that the whole family, including children, has to work to earn enough to live on.

Tijuana. I also thought of writer Alfie Kohn's admonition after the Sept. 11 attacks: "Schools should help children locate themselves in widening circles of care that extend beyond self, beyond country, to all humanity." One story that can help do this is Pam Muñoz Ryan's "First Crossing" (see p. 87), from a book with the same title edited by Donald Gallo (Candlewick Press, 2004). In the story, 14-year-old Marco attempts to cross the Tijuana–San Diego border with his father. As they embark on their dangerous journey, they encoun-

---

SECTION 4 PHOTO: AP PHOTO

A Mexican man hides his face from the camera as he rows his raft with three immigrants across the Rio Grande into the United States. The man hires out his raft to take people across the river.

ter *coyotes* (people smugglers), the Border Patrol, and Marco's fear of separation from his father and his family in Mexico.

I teach in a two-way Spanish-English bilingual elementary school and many of my fifth graders belong to immigrant families. I decided to use "First Crossing" at the beginning of the year to initiate our year-long discussion of immigration and to begin to break down the barriers of "self" and "country" that Kohn warns against. Like Kohn, I want my fifth graders to regard themselves as part of a broader human family and to think critically about the border and the way it legitimates "us" and "them" divisions. I thought that "First Crossing" might be a good way to honor the experiences of some of my immigrant students, and perhaps be an invitation to them to share their stories in a supportive environment.

Before we read Muñoz's story, I asked the students what they knew about immigration, and if they had any questions we might address throughout the year. The students' knowledge ranged broadly. They knew there were lots of immigrants, "especially Hispanics and Russians" (there's a growing Russian immigrant community in Milwaukee), that some were "illegal," some "without papers," and some stayed and some returned home. One immigrant student explained that "the *migra* kicks people out of the country." I asked what he meant by "the *migra*" and he said, "the border police." I noted that for many people "the migra" referred to any government official involved in immigration enforcement and was not limited to just border officials.

When I asked why they thought people left their home countries, students said that people wanted "more space," "jobs," "a home," "because they don't get paid a lot [in their home country]" and "to start new lives."

The questions they had about immigration were varied and thoughtful. They ranged from "Why is there a border between Mexico and the United States?" to "What are documents for?" to "How many people immigrate to the United States?"

I told students that the story we would read over the next three days wouldn't answer all their questions, and in fact might elicit more. I explained that we'd start by looking at immigration from the point of view of a boy about their age. We could have read the story more quickly, but I wanted to give my students time to enter into the difficulties and choices faced by Mexican immigrants. I hoped that the longer my students spent with Marco and his father, the greater the likelihood of nurturing their empathy.

I explained that Marco's father has crossed the border into the United States illegally several times to make money to support his family in Mexico. This time he is taking his son with him. It could be dangerous.

I then said, "I want you to pretend that you are Marco. Get inside his thoughts and write down what he might be thinking. Write as if you were Marco, so use the word 'I' in your writings." I also asked them to predict what might happen, reminding them, "When you make predictions and think about a character, your reading comprehension — your understanding of the story — improves."

POLYP

The students wrote in their reading-response journals and then shared in pairs. Many wrote that they were "scared" and already "miss home." Many predicted the police or Border Patrol would catch Marco. One wrote: "I don't know if I really want to be here. But what choice do I have? I need to go with my papa so we can have a better life. I'm scared."

I distributed copies of "First Crossing" and we started reading together as a class. Early on, Marco explains that his father originally left Mexico to help his family survive. Marco thinks back to the time when "six days a week, Papá had carried 50-pound bags of rock and dirt from the bottom of a crater to the top of a hill" for a "pitiful $5 for his nine hours." We paused and figured out how much per hour Marco's father earned in Mexico and then compared it to Marco's father's statement that in the United States he makes "$30, $40, $50 a day, maybe more."

I had students calculate the difference between the two wages in terms of a day, a week, and a year — at first by themselves and then as a class. The students figured out that in the United States Marco's father could earn in one day what it took him a week to earn in Mexico.

"That's not fair!" exclaimed one student. "No wonder people want to come here," said another.

Stopped by the Border Patrol

Marco and his father travel standing up in the back of a van so full of people they can barely breathe. I paused to point out Muñoz Ryan's descriptive language, "Their bodies nested together, faces pressed against faces, like tightly bundled stalks of celery. Marco turned his head to avoid his neighbor's breath and found his nose pressed against another's ear."

I had taped off an area in the classroom to demonstrate the approximate dimensions of the van. I asked a dozen student volunteers to stand in the "van" while we reread that part. I then asked for a few more volunteers to act out the van being stopped by Border Patrol agents, the migrants being taken in and fingerprinted. The students particularly enjoyed giving false names as Marco did in the story.

In the short story, the Border Patrol sends Marco and his father to Tijuana where they find their way back to the coyote. They now try a different way to cross the border, one even more brazen than the first. They are to hide under the hood of a car that has a platform inserted next to the engine. They must travel one at a time and

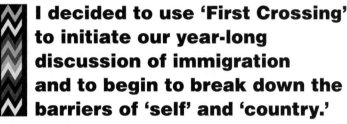

I decided to use 'First Crossing' to initiate our year-long discussion of immigration and to begin to break down the barriers of 'self' and 'country.'

are to meet across the border.

Again, I paused and asked students to write a brief interior monologue.

Mario* wrote, "I feel very scared because I want to see my dad again. Maybe the migra will send him to a different place and then where am I going to go?" Tonya wrote: "I am scared because I might get burned by the engine, or I could get caught by the migra, I am also scared because my dad might not be there when I get there, if I can get there. I wonder if I am ever going to see my hometown and my mom and sisters again. … I wish I could go home to see my mama and sister and never come back."

A student who speaks limited English and whose family has had immigration problems wrote in Spanish: *"Marco tiene miedo de crusar la frontera porque puede estar la migra y lo puede regresar a México y su familia tambien tiene mucho miedo."* [Marco is afraid to cross the border because the migra might be there and they might return him to Mexico and his family is very afraid too.]

Miguel referred back to the time Marco was waiting in the coyote's house watching an *Aladdin* video and wrote, "I feel nervous my dad is going to get caught; I wish I had a magic carpet too."

Others were optimistic. Jaime wrote, "I feel good 'cause we're going to the United States. I will be happy because we gonna live more, save, and work and we can go shopping for clothes and some shoes and go to parties."

'Scrunched Like Sardines'

When we got to the section of the story when the coyote demands that Marco lie quietly in the car next to the motor, I asked for a volunteer to do the same in a taped off section on the floor. While we read this excerpt very slowly, Jaime lay absolutely silent. The children watched Jaime lie without motion and followed along in their copies.

After getting up from the floor, I asked Jaime how he'd felt. Jaime said it was hard to lie that still and that he had pretended to hear the car engine. "It would have been worse," he told some kids, "if I had been really inside that car." Time didn't permit the many other volunteers who wanted to lie silently on the floor, although I did compliment Jaime again and playfully reminded other students that such stillness could be practiced any

* All students' names have been changed.

time in a seated position during a lesson.

After we completed the story, for homework I asked students to choose an event in the story, draw a picture of it, and write a caption.

Many children drew the van and coyote when they "were scrunched like sardines." One student wrote: "I drew Marco and his dad when they were going to cross the border but the police caught them." Others drew "when Marco was to hide in the engine."

Others stressed the positive: "This is the dad crossing the border [where he is] going to make more money." One Mexican-American student drew a picture of a car with a Mexican flag in the wind, with the caption, "This is when they get to buy a new car in the United States."

I found it interesting that while students seemed to express real empathy for Marco — either in writing or in discussion — students of immigrant families were more likely to speak about the economic benefits of coming to this country.

As a final in-class activity, I asked students to write Marco a letter of advice. I encouraged those who had come to this country as immigrants or moved to a new school to draw on their own experiences.

Students' advice ranged from how to get along in school, to dealing with a new language and how to deal with the migra. Some students clearly recognized that undocumented families must be vigilant. The personal nature of the letters and the sensitive advice showed that students cared for Marco.

A Mexican-American girl whose family immigrated to the United States wrote, "My advice for you is to fake to be somebody else and try not to get caught. And if you do just take a break and wait for a couple of weeks or months. After that you can go back and fake you are somebody else and if you get past I would be really happy for you. Good luck. Sincerely, your friend."

Lucy, who has complained about living with her strict grandfather after her mother abandoned her, wrote, "Dear Marco, You are a brave and courageous boy. You did not cry when you were in the hood of the car. Let me tell you now I would have cried until my eyes were swollen. You are just like me, I wonder when my magic carpet will come!"

Tonya, who is African-American, wrote, "Dear Marco, I hope you don't get caught. I am rooting for you and I also support you. Do you want to go home to see your mama? How did you feel when you finally crossed the border? If I were you I'd want to go home. I wish you good luck Marcos and papa! Buena suerte!"

Roberto, who had pointed out that as a Puerto Rican he didn't have trouble going back and forth to "my country," wrote, "I think [your story] was great. I was sometimes sad, sometimes happy and sometimes anxious.

Don't you wish your family had papers?"

Jaime related his own immigration story to Marco's writing: "I've been thru those problems too. I don't have papers but I came here thru the desert. There was hot water [to drink] but I really didn't care. Then I almost got caught with a coyote in a van with seats and they told me and my mom to stay quiet under them. The coyote had them covered so they won't see us. They asked the coyote what is that (the seat covers) for and he said so the seats stay clean."

New Respect

After Jaime shared part of his story, it seemed that students gained new respect for him, as other class members encouraged him to share more. He declined, at which point one girl, hoping for more stories, said, "Why don't we have all the people in the class who don't have papers raise their hands?" A few students agreed saying, "Yeah!" I quickly vetoed the idea, pointing out that it was a personal matter for each student and their family and there was no need for people to share that information if they didn't want to. I said, "In our classroom we treat people the same regardless of whether they have papers or not." One student seated close to where I was standing said to students seated nearby, "The government oughta do the same."

As we concluded our reading of the story, the students were indignant not only at Marco's treatment at the hands of the Border Patrol, but also at me when they realized that it was the *end* of the story. Because I had shown students the whole book, entitled *First Crossing*, they had assumed that we had read only the first chapter, and would be able to continue the story in subsequent chapters.

As I mentioned earlier, I had limited goals in using "First Crossing." Later in the year, we will explore some of the causes of migration from Mexico and look at aspects of the origins of the border. And we'll look more at the immigrant experience in the United States. I wanted to begin this inquiry with a story that gently but profoundly calls into question the outlawing of people who were born on the "wrong" side of a national boundary. Should Marco and his father (who, of course, represent millions of other undocumented migrants) be captured and deported to Mexico? That's a political and a moral question that students will confront later in the year. But answering it should begin from an appreciation of our shared humanity. ■

Bob Peterson (repmilw@aol.com) teaches at La Escuela Fratney in Milwaukee. He is an editor of *Rethinking Schools* magazine.

More stories about immigration-related themes can be found in Resources, p. 132.

BY PAM MUÑOZ RYAN

First Crossing

Revolution Boulevard in downtown Tijuana swarmed with gawking tourists who had walked over the big cement bridge from the United States to Mexico. Shop owners stood in front of their stalls calling out, "I make you good deal. Come in. I make you good price." Even though it was January, children walked the streets barefooted and accosted shoppers, determined to sell gum or small souvenirs with their persistent pleas: "Come on, lady, you like gum? Chiclets? Everybody like gum." Vendors carried gargantuan bouquets of paper flowers, hurrying up to cars on the street and trying to make sales through open windows. It appeared that no one ever accepted the first rebuff from tourists. The Mexicans simply badgered them until they pulled out their wallets. With its shady, border-town reputation, Tijuana maintained an undeniable sense of mystery, as if something illegal was about to transpire.

Marco added up the hours he'd been riding on buses from his home in Jocotepec, Jalisco, in order to reach Tijuana. Eighteen hours? Twenty-three hours? It was all a blur of sleeping and sitting in stations and huddling as close to his father as possible so he wouldn't have to smell the sweat of strangers. Now, even though they were finally in the border town, their journey still wasn't over. Papá pointed to a bench in front of a liquor store, and Marco gratefully dropped onto it. Even though it wasn't dark yet, a neon sign flashed TEQUILA and KAHLÚA in the liquor store window. Marco felt conscious of himself, as if everyone who passed by knew why he was there. For some reason he felt guilty, even though he hadn't yet done anything wrong.

"No te apures. Don't worry," said Papá, reaching into a brown bag for a peanut. He calmly cracked and peeled it, letting the shells drop onto the sidewalk.

Marco looked at him. Papá had an eagle's profile: a brown bald head with a bird-of-prey nose. Once, when he was a little boy, Marco had seen a majestic carved wooden Indian in front of a cigar store in Guadalajara and had said, "Papá, that's you!" Papá had laughed but had to agree that the statue looked familiar. Marco looked just like Papá but with 10 times the hair. They had the same walnut-colored skin and hooked noses, but Papá's body was muscular and firm while Marco's was skinny and angular, all knees and elbows.

"How do we find the *coyote?"* asked Marco.

"Do not worry," said Papá. "The coyote will find us. Like a real animal stalking its next meal, the coyote will find us."

Marco took off his baseball cap and ran his fingers through his thick, straight hair. He repositioned the hat and took a deep breath. "Papá, what happens if we get caught?"

"We have been over this," said Papá, still cracking peanuts. "We will have to spend a few hours at the border office. We stand in line. They ask us questions. We give them the names we discussed. They take our fingerprints. Then we come back here to Tijuana. The coyote will try to move us across again, tomorrow or the next day or even the next. It could take two attempts or a dozen. Eventually, we make it. It's all part of the fee."

"How much?" asked Marco.

"Too much," said Papá. "It is how it is. They are greedy, but we need them."

Stories of Danger

Marco had heard stories about coyotes, the men who moved Mexicans across the border. Sometimes they took the money from poor peasants, disappeared, and left them stranded in Nogales or Tecate with no way home. Coyotes had been known to lead groups into the desert in the summer, where they would later be found almost dead and riddled with cactus thorns. And then there were the stories about scorpion stings and rattlesnake bites after following a coyote into a dry riverbed. Just last week, Marco overheard a friend of Papá's tell about a group of people who hid in a truck under a camper shell, bodies piled upon bodies. The border patrol tried to stop the truck, but the coyote was drunk and tried to speed away. The truck overturned, and 17 Mexicans were killed. Since then, Marco's thoughts had been filled with his worst imaginings.

Papá saw the wrinkle in Marco's forehead and said, "I have always made it across, and I wouldn't keep doing this if it wasn't worth it."

Marco nodded. Papá was right. Everything had been better for the family since he'd started crossing. His father had not always worked in the United States. For many years, before Marco was 10, Papá had gone to work at a large construction site in Guadalajara, 30 miles away from their village of Jocotepec. Six days a week, Papá had carried 50-pound bags of rock and dirt from the bottom of a crater to the top of the hill. All day long, up and down the hill.

Marco had asked him once, "Do you count the times you go up and down the hill?"

Papá had said, "I don't count. I don't think. I just do it."

Papá's frustration had grown as the years went by. He was nothing more than a *burro*. When the hole in the ground was dug and the big building finished, he had been sent to excavate another hole. And for what? A pitiful $5 for his nine hours? The day that one of *los jefes* spat on his father as if he was an animal, Papá set the 50-pound bag down and began to walk away.

The bosses laughed at him. "Where are you going? You need work? You better stay!"

Papá turned around and picked up the heavy bag. He stayed for the rest of the day so that he could collect his pay and get a ride home, but he never went back.

He told Mamá, "My future and the children's future are marked in stone here. Why not go to the other side? There, I will make $30, $40, $50 a day, maybe more."

or the past four years, Marco had seen Papá only twice a year. He and his mother and younger sisters had moved into another rhythm of existence. He woke with the roosters, went to school in the mornings, and helped Mamá with Maria, Lilia, and Irma in the afternoon. During harvest, he worked in the corn or *chayote* fields and counted the days until Papá would come home.

The money orders always preceded him. They made Mamá happy and made Papá seem godlike in her eyes. They still did not own a house, but now they were able to pay the rent on time and had plenty left over for things like a television and the clothes and games Marco's sisters always wanted. They had money for the market

and food, especially for the occasions when Papá came home and Mamá cooked meat and sweets every day. The first few nights were always the same. Mamá made *birria,* goat stew, and *capirotada,* bread pudding. Then Papá went out with his *compadres* to drink and to tell of his work in *Los Estados,* the States. The family would have his company for a month, and then he would go back to that unknown place, disappearing somewhere beyond the vision of the departing bus.

"What is it like, Papá?" Marco always asked.

"I live in an apartment above a garage with eight messy men. We get up early, when it's still dark, to start our work in the flower fields. In the afternoon, we go back to the apartment. We take turns going to the store to buy tortillas, a little meat, some fruit. There is a television, so we watch the Spanish stations. We talk about sports and Mexico and our families. There is room on the floor to sleep. On weekends we sometimes play *fútbol* at the school and drink a few *cervezas.* Sometimes we have regular work, but other times we go and stand on the corner in front of the gas station with the hope we will be picked up by the contractors who need someone to dig a ditch or do some other job a *gringo* won't do. It goes on like this until it's time to come back to Mexico."

For several years, Marco had begged to go with Papá. His parents finally decided that now that he was 14, he was old enough to help support the family. With both Marco and Papá working, the family could buy a house next year. Mamá had cried for three days before they left.

When it was time to board the bus to Guadalajara, Marco had hugged his mother tight.

"Mamá, I will be back."

"It will never be the same," she'd said. "Besides, some come back and some do not."

Marco knew he would return. He already looked forward to his first homecoming, when he would be celebrated like Papá. As the bus pulled away from Jocotepec, Marco had waved out the small window to the women, and for the first time in his life, had felt like a man.

Marco leaned back on the hard bench on the Tijuana street and closed his eyes. He already missed Jocotepec and his sisters playing in the corn fields behind the house. He even missed the annoying neighbor's dog barking and Mamá's voice waking him too early for mass on Sunday morning when he wanted to sleep.

Papá nudged him. "Stay close to me," he said, grab-

"Welcome to the United States." A pickup truck passes over the Rio Grande while crossing the border into El Paso from Juárez.

bing Marco's shirtsleeve.

Marco sat up and looked around. There was nothing unusual happening on the street. What had Papá seen?

The Coyote

A squat, full woman wrapped in a red shawl came down the sidewalk with a determined walk. Marco thought her shape resembled a small Volkswagen. Her blue-black hair was pulled back into a tight doughnut on the top of her head, not one strand out of place. Heavy makeup hid her face like a painted mask, and her red mouth was set in a straight line. As she passed, she glanced at Papá and gave a quick nod.

"Let's go," he said.

"That's the coyote?" said Marco. "But it is a woman."

"Shhh," said Papá. "Follow me."

Papá weaved between the tourists on the street, keeping the marching woman in his sight. She pulled out a beeping cell phone and talked into it, then turned off the main avenue and headed deeper into the town's neighborhood. Others seemed to fall in with Papá and Marco from doorways and bus stops until they were a group of eight: five men and three women. Up ahead, the coyote woman waited at a wooden gate built into

the middle of a block of apartments. She walked in and the little parade followed her. They continued through a dirty *callejón* between two buildings, picking their way around garbage cans until they reached a door in the alley wall.

"In there," she ordered.

Marco followed Papá inside. It seemed to be a small basement with plaster walls and a cement floor. Narrow wooden stairs led up one wall to someplace above. A light bulb with a dangling chain hung in the middle of the room, and in a corner was a combination television and video player with stacks of children's videotapes on the floor. The woman came inside, shut the door, and bolted it. The men and women turned to face her.

"Twelve hundred for each, American dollars," she said.

Marco almost choked. He looked around at the others, who appeared to be peasants like him and Papá. Where would they have gotten that kind of money? And how could Papá pay $2,400 for the two of them to cross the border?

The transients reached into their pockets for wallets, rolled up pant legs to get to small leather bags strapped around their legs, unzipped inside pouches of jackets,

REUTERS/JEFF MITCHELL

U.S. Border Patrol agents question an immigrant caught crossing the Rio Grande illegally near Eagle Pass, Texas.

and were soon counting out the bills. Stacks of money appeared. The coyote walked to each person, wrote his or her name in a notebook, and collected the fees. Papá counted out 120 bills, all 20s, into her chubby palm.

In his entire life, Marco had never seen so much money in one room.

"*Escucha*. Listen. Since Sept. 11, I have had trouble trying to get people across with false documents," she said, "so we will cross in the desert. I have vans and drivers to help. We'll leave in the middle of the night. If you need to relieve yourself, use the alley. The television does not work, only the video." Her cell phone beeped again. She put it to her ear and listened as she walked up the stairs, which groaned and creaked under her weight. Marco heard a door close and a bolt latch.

It was almost dark. Marco and Papá found a spot on the concrete floor near the video player. Marco put his backpack behind him and leaned against it, protecting himself from the soiled wall, where probably hundreds of backs had rested.

One of the women, who was about Mamá's age, smiled at Marco. The others, tired from their travels,

settled on the floor and tried to maneuver their bags for support. No one said much. There was murmuring between people sitting close to each other, but despite the obligatory polite nods, anxiety prevented too much interaction.

A man next to Papá spoke quietly to him. His name was Javier, and he'd been crossing for 12 years. He had two lives, he said: one in the United States and one in his village in Mexico. The first few years of working in the States, he dreamed of the days he would go home to Mexico and his family, but now he admitted that he sometimes dreaded his trips back. He wanted to bring his wife and children with him to work and live in the U.S., but they wouldn't come. Now he went home only once a year. What worried him was that he was starting to prefer his life on the other side to his life in Mexico.

Papá nodded as if he understood Javier.

Marco said nothing because he knew that Papá was just being polite. He would never prefer the United States to Mexico.

Marco was too nervous to sleep. He reached over and took several videotapes from the pile. They were all cartoon musicals, luckily in Spanish. He put one in the machine, *The Lion King,* and turned the volume down low. Trancelike, he watched the lion, Simba, lose his father.

"*Hakuna matata*," sang the characters on the video. "No worries."

A series of thoughts paraded through Marco's mind. The desert. Snakes. The possibility of being separated from Papá. Drinking beer with the men in Jocotepec after eating goat stew. A woman coyote. Scorpions. He closed his eyes, and the music in the video became the soundtrack of his piecemeal nightmare.

Hours later, Papá woke Marco. "Now, *M'ijo*. Let's go."

Marco, jarred from sleep, let Papá pull him up. He rubbed his eyes and tried to focus on the others, who headed out the door.

Crammed Together

A man with a flashlight waited until they all gathered in a huddle. He wore all black, including his cap, the brim pulled down so far that all that was apparent was his black moustache and a small, narrow chin.

They picked their way through the alley again, following the direction of the man's light. At the street, a paneled van waited, the motor running. The door slid open, and Marco could see that the seats had been removed to create a cavern. It was already filled with people, all standing up. Men and women held small suitcases and had plastic garbage bags next to them filled with their belongings.

There didn't seem to be an inch of additional space until the flashlight man yelled, "*¡Mueva!*" Move!

The people in the van crammed closer together as each of the group of eight climbed inside.

"*¡Más!*" said Flashlight Man. The people tried to squash together. Papá jumped inside and grabbed Marco's hand, pulling him in, too, but Marco was still half out. The man shoved Marco as if he were packing an already stuffed suitcase. The others groaned and complained. The doors slid shut behind Marco. When the van surged forward, no one fell because there was no room to fall. Their bodies nested together, faces pressed against faces, like tightly bundled stalks of celery. Marco turned his head to avoid his neighbor's breath and found his nose pressed against another's ear.

When the van surged forward, no one fell because there was no room to fall. Their bodies nested together, faces pressed against faces.

The van headed east for a half hour. Then it stopped suddenly, the door slid open, and Flashlight Man directed them into the night. His cell phone rang to the tune of "Take Me Out to the Ballgame," and he quickly answered it.

"One hour. We will be there," he said into the phone. Then he turned to the small army of people and said, "Let your eyes adjust to the night. Then follow me."

Marco and Papá held back. They were the last in the group forming the line of obedient lambs walking over a hill and down into an arroyo. There was no water at the bottom — just rocks, dirt, and dry grasses. Visions of reptiles crowded Marco's mind. He was relieved when they climbed back up and continued to walk over the mostly barren ground. They crossed through a chain-link fence where an opening had been cut.

"Are we in the United States?" asked Marco.

"Yes," said Papá. "Keep walking."

They walked along a dirt road for another half hour, and in the distance, headlights blinked. Flashlight Man punched a number into his cell phone. The headlights came on again.

"That's it," said Flashlight Man, and they all hurried toward the van, where they were again sandwiched together inside.

That wasn't so bad, thought Marco, as the van sped down a dirt road. A tiny bud of relief began to flower in his mind. No worries.

Within five minutes, the van slowed to a crawl and then stopped. Marco heard someone outside barking orders at the driver. Suddenly, the van door slid open and Marco met la migra.

Four Border Patrol officers with guns drawn ordered them out and herded them into two waiting vans with long bench seats. *A small consolation,* thought Marco. They rode back to the Border Patrol station in silence. Inside, it was exactly as Papá had said. They stood in line, gave false names during a short interview, were fingerprinted, and released.

"Now what?" asked Marco, as they stood in front of the Border Patrol building on the Mexico side.

"We walk back to *la casa del coyote*," said Papá.

It was seven in the morning as they walked down the narrow streets. Most shops weren't open yet, and bars and fences enclosed the vendors' stalls, which were filled with piñatas, leather goods, ceramics, and sombreros. Papá bought premade burritos and Cokes inside a corner *tienda* before they turned down the street that led to Coyote Lady's house.

Many of their group had already found their way back to the basement room off the alley. Papá and Marco found a spot against the wall and fell asleep. They woke late in the afternoon, went to the taco vendor on the corner for food, and came back and watched the video *The Little Mermaid*.

Marco listened to the fish maiden's song. She wanted to be free to go to another world. *Like me,* he thought. It seemed *everyone* wanted to get to the other side.

In the middle of the night, they were roused and put in a van for another attempt to cross over. Again, the Border Patrol sat in wait and ambushed them, as if they had known they were coming. Each night the van took them a little farther east into the desert, but after five attempts, they were no farther into the United States than they'd been the first night.

Early Sunday morning, Coyote Lady came down the stairs into the basement room. She wore a dress like the ones Marco's mother wore for church, a floral print with a white collar, although it was much bigger than any dress his mother owned. Her face was scrubbed clean of makeup, and she looked like someone's aunt or a neighborhood woman who might go to mass every day.

"Today is a big football game, professional, in San Diego. La migra will be eager to get people into the U.S. in time for the game. We start moving you in one hour, one at a time. The wait will not be bad at the border this morning. But later today, closer to game time, it will be horrible."

Marco looked at Papá. He did not want to be separated from him.

Papá said, "How?"

"In a car," said Coyote Lady. "We hide you. If I take only one across at a time, the car doesn't ride low in the back and does not look suspicious. I drive in a different lane each time. As you can see, we are having trouble with the usual ways, so we try this. It has worked before, especially on a busy day."

Marco didn't like the idea of being away from Papá. What would happen if Papá got across and he didn't? Or what if he couldn't find Papá on the other side? Then what would he do? He didn't like this part of the journey. Suddenly, he wished he'd stayed home for another year in Jocotepec.

Suddenly, Marco wished he'd stayed home for another year in Jocotepec.

As if reading his mind, Papá said, "I will go before you, Marco. And I will wait for you. I will not leave until you arrive. And if you don't arrive, I will come back to Tijuana."

Marco nodded.

Coyote Lady gave orders and told a woman to get ready to go. Every hour she stuck her head inside the room and called out another person.

Papá and Marco were the last of the group to go. They walked outside.

In the alley, the trash cans had been pushed aside to make room for an old car, a sedan. Flashlight Man waited beside the car, but he wasn't wearing his usual black uniform. Instead, he had on jeans, a blue-and-white football jersey, and a Chargers cap. He lifted the hood.

Inside, a small rectangular coffee table had been placed next to the motor, forming a narrow ledge. Two of the wooden legs disappeared into the bowels of the car and two of the legs had been cut short and now provided the braces against the radiator and motor.

"Okay," he said. "You lie down in here. It only takes a half hour. There is a van waiting for you in Chula Vista that will take you to your destinations."

Papá's Turn

Papá climbed up. Flashlight Man positioned his feet and legs so they would not touch the motor. Papá put his head and upper body on the tiny tabletop, curling his body to make it smaller. For an instant before the hood was closed, Papá's eyes caught Marco's.

Marco turned away so he wouldn't have to see his

father humbled in this manner.

"*Vámanos*," said Coyote Lady, and she wedged into the driver's seat. Flashlight Man sat on the passenger side. A Chargers football banner and blue pompoms sat on the dashboard as further proof of their deception. The car backed out of the alley and left. Marco closed the gate behind them.

He paced up and down the alley. They had said it would take an hour roundtrip. The minutes crawled by. Why did Papá agree to do this? Why did he resign himself to these people? "It is the way it is," Papá had said. Marco went back into the basement room and walked in circles.

After one hour, he put in a tape, *Aladdin,* and tried to pay attention as the characters sang about a whole new world. It was so easy in the video to get on a flying carpet to reach a magical place. *Where is this new world? Where is Papá? Did he get through?* Marco had never once heard a story of someone crossing over under the hood of a car. He tried to imagine being inside, next to the engine. His stomach churned. *Where is my magic carpet?*

The door opened suddenly. Flashlight Man was back. "Let's go," he said.

The car was already positioned in the alley with the hood up. Coyote Lady took Marco's backpack and threw it in the trunk. Marco climbed up on the bumper and swung his legs over the motor, then sat on the makeshift ledge. Flashlight Man arranged Marco's legs as if he were in a running position, one leg up, knee bent. One leg straighter, but slightly bent. Marco slowly lowered himself onto his side and put his head on the tabletop. Then he crossed his arms around his chest and watched the sunlight disappear to a tiny crack as the hood was closed.

"Don't move in there," said Flashlight Man.

Don't worry, thought Marco. *My fear will not permit me to move.*

The motor started. The noise hurt his ears, and within minutes it was hot. The smell of motor oil and gasoline accosted his nostrils. He breathed through his mouth, straining his lips toward the slit where the light crept through for fresh air. The car moved along for about 10 minutes until they reached the lanes of traffic that led to the border crossing. Then it was stop and go. Stop and go. Marco's legs began to cramp, but he knew not to move one inch. He tried not to imagine what would happen if he rolled onto the inner workings of the car.

The car lurched and stopped, over and over. Marco wanted to close his eyes, but he was afraid that he would get dizzy or disoriented. He watched the small crack between the car and hood as if it were his lifeline. A flash of color obliterated his line of sunlight as a flower vendor stopped in front of the car, trying to make one last sale to those in the car next to them "*¡Flores, flores!* You buy cheap."

The line of cars started to move again, but the flower vendor continued to walk in front of their car. Coyote Lady pressed on the horn. Marco's body trembled as the sound reverberated through his body. He inched his hands up to cover his ears. The vendor stepped out of the way, and the car began to move faster.

arco never knew when they actually crossed the line. He only knew when the car began to speed up on the freeway. His body pulsed with the vibrations of the car. Afraid to close his eyes, he watched beads of moisture move across the radiator, as if they had the ability to dance. Marco could not feel his right foot. It had fallen asleep. Panic crept into his chest and seized his muscles. He slowly pressed his hand back and forth across his chest to relieve the tightness. "No worries," he whispered. "No worries."

The car stopped and shook with a door being slammed. Marco heard someone fiddling with the hood latch. Light streamed into his eyes, and he squinted. Flashlight Man pulled him from the car and handed over his backpack. Marco stumbled from his dead foot, and his body still rocked with the feeling of the moving car. He looked around. He was in a parking lot behind an auto shop. Papá was waiting.

"We made it," said Papá, clapping Marco on the back. "We're in Chula Vista."

Marco said nothing. He couldn't hear what Papá had said because of the noise in his ears, as if they were filled with cotton and bees. He felt as if he'd been molested, his body misappropriated. He pulled away from Papá's arm and climbed into the waiting van, this one with seats and windows. The door slid shut. Marco turned his face to the window and saw Coyote Lady and Flashlight Man driving away.

The others in the van smiled and talked as if they'd all just come from a party. The relief of a successful crossing seemed to have unleashed their tongues. Marco listened as they talked of their jobs in towns he'd never heard of before: Escondido, Solana Beach, Poway, Oceanside. Papá told them that he and his son were going to Encinitas to work in the flower fields and that

it was his son's first time crossing over. Faces turned toward Marco.

Marco cringed, his discomfort showing. *Why did he have to mention me?*

One of the men laughed out loud. "At least you were not rolled in a mattress like I was on my first time!"

"Or like me," said a young woman, grinning. "They dressed me as an *abuelita,* a grandmother, with a wig and old clothes and had me walk across with another woman's identification. I was shaking the entire time."

Marco could only force a smile, but everyone else laughed.

Stories spilled from their lips about their first times or their friends' or family members': hiding inside hollowed-out bales of hay, cramped inside a hide-a-bed sofa from which the bed frame had been removed, buried in the middle of a truckload of crates filled with cackling chickens. Marco found himself chuckling and nodding in co-misery. An almost giddy air seemed to prevail as they all reveled in one another's bizarre stories and sometimes life-threatening circumstances.

He found himself eager to hear of each exploit and began feeling oddly proud and somehow connected to this unrelated group. A strange camaraderie seemed to permeate the air, and when one man told how he was hidden in a door panel of a truck, smashed in a fetal position for one hour, and thought he might suffocate, Marco laughed the hardest.

As the people were dropped off in towns along the way north, they shook hands with Marco and Papá and left them with the words "*Buena suerte,*" good luck. When Papá and Marco were the only ones left in the van and the driver finally headed up Freeway 5 toward Encinitas, Papá grinned at him. "OK now?"

Marco nodded. "OK." He looked out the window at the people in the cars on the freeway. They were all headed somewhere in the United States of America. Marco wondered how many were headed to a whole new world. ∎

Pam Muñoz Ryan's maternal grandparents immigrated to the United States from Aguascalientes, Mexico, during the Great Depression. Her grandmother's life was the inspiration for Ryan's book *Esperanza Rising.* Ryan's other books include the historical *Riding Freedom,* the biography *When Marian Sang,* and several picture books, among them *Amelia and Eleanor Go for a Ride, Mud Is Cake,* and *Hello, Ocean.*

Life on the Border

BY LINDA CHRISTENSEN

Reading Chilpancingo

"The border" is not simply a wall, nor just a site for foreign investment. It's where people live. In "Reading Chilpancingo," English teacher Linda Christensen describes a visit to the Chilpancingo colonia in Tijuana and how she uses this experience to craft critical reading activities for her students.

When I met Lourdes Lujan and saw her contaminated river, I knew I had to teach about Chilpancingo, a Tijuana neighborhood where corporations' toxic presence and women's organizing against the monster in their backyards make for David and Goliath teaching lessons.

When our Rethinking Schools–Global Exchange tour first entered Colonia Chilpancingo and descended downhill to where the waste from hilltop factories bubbled into Río Alamar, the stench of burning rubber and untreated garbage filled the air. Lourdes Lujan, local activist,

 **Thousands of tons of abandoned, hazardous chemicals have unleashed a horror on this Tijuana neighborhood.**

walked down from her home perched above the river. "When I was growing up, I played and fished in this river," she said. "My family had picnics at that park." She pointed to a sandy, trash-filled triangle at the edge of the river filled with discarded tires, pop cans, plastic bottles, baby diapers, and a lone picnic table. Her arms are pocked with rashes.

"Now, when the stream starts to flow, and it isn't even the rainy season, the kids play in the puddles. You know how kids are. They play in the water, and get blisters all over their feet."

Lourdes Lujan is part of a collective that works with

women in their local communities and across the U.S. border to battle the giant corporations and their governments that have made her home a nightmare. But the horror story unleashed by Metales y Derivados, a U.S.-owned battery recycling company whose owner abandoned thousands of tons of hazardous chemicals that contaminated Colonia Chilpancingo, didn't stop with rashes and blisters. Lourdes described children born without brain stems, children whose parents slept with them at night, fearful they would drown in their own blood from spontaneous nose bleeds, maquila workers who suffered miscarriages and birth defects, neighbors with abnormally high rates of cancer. She pointed to the buildings on the ridge above Chilpancingo and explained how Santa Ana winds blow contaminated waste down into her village, how the rains sluice down the side of the mesa and pool in the grade school at the bottom of the hill.

I watch two boys walking on a muddy path, heading to their homes constructed from wooden pallets and tarps, homes without running water or sewage connections. The men, women, and children who seek shelter along this toxic riverbed have traveled from southern Mexico, hoping to find work on the maquila-saturated hilltop and a toehold into a better life. We ask Lourdes if they know about the contamination. She shrugs. It's hard to get people to care about potential harm when daily they worry about getting enough food for their children.

Later, we learn about elevated lead counts, the high price of lead tests compared to maquila wages, and the long fight that Lujan and her group have waged to edu-

---

Two men listen to a prayer near the U.S.-Mexico border fence before a march to mark the 10th anniversary of Operation Gatekeeper and to commemorate the 3,200 migrants who died crossing into the United States during its first 10 years. The crosses indicate "No olvidado" — Not forgotten.

cate their neighbors about the factories' toxic waste. We learn about the lawsuits they've sponsored to make Jose Kahn, the San Diego-based owner of Metales y Derivados, and the U.S. and Mexican governments clean up the poisons surrounding Chilpancingo.

Back Home

To bring the lesson back to my junior students at Grant High School in Portland, Ore., I start with a photograph of the hill opposite Chilpancingo that includes a shot of the makeshift housing for maquila workers and a polluted stream. Eventually, they will read an article about the toxic waste, but I use the photograph to stir their interest. My students are a delightful mix of colors, attitudes, and ambitions. What unites them is that they didn't choose to be in any of the honors, AP, or advanced English classes that Grant High School offers. Many struggle with reading and writing; about a third spend at least one period of the day in special education classes or they have a case worker; others have sophisticated literacy skills, but have disengaged from school for a variety of reasons. Any lesson I bring to my class must include reading and writing strategies for this diverse group. I've discovered through our lessons on race, class, and Hurricane Katrina that they care about the world beyond their cell phones. I attempt to build units that teach literacy skills embedded in larger world issues, and I try to find places where they can learn to read critically, but that also give them examples of how people have worked together to confront oppression. Chilpancingo fits my criteria.

I put the photograph of Chilpancingo on the overhead. (See photo, p. 99. This photo in color can be downloaded at www.rethinkingschools.org/mexico.) I tell students: "Reading a picture is like reading a text. You read on a number of levels. I want you to read the picture first. Just make a list of everything you see in the photo. Don't make any judgments about what's there. Make a list." My students verbalize while they work. Perhaps not everything they think comes out of their mouths, but they are not a quiet group: "Shacks," one student says.

"Wait. Wait. You're making a judgment," I tell them. "Just write what you see. Someone give me an example." Ann Truax, an outstanding Portland ESL teacher, taught me to begin reading lessons with visual texts to draw students in, but also to give English language learners pictures in their heads as they encounter new vocabulary. I've discovered this strategy works with all students as a pre-reading strategy.

The students catalogue details in the picture: Water. Bottles. Cans. Dead tree. Shadow. Smoke. Blue tarps.

Water. Gray skies. Truck. Houses. Rust. Their lists grow long. They crowd around the overhead to get a better look. Later, I see that Charlie has written, "Sedges, a small weed-like plant that grows by water."

Students share their lists with a partner. Then we go around the class with everyone adding items from their lists. When Dontay calls out, "Dirty water," I stop the shout-out.

"Wait. That's a judgment. Where's your evidence? How can you tell that the water is dirty?"

Dontay looks back at the picture. "See the bottles and paper in the water? That's what makes it dirty."

"OK. Now when you do that in reading, it's called an inference. You gather up information, then you make a judgment about it. For example, if you read about a man who slapped his child in the grocery store; what kind of inference would you make about him?"

"Child abuser," Alley shouts.

I admit. I am shamelessly didactic, but too many of my students have bought into the idea that they can't read. My job is to show them that they are "reading" all the time. I want to name their reading strategies, so when they read word texts, they can remember that they know how to do this.

"Now, I want you to list your questions." When no one writes, I ask, "Who has a question?"

Josh starts, "The five w's. Where is the picture taken? What is in the picture? When was it taken? Why was it taken? Who took the picture?"

"What's in the river?" Katie asks.

"Is there piss in the river?" Vernell jokes to get a laugh.

"Now, on your own." I use this question technique prior to introducing the reading because often my poor readers read the surface of words. They skim over the paragraphs, forgetting what they've read as soon as their eyes have passed the words. They even talk about their "comprehension problems." I use activities like this one to teach them how to read with questions in their heads to provide hooks to slow them down, but also to capture images, facts, and ideas that slide by when they read without purpose.

"When we share out, I want you to write down other people's questions. When you read the article about this place, I want you to read to answer all of these questions." I've found that it's not enough to practice strategies without discussing them with my students. When I make my reasons for using the strategies transparent, they understand what I'm doing, so they can transfer the process. At parent conferences, I was pleased when the parent of one of my mainstreamed special education students explained how her son was transferring the strategies he'd learned in my class to his history class. He showed her how he highlighted and wrote

Portland, Ore., teacher Danica Fierman took this photo in the Chilpancingo colonia of Tijuana during a Rethinking Schools–Global Exchange tour. Linda Christensen uses the photo in one of the "Reading Chilpancingo" activities.

marginal notes and told her that it helped him retain the information.

After students review their questions with a partner, we share in the large group again. I write the questions on the overhead as students call them out. It's clear that they've started caring more about what's happening in the picture. Their cute, glib remarks are gone. "Who lives there? Is this human's destruction or nature's? Where did the garbage come from? Why doesn't someone clean it up? What caused this mess? Where is the water coming from? Are there any dead bodies? Is this a dumpsite? Do people live there? Why is that tree dead? What is in that mound? Is this a wetland? Is that a neighborhood behind the trees and shrubs? Do people drink the water? What are they trying to show with the picture? Why don't the people move to a better place?"

Making Connections

I move to the next pre-reading strategy — connecting new information to previous knowledge. Skilled readers and learners do this automatically, but struggling readers don't. "Now, I want you to make connections between the picture and your lives. Does this remind you of any place you've been? Movies? News programs? Something you've read? Who can make a connection?"

No one answers. "Does it look like a spot on the way to the Oregon coast?" Still no answer. I continue, "When I showed this picture to a group of teachers, one of them said that it looked like a field where he and his friends hung out in high school. It kind of reminds me of Beggar's Tick, the site where my daughter Gretchen took water and soil samples when she was in Mr. Street's environmental science class."

"It looks like the off ramp to the dump," Ethan says.

"Great. The reason you want to make connections between the picture and your life is that when you make a connection, your brain finds a way to remember it. This is the same thing you do when you read. But it's also to think about the similarities in their lives and ours — as well as the differences."

Calais raises her hand, "This reminds me of Tijuana when Heather and I went there last summer with our church group to build a playground."

"OK, now write your connections."

Thomas writes that it reminds him of the ads about adopting poor children. "They always show them surrounded by trash." Other students write: a relative's backyard, New Orleans after the hurricane. Charlie writes that it reminds him of the "crap Tim Robbins had to crawl through at the end of *Shawshank*

Redemption." Brittany writes, "Driving through L.A. in September."

"Now, it's time to read about this place. All year, we've been keeping two ideas in front of us as we read: injustice and hope. When we read about Hurricane Katrina, we examined where there was injustice, and where we found hope. When we read _Thousand Pieces of Gold,_ we talked about the injustice that Lalu faced, and where she found hope. Now, I'm going to give you an article that was published in the _Washington Post;_ I want you to read to identify both the injustice and the hope in this situation. I also want you to use the same strategies we used to 'read' the picture while you are reading the article. Keep those questions in front of you as you read."

BOB PETERSON

Chilpancingo's Río Alamar area has no running water or other services. Water is delivered by trucks. Filling a 55-gallon barrel costs about $1.50 — roughly 12 times as much as public water in Portland, Ore.

The class moves into their work groups. In this class of diverse abilities, I strategically place strong and weak readers together. I hang group members' names on the sides of the room where I've clustered their desks. I distribute highlighters and copies of Kevin Sullivan's article (see p. 102). This is a difficult read for many of my students.

"Feel free to read this out loud in your group. Highlight places in the article that answer your questions. Write new questions that the article raises for you in the margins. Find the justice and the hope." Students' outrage is immediate. I can hear Ethan cursing in his corner overlooking the soccer field. I hear Ryan, "Damn, man, this is cold." The bell rings before we can discuss the article.

Adding Details

The next day I draw a circle on the overhead; I write Chilpancingo in the middle and ask students to return to their articles and notes. "Let's review the reading from yesterday. What key pieces of information should I add to the 'map' of the article?"

Hillary says, "You need a section for birth defects."

Russell adds, "You need a part for effects of the toxic waste on the people who live there."

"How about a section on what happened to the environment?"

The overhead fills up as students tell me where to add details. Josh points to the overhead, "By birth defects you want to add still births, born without lower body and without skulls."

Katie adds, "By the environment, you need to add toxic waste; Metales; Jose Kahn, the owner of Metales."

I had worried that students wouldn't understand the article, but without even looking back at their notes, they were shouting out answers. When they did return to the article, they looked for specific numbers — the amount of waste left behind, the cost of the cleanup.

"Now, tell me what new questions came up for you in your reading? What do you still want to know that this article didn't answer?" I wind the overhead to a new sheet as students call out their questions. "You write them down too," I say, "because we will read more articles about Chilpancingo."

I list their questions on the overhead: What happened to the children? Did Jose Kahn ever clean up the waste he left behind? Are there still birth defects? Who helped clean it up? What happened to Carmen's new baby? Their questions are specific. Pointed. They want to know what happened to these people.

"I want you to get back into your groups. Each person in your group is going to read a different article that gives more information. In order to answer your questions, you will each need to read carefully, take notes, and then share your information with your group."

I distribute color-coded articles written from different perspectives about Chilpancingo. (These articles are online at www.rethinkingschools.org/mexico.) For example, I give one student in each group Mariana Martínez's article "Empowerment Brings Change." This article describes how Factor X, a Tijuana women's group that provides education to maquila workers, teaches women how to advocate for themselves and their communities. As Martínez explains:

> Little by little people are learning to speak out, and become an agent of change. An example of the people taking charge was the case against Metales y Derivados, a company owned by New Frontier Company in San Diego. After many complaints from the community to the Mexican environmental authorities, after gathering over 500 signatures and organizing protests, the case was finally brought to the attention of the Environmental Cooperation Committee, which was established as part of the Free Trade Treaty [NAFTA], who ... established that the chemicals that this company manages are of "grave danger to human health" and that "Mexican authorities had failed to enforce their own environmental laws."

I give the article "Environmental Health and Toxic Waste" to my struggling readers because it contains pictures of Lourdes Lujan and Magdalena Cerda, an activist from San Diego, as well as pictures of the Metales plant. It has shorter passages, but it provides some relevant information about how the toxic waste generated in Tijuana doesn't stay there:

> The air and water are shared. The runoff from the Industrial City flows into a stream in Colonia Chilpancingo. ... The pollution produced in Tijuana equally affects the people of San Diego. In addition, the capital which comes to Tijuana is American capital, which for the people here produces only a little money and a lot of pollution. People in Mexico need this work desperately, but it doesn't allow them to live in dignity or comfort. This type of injustice is not tolerable, and this is why we work together.

I realize that I didn't clarify to students that the second round of readings would contain overlapping informa-

tion with the first. I also didn't point out the different dates on the readings, so they were not as alert to the changes within each article as I hoped they would be.

"When you finish your reading, share your information with your group. Add this new information to your map. Then write a paragraph summarizing what you learned about injustices in Chilpancingo and where you find hope."

Most expressed both outrage and hope about the environmental destruction wreaked on this community. Charlie's anger at Jose Kahn was echoed by his classmates, but he did find hope in the community's organizing:

> I believe what Jose Kahn did was horrible and the United States should make him pay for the cleanup. The community around the pollution is paying instead. There is a lot of hope in that community, along with a lot of strength. They have come together and formed programs to educate themselves on how to deal with the problem. Meanwhile, the U.S. needs to do the right thing and make Jose Kahn pay.

Brittany blamed Jose Kahn as well, but again found hope in the neighbors organizing:

> It was definitely wrong for Jose Kahn to just leave all that toxic waste in Chilpancingo. It was killing all of the residents. Not immediately, but slowly and painfully. ... Jose didn't have to pay because he crossed the border. But what is cool is that the residents are being informed and informing each other about how to protect themselves and deal with the toxins. There is a five-year project to clean up Chilpancingo.

My students didn't travel to Mexico with me. They didn't stand on the banks of Río Alamar, smell the acrid odor of a town drowning in toxins, see the rash on Lourdes's arms. But sitting in a classroom near the banks of the Columbia River, they learned how to step into a picture and connect with a community on the other side of the border and question why it's OK for a U.S. corporation to leave toxic waste behind, and discover how women organizing in local communities can tackle giants — and win. ∎

My students didn't stand on the banks of Río Alamar and smell the acrid odor of a town drowning in toxins. But they learned how to step into a picture and connect with a community on the other side of the border.

Linda Christensen (lchrist@aol.com) is an editor of *Rethinking Schools* magazine. She is author of *Reading, Writing, and Rising Up: Teaching About Social Justice and the Power of the Written Word.*

BY KEVIN SULLIVAN

A Toxic Legacy on the Mexican Border

TIJUANA, Mexico — Andrea's monster lives up here.

It breathes lead dust that coats her windows and her baby toys. It sweats rivers of arsenic and cadmium and antimony that seep into her water and the soil where her children play. It squats on a hilltop above her home, horrible and poisonous.

"There it is," says Andrea Pedro Aguilar, breathing heavily from the hike up the hill.

She is standing in front of her monster, the derelict remains of a lead smelter that everyone here calls Metales. For more than a decade, an American-owned company, Metales y Derivados, took in thousands of U.S. car and boat batteries, cracked them open to extract their lead, melted it into bricks and shipped the bricks back to the United States.

The toxic dump here exemplifies how much of the border area is a no man's land, a place where international companies have polluted the environment.

Mexico shut the plant in 1994 and the next year its owner, a U.S. citizen named Jose Kahn, crossed the border back into San Diego. Mexican arrest warrants were outstanding, charging him with gross environmental pollution. He still lives in a comfortable neighborhood of San Diego.

According to the Mexican government, he left behind up to 8,500 tons of toxins from battery guts that lie strewn over three acres, in open piles, rusted barrels, and rotted bales. Every time the wind blows or the rain falls, more of the toxins end up in Colonia Chilpancingo, a worker's village of 10,000 people directly below the plant.

According to Mexican environmental officials and the U.S. Environmental Protection Agency, the toxic dump here exemplifies how much of the border area is a no man's land, a place where international companies have polluted the environment.

When the Metales furnaces were still burning in 1990, a Mexican university study found levels of lead more than 3,000 times higher than U.S. standards and levels of cadmium more than 1,000 times higher in a stream that runs through the community and eventually flows north over the border into the United States. A 1999 study by the enforcement division of Mexico's environment ministry found lead concentrations in the soil near the plant 50 times higher than the limit set by Mexican law. That report called the Metales site a "major health risk."

A cleanup of the site could cost $6 million or more. In 2002, the state of Baja California and Kahn filed a joint loan request for $800,000 from the North American Development Bank, which was created as part of the 1994 North American Free Trade Agreement (NAFTA). A bank official said the unusual request — coming amid rising demands from residents for a cleanup — is being reviewed. He said one concern is that the loan might not cover the cost of the cleanup.

In the meantime, the toxins bake in the sun and blow in the wind. The pollution keeps flowing into Chilpancingo, from Metales and from some of the other 130 factories, known as maquiladoras, in the huge industrial park, Otay Mesa, where it sits.

"Danger, hazardous waste" is stenciled on the concrete wall that partially surrounds Metales. But the place is still a favorite for dare-taking kids who scoot through holes in a fence into the forbidden site.

Reached by telephone, Kahn, who is in his late 80s, said, "We are negotiating a loan to clean up the place. I really can't tell you anything more than that." He declined further comment on Friday. In an interview published in the *San Diego Union-Tribune*, Kahn said the loan request shows that he is serious about cleaning up Metales: "We all want a solution. No one wants to

AP PHOTO/LENNY IGNELZI

Toxic remains of the U.S.-owned Metales y Derivados plant above Chilpancingo.

walk about without a cleanup."

It hasn't rained in Chilpancingo for nearly two months, but dirty water still runs down the middle of Andrea's street. It starts in a gaping drainage pipe that emerges from beneath the industrial park that emits a milky white flow of God-knows-what that flows downhill to Andrea's neighborhood. Factories there are required by law to treat their own hazardous waste, but state environmental officials say many still dump illegally.

"I don't know what they were thinking," says Andrea, who had two feet of acrid, filthy water in her living room when heavy rains caused flooding last year. "People live down there."

Neighbors like her kids. Lupita is 4 and Ivan is 6. They ride scooters in their living room and watch *Monsters, Inc.* and *Rugrats* for hours on end. Andrea thinks it's safer for them to be inside even though her little lead-testing kits have turned up elevated levels of the toxin on her dishes and on the sill of her kitchen window. Outside, the fruit trees and grass that her mother planted 20 years ago have all died.

Just before Christmas, 20 Chilpancingo children under the age of 6 were tested for lead. Officials from the Environmental Health Coalition, a San Diego-based organization, said that all the results showed significant and potentially dangerous levels of lead in their bloodstreams. Lupita's blood had the highest level, 9 micrograms of lead per deciliter, just under the level of 10 micrograms per deciliter, classified as elevated for children by the U.S. Centers for Disease Control and Prevention. Lead, especially in children, can damage organs and severely retard mental development, and studies suggest it may cause cancer and birth defects.

Officials at the CDC said arsenic, cadmium, antimony and other byproducts of the smelting process are carcinogens. CDC officials also said that exposure to those metals can cause skin rashes, nosebleeds and hair loss.

Lupita's hair slips out by the brushful every day, and she has suffered spontaneous bleeding in her nose and throat for the past couple of years. It got so bad in November that Andrea and her husband slept with Lupita, out of fear that she might drown in her own blood. Andrea says they did not know what was causing her problems. Then her lead test came back positive.

Now Andrea stands before the monster, a mile south of the U.S. border, shaking her head in disgust.

Wenceslao Martínez, a physician, runs a health clinic a few blocks from Andrea's house. He says he constantly sees patients with suspicious diseases, from chronic rashes to cancers to fatal birth defects.

"For a colonia of only 10,000 people, what we see here is very strange," he said. "There is definitely a link to the maquiladoras. But it's hard to prove. So who gets

ENVIRONMENTAL HEALTH COALITION

The remains of the Metales y Derivados site. The sign reads, "Danger: Contamination."

the blame? Nobody."

He treated Margarita Jaimes's 3-year-old son, Serafin Vidrio, who turned up one day in July 2002 with swelling in his neck and eyes. He was diagnosed with acute leukemia on Aug. 6. He died on Aug. 24.

Margarita, like the others, is frustrated no one has spent the money to study whether the illnesses around these factories are linked to the toxins they have dumped. As she talks, her daughter, Eva Paulette, 6, sits on her lap. She has been having nosebleeds. Her hair is falling out in clumps. The doctors cannot explain it.

Carmen Garcia used to walk to work every day past Andrea's house, past the open piles of sludge at Metales to a factory where she assembled stereo speakers. When she became pregnant, she knew her factory was not the best environment, because in the previous two years three of her co-workers had delivered stillborn babies.

Then on Nov. 3, 2000, Carmen delivered Miguel Angel, who suffered from anencephaly, a fatal defect in which babies are born with little or no brain or skull. Miguel Angel's empty skull was open wide like a tulip. He survived for two months.

"It's like a trap here," Carmen said. She's pregnant again. "I'm so scared."

A CDC spokesperson estimated that anencephaly occurs in two to four of every 10,000 births in the United States; hydrocephaly, a related disorder, occurs in about six of 10,000 births.

The state of Baja California, which includes Tijuana, is now conducting its first major study of those two birth defects. Moises Rodríguez Lomeli, the state's chief epidemiologist, said the study was launched after state officials realized the rate of those birth defects in the state was abnormally high. In one two-block area of Chilpancingo, residents count eight babies born with those two defects in recent years.

Andrea and other community leaders, working with the Environmental Health Coalition, filed a complaint about Metales with the Commission for Environmental Cooperation, NAFTA's environmental watchdog agency. The commission issued a report in 2002 noting that "exposure to these heavy metals can severely harm human health" and called the site's cleanup "urgent."

In the commission's 154-page report, the enforcement division of Mexico's environment ministry said that "with alarming regularity" foreign-owned factories are being abandoned, with their hazardous waste left behind. It also said the EPA viewed the Metales situation as "exemplifying a critical public policy issue in the border region: the use of the border as a shield against enforcement." The Mexican government has been reluctant to clean up foreign-made messes, and when the foreigners return home they are beyond the reach of Mexico's laws.

Black smoke is rising from a burning car behind Andrea's house. She's standing in her fenced-in yard, where she rents out a couple of small shacks to make a little money. The woman who lives in one of them gave birth a few months ago to a baby missing most of its lower body. The previous tenant in the same house woke up with her neck swollen like a bullfrog's. "Two months later, she was dead," Andrea says. "Nobody ever knew why."

Andrea and other women in the community, with help from the Environmental Health Coalition, are now trying to educate residents about the hazards around them. They pass out lead-testing kits and arrange blood tests for children. They write to government officials and hold all-night vigils outside their offices. They marched on Kahn's office in San Diego, holding up signs with such messages as: "Jose Kahn: You forgot something in Tijuana."

A couple of unhurried firemen arrive to begin hosing down the burning car. Andrea, who is pregnant again, says she dreams of the day when all the toxic pollution is gone, when Chilpancingo is clean and healthy, filled with flowers and trees, the way she remembered it as a girl.

Then she closes her eyes against the thick, black smoke.

The Transnational Capital Auction

After NAFTA took effect, according to the Institute for Policy Studies, maquiladora employment in Mexico shot up from 550,000 in 1994 to 1.3 million in 2000. But then it slumped to 1.07 million in 2004. Corporations that had migrated from the United States to Mexico, seeking lower wages and a more favorable "investment climate," continued to sniff out better opportunities around the globe. As "efficient as Mexican laborers have proven to be in global competition, they fall far short of Chinese workers in the low wage department," one writer pointed out. U.S. investment in Mexico started heading to Asia. Like it or not, Mexico was a player in a worldwide bidding war to attract capital.

I wrote this simulation game, "The Transnational Capital Auction," because I wanted students to grasp some aspects of capital (i.e., foreign investment), as a force in today's world — to help them see that social conditions in poor countries need to be viewed in terms of a global capitalist system. The game is a metaphor for the auction that capital holds to determine who in the world will make the most attractive bid for its "services." Students engage this dynamic from the standpoint of Third World elites, and simulate a phenomenon that has been called the "race to the bottom," whereby these elites compete against one another to attract capital. The game's "punch line" is an examination of the social and ecological consequences of the auction. The activity helps anticipate students' key question in the Mexico Border Improvisations (p. 113): "Why does the Mexican government allow Mexican workers on the border, and the environment, to be so mistreated?"

Note: If any of what follows starts to feel complicated, don't worry. The game has been used by lots of teachers, with excellent success. It's simpler than it may appear.

Materials Needed

- Several desirable candy bars — at least six.
- Copies of the student handout "The Transnational Capital Auction Game" — one for each student in the class.
- Copies of the "Transnational Capital Auction 'Friendly to Capital' Credit Sheet" — a minimum of seven, enough so that each country group can have at least one.
- A minimum of 35 copies of the "Bids to Capital" slips so that each group has one per round (seven groups, five auction rounds).

Time Required

It's best to have a block period of 80 or 90 minutes to complete this. I've done it in shorter periods of time by reducing the number of rounds to three or four.

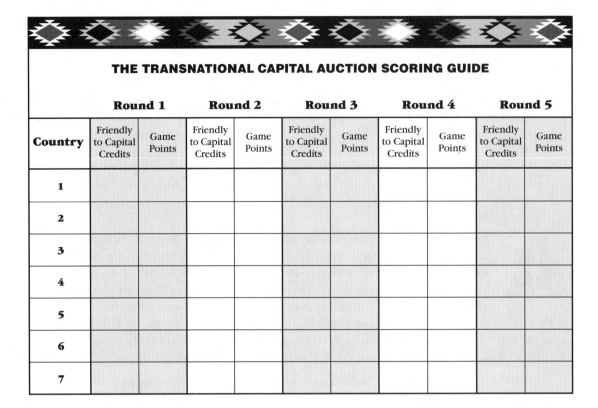

THE TRANSNATIONAL CAPITAL AUCTION SCORING GUIDE

Country	Round 1		Round 2		Round 3		Round 4		Round 5	
	Friendly to Capital Credits	Game Points	Friendly to Capital Credits	Game Points	Friendly to Capital Credits	Game Points	Friendly to Capital Credits	Game Points	Friendly to Capital Credits	Game Points
1										
2										
3										
4										
5										
6										
7										

Suggested Procedure

1. Before the activity, create the auction scoring guide on the board or on an overhead transparency. It should look something like the chart above.

2. If you have at least 21 students in your class, divide them into seven groups. Ask the groups to form around the classroom, as far away from one another as possible.

3. Distribute copies of "The Transnational Capital Auction Game," "Transnational Capital Auction 'Friendly to Capital' Credit Sheet," and the "Bids to Capital" slips (each group should receive five "Bids to Capital" slips, one for each round). Read aloud with students the full handout "The Transnational Capital Auction Game" (both the "Introduction" and "Rules of the Game"). It should be obvious, but emphasize the distinction between Friendly to Capital credits and game points.

   Answer any questions students might have. Review the "Transnational Capital Auction 'Friendly to Capital' Credit Sheet." Point out that a group earns more credits the friendlier it is to capital. Show them the candy bars and announce that the three groups with the most game points will win all the candy bars. (If you like, before the game begins, you can suggest that students name their countries instead of just using a number.)

4. Begin the first round: Tell students to make their bids in each of the categories and to total up their Friendly to Capital credits on the "Bids to Capital" slips. Note that this is really the hardest round because students don't have any way of knowing what the other groups are bidding.

   I play "Capital" in the game, and wander the classroom as the small groups decide on their bids, urging them to lower the minimum wage, taxes on corporate profits and the like. I prod them with comments like, "Come on, show that you really want me!"

5. After each group has submitted its bid, write these up on the board or overhead. Award the first game points based on the results — again, 100 game points for the third highest number of Friendly to Capital credits, 50 for the second highest and 25 for the first. (This is explained in the handout that includes "Rules of the Game"). After this first round has been played, and the points are posted, I scoff at the losers and urge them to get with the program and start

making some bids that will attract Capital.

From this point on, for better or for worse, the competition to "win," or for candy bars, takes over, and students "race to the bottom" of conditions for their respective countries. Sometimes they even realize what they're doing as they decide on their bids. "This is like 'The Price Is Right,' oppression style," I overheard one of my students say one year.

6. After each round of bids, continue to post the Friendly to Capital credit scores and award game points for that round. Keep a running total of each country team's game points. As Capital, I continue to urge students lower and lower: "Country five, you think I'm going to come to your country if your tax rate is 30 percent? Come on, next round let's get that way down."

7. For the fifth and final round, ask each student to write down their group's last bid, separate from the "Bid to Capital" slips — not just the number of credits, but the actual minimum wage, the child labor laws, etc. For their homework writing assignment, each student needs to know the specific social and environmental conditions created by the auction in their pretend country.

Award candy bars to the "winners." For homework, or in class, ask students to write on two questions:

- Look over your auction "bids" for the fifth and final round of the Transnational Capital Auction — on minimum wage, child labor, worker organizing, taxation rates, and environmental laws. If Capital were to accept your "bid" and come to your country, what would be the real human and environmental consequences there?
- How might this activity relate to what's going on in Mexico today?

8. Some additional discussion questions to raise:

- What would be the social effects of such low wages? (You might list these on the board or overhead.) How would families be able to survive? How could a family supplement its income? You might point out that even if a country did have child labor laws, the low wages for adults would put pressure on a family to send its children to work.
- Why did you keep driving down conditions in your country? Why didn't you get together and refuse to bid each other down?
- How are the "transnational capital auction" and the "race to the bottom" related to high rates of immigration from poor countries to wealthier countries? to the conditions in the Chilpancingo colonia of Tijuana?
- In what way, if any, is NAFTA related to the "transnational capital auction"?
- Is corporate investment always a good thing? (You might make two columns on the board or overhead and ask students to list possible benefits of investment and some of the harmful effects of investment and how it is attracted.)
- Who benefits and who doesn't benefit from the "race to the bottom" we simulated in class? How could people in various countries get together to stop attacks on their social and environmental conditions?
- What could we do in this country to respond to the global "race to the bottom"?

9. One option would be to give students an opportunity to play the Transnational Capital Auction all over again, except this time they could represent labor and environmental activists instead of a country's elite.

It's important that, if possible, students not be left with the sense that the downward leveling they experience in the auction is inexorable. Students need to see "big pictures" in order to recognize how countries as diverse as the United States and Mexico are linked in global "auctions" simulated here. But we also need to highlight those groups that seek alternatives and attempt to build alliances across borders to challenge the race to the bottom, as is the case, for example between the San Diego-based Environmental Health Coalition and the Colectivo Chilpancingo Pro-justicia Ambiental in Mexico.

The Transnational Capital Auction Game

Introduction

You are leaders of a poor country. Each of your countries was either colonized by European countries or dominated by them economically and militarily. You need to attract foreign investment (capital) from transnational corporations for many different reasons. Of course, not all of your people are poor. Many, including a number of you, are quite wealthy. But your wealth depends largely on making deals with corporations that come to your country. You get various kickbacks, bribes, and jobs for members of your families. Some of this is legal, some not. But in order to stay in power you also need to provide jobs for your people, and the owners of capital (companies like Nike, Disney, Coca-Cola, Hyundai, Panasonic, Levi Strauss, etc.) are the ones who provide thousands of jobs in their factories. The more jobs you can bring into your country, the more legitimacy you have in the eyes of your people. *And,* your government collects taxes from these companies, which help keep your government working, and also help you pay back loans to the International Monetary Fund and other foreign-owned banks. **The bottom line is this: You badly need these companies to invest capital in your country.**

But here's the problem: You must compete with other poor countries that also need capital. Corporations are not stupid, and so they let you know that if you want their investment, you must compete with other countries by:

- Keeping workers' wages low.
- Having few laws to regulate conditions of work (overtime, breaks, health and safety conditions, age of workers), or not enforcing laws that *are* on the books.
- Having weak environmental laws.
- Making sure that workers can't organize unions; having low taxes on corporate profits, etc.

Basically, companies hold an auction for their investments. The countries that offer the companies the most "freedom" are the ones that get the investment.

Rules of the Game

The goal is to win the game by ending up with the most *game points* after five auction rounds. Each country team's goal is to "win" by attracting capital. The team that bids *the third highest number* of "Friendly to Capital" credits in a round is *awarded 100 game points;* the team with *the second highest number of Capital credits is awarded 50 game points;* and the team with *the highest number of Capital credits is awarded 25 game points.* The other teams get **no** points for the round. The auction is "silent" — you don't know until the end of each round who has bid what.

Again, Capital will go where the people are "friendliest" to it. However, the "friendlier" you are to Capital, the angrier it may make your own people. For example, Capital wants workers to work for very little and to not worry about environmental laws. But that could start demonstrations or even rebellions, which would not be good for Capital or for you as leaders of your country. That's why the team bidding the highest number of Capital credits does not get the highest number of game points. **Last rule:** Your team may be the highest (Capital credit) bidder *twice* and not be penalized. But for each time you are highest bidder more than twice, you lose 10 game points — 10 the first time, 20 the second, etc. This is a "rebellion penalty." Good luck.

The Transnational Capital Auction Game
'Friendly to Capital' Credit Sheet

Minimum Wage/Hour Credits

Wage/Hour	Credits
$5.00	0
$4.75	10
$4.50	15
$4.25	20
$4.00	25
$3.75	30
$3.50	33
$3.25	37
$3.00	40
$2.75	43
$2.50	46
$2.25	49
$2.00	52
$1.75	55
$1.50	58
$1.25	61
$1.00	64
$0.85	67
$0.75	70
$0.65	73
$0.55	76
$0.45	79
$0.35	82
$0.30	85
$0.25	88
$0.20	91
$0.15	94
$0.10	97
$0.05	100

Child Labor Credits

	Credits
Child labor below 16 is illegal/enforced	0
Child labor below 16 is illegal/weakly enforced	15
Child labor below 16 is illegal/not enforced	30
Child labor below 14 is illegal/enforced	50
Child labor below 14 is illegal/weakly enforced	70
Child labor below 14 is illegal/not enforced	85
No child labor laws	100

Worker Organizing Credits

	Credits
Unions fully legal/allowed to organize	0
Unions fully legal/some restrictions on right to strike	15
Only government approved unions legal/some restrictions	30
Only government organized unions allowed	45
Unions banned/no right to strike	60
Unions banned/no right to strike/military stationed in factories	85
Unions banned/no right to strike/military stationed in factories/suspected union organizers jailed/military used against strikes	100

Environmental Laws Credits

	Credits
Strict environmental laws/enforced	0
Strict environmental laws/weakly enforced	15
Strict environmental laws/not often enforced	30
Some environmental laws/enforced	50
Some environmental laws/weakly enforced	70
Some environmental laws/not often enforced	85
Almost no environmental laws	100

Taxation Rate on Corporate Profits

Rate	Credits	Rate	Credits	Rate	Credits
75%	0	50%	25	20%	70
70%	5	45%	30	15%	75
65%	10	40%	35	10%	80
60%	15	35%	40	5%	90
55%	20	30%	50	0% (no taxes)	100
		25%	60		

The Transnational Capital Auction: Bids to Capital Slips

BIDS TO CAPITAL

Round #_____

Country _____

    Minimum wage credits . . . . . _____

    Child labor credits. . . . . _____

    Worker organizing credits. . . . _____

    Taxation rate credits. . . . . . . _____

    Environmental laws credits . . . _____

Total credits this round . . _____

BIDS TO CAPITAL

Round #_____

Country _____

    Minimum wage credits . . . . . _____

    Child labor credits. . . . . _____

    Worker organizing credits. . . . _____

    Taxation rate credits. . . . . . . _____

    Environmental laws credits . . . _____

Total credits this round . . _____

BIDS TO CAPITAL

Round #_____

Country _____

    Minimum wage credits . . . . . _____

    Child labor credits. . . . . _____

    Worker organizing credits. . . . _____

    Taxation rate credits. . . . . . . _____

    Environmental laws credits . . . _____

Total credits this round . . _____

BIDS TO CAPITAL

Round #_____

Country _____

    Minimum wage credits . . . . . _____

    Child labor credits. . . . . _____

    Worker organizing credits. . . . _____

    Taxation rate credits. . . . . . . _____

    Environmental laws credits . . . _____

Total credits this round . . _____

BY AMALIA ORTIZ

The Women of Juárez

AT THE WEST TIP OF TEXAS
a line divides us from them
and on the other side
they all look like me
yet on my side we sit passively nearby
while the other side allows a slow genocide

500 missing women
some claim more
some less
some dismissed as runaways
against parents' protest
hundreds found dead
hundreds still missing
the exact count is a mystery
and those disappearing daily
they all look like me

I am a dead ringer
for an army of the dead
Mexico's slaughtered sisters
all slim
long dark hair
petite
some say pretty
my family would in my absence
all young
all lost
or dead
and they all look like me

some foolishly search for one serial killer
when bus and cab drivers
even cops are under suspicion
while the ever growing numbers reflect an entire
society
where young women are expendable
young women like me

mothers recognize raped and mutilated remains
daughters' clothes with mismatched human bones
DNA that doesn't match
those are her shoes
but that's not her hat
this shirt is my sister's
but those aren't her slacks
dumped like trash
burnt to ash
in the desert that keeps its secrets

one body found in the middle of the street
in a neighborhood not unlike mine
on this side of the line
I am alive
and my father reclines
in his retired military easy-chair bliss
of Ft. Bliss

Mom and Dad warn to be careful
but aren't overly concerned
when my brothers and I
cross from El Paso to Juárez
for late-night cheap college drink-a-thons

continued on next page

Amalia Ortiz grew up on the border and is now a performance poet, actor, director, and activist in San Antonio. She has performed throughout the United States and on HBO's *Def Poetry Jam.* Ortiz also teaches workshops in elementary schools.

as long as we stay on the touristy paths
that may exploit
but do protect Americans and our American
    dreams

we are different
and even my parents don't seem to see
all those missing women
they all look like me

but I am told I am different
less Mexican
less poor
American thus worth more
different

similarities
they all worked like I do
so many last seen
going to or coming from work
at U.S. corporate-owned maquiladoras
but I'm told this isn't an American issue
and I'm lucky here on the safe side

safe
yet not quite out of earshot of distant cries
of families searching ditches and roadsides
bearing snapshot after snapshot
of my brown eyes

Have you seen this girl?
She is my sister
La has visto?
Es mi niña
my baby
mi hermana
my wife
Have you seen her?
This face? *Esta cara?*

When you fit the profile of a predator's prey
you can't help but take the crimes personally

I am a symbol of those who survive
mouth open in defiance of their silence
spared by a line in the sand
drawn between their grandfather
and mine
and if that line had fallen closer to home
somewhere between you and I
who would I be?
what would my worth be then?
and if silenced who would speak for me?

See "More Teaching Ideas," p. 126, for ideas on using this poem and background information about the issues raised.

Mexico Border Improvisations

The NAFTA role play and "The Transnational Capital Auction" help students grasp some of the broad economic forces shaping Mexican society. These are "big picture" role plays, but they don't necessarily help students appreciate the intimate ways that these forces ripple through people's lives. Improvisations are one way to bring social analysis to a human level. For the most part, the situations in this lesson are based on stories I collected during my five trips to the border between February 2003 and March 2005.

In the lesson, students meet in small groups to discuss how to perform the improv situations for other class members. After each performance, the class discusses as a large group and then proceeds to the next improv. At the conclusion, students choose one of the situations to write from. There is no "correct" response in any of these. The aim is for students to appreciate the dilemmas presented here, not to imitate what actually happened. I want them to see that people's choices do make a difference — albeit in circumstances that they don't choose.

Materials Needed

- Copies of the 14 Mexico Border Improvisations for each student.
- A thin dust mask as a prop for improvisation #3, "Poisonous Fumes and Pregnancy."
- Language identification cards for improvisation #7, "Speak Spanish!"

Time Required

A minimum of 20 minutes or so for preparation, at least an hour for performances and discussion (although more is preferable), 15 minutes to write afterwards, and time to share and discuss after students have completed the writing.

Suggested Procedure

1. Divide the class into seven groups and have each group cluster around the classroom.

2. Distribute copies of the "Mexico Border Improvisations" to all students. (Alternatively, cut out improvisations and give two to each group.) Explain that they are going to perform improvisations based on actual situations confronted by Mexicans, mostly those living at the border. Make sure students know that an improvisation is not like a scripted play, where each individual has prepared lines. Read one from the handout as an example. Improv #8, "Cheated," is short and can help students grasp the activity. In this situation, there are four individuals: three Mexican workers, only one of whom speaks English, and a U.S. employer who has cheated them out of wages they'd been promised. Point out that in this improv, participants decide which of them would play which character. Then they might talk out how their characters will respond to the situation, but they needn't work out line by line what they will say. Explain that the aim of the activity is to explore some of the real-life daily choices that migrants experience.

3. Assign each group two improvs to perform. They are not in any particular order, so it doesn't matter which groups get which improvs. Let students know that they can bring additional characters into an improv and change it in ways that make sense to them. They should be

faithful to the premise of the improv, but they needn't be chained to it. For example, in "Cheated," they might bring in a police officer or even a bystander, or they might have only two workers. Let students know that there is no correct answer for any of these but that it is important that they try to play these as realistically as they can.

4. Give students sufficient time to plan their improvs. Circulate among the different groups and help them think about some of their characters' choices.

5. If you are able to arrange it, seat the class in a circle, with a gap at one end of the classroom for the "stage." Students should sit with their respective groups. It's important that students take the improvs seriously or they won't get anything out of them. On the other hand, inevitably students will find lots of the situations amusing and watching their peers perform will generate occasional laughter. The trick is to balance serious with playful. I begin by talking about this dynamic with students, saying something like, "It's important that we try to take the improvisations seriously. These are about real people's lives, and many of the situations that people find themselves in are painful and difficult. The more we recognize this, the more we'll learn. If we laugh during these, we should remember that it's not because we think the situations themselves are funny. It's because we're not used to seeing each other in different roles. And sometimes laughter is a way to distance ourselves from painful circumstances."

6. Before we begin, I tell students that at the conclusion of the improvs they'll be writing an interior monologue or poem based on one of the performances, so they should listen to the dialogue and "steal language" for their writing. They can write either from a situation that they performed or one that other students performed.

7. I begin by calling on a group that I have confidence will get the class off to a good start. We proceed one group at a time (performing only one of their two assigned improvs) and then if time allows, we'll come back through each group again. After each improvisation, I encourage applause, and ask the performing group to remain in place so that we can discuss. I ask the class if anyone has a question that they would like to ask of any of the characters in the improv. For example, in the "Cheated" improv mentioned above, a student might ask one of the characters, "Didn't you worry about whether the employer would call immigration officials and have you deported? He probably knew that you didn't have papers." And the student would respond in character.

8. Here are some details about each of the improvisations that might be helpful in leading a discussion:

    ◆ **#1 "Where to Live?"**
    This situation is based on visits to Chilpancingo, a working-class colonia (neighborhood) in Tijuana. (See "Reading Chilpancingo," p. 97, and "A Toxic Legacy on the Mexican Border," p. 102.) Conditions in the Río Alamar area are grim, but Chilpancingo proper is no paradise either. It sits below the factory-dense Otay Mesa, and wind and rain blow pollution to both the established Chilpancingo colonia, and to the riverbed. Students can do the math, but obviously saving up for a coyote to help guide a family to the United States, which could cost $1,500 a person, would take a lot longer if a family chose to spend more on housing in Tijuana. Often, students will assume that the only route to happiness is finding a way to the United States. But I've spoken to countless people in Tijuana who have no intention of leaving Mexico and are not there merely in transit to the north. This is something that may be worth exploring in students' improvisations and conversations: Do they assume that the only way to lead a decent life is by fleeing Mexico? If so, why?

    ◆ **#2 "Forced Birth Control"**
    During my most recent trip to the border, our Rethinking Schools–Global Exchange group met with the U.S. owner of a maquiladora, who also works as a consultant for larger firms like Sanyo, Sony, and Pepsi. It was a national holiday, Benito Juárez's birthday, so no workers were around, and the owner seemed in a talkative mood. He openly discussed with us a range of management strategies at the maquila. I decided to ask him

directly, but politely, about rumors we'd heard that some maquilas require pregnancy tests for prospective workers. He didn't hesitate: "We do a pregnancy test for all women." He explained that he didn't want pregnant workers, that if he hired a woman when she was pregnant then he'd be responsible for her pregnancy leave. Further, he volunteered that he has a doctor at the factory for five hours every Monday, and that they offer every kind of birth control available: condoms, birth control pills, Norplant, etc. He explained that his workers are mostly from rural areas in southern Mexico and unfamiliar with birth control practices, so he sees himself as a kind of teacher. Afterwards, Mago, a maquila worker affiliated with the Workers' Information Center, told us that it is illegal to force women to take a pregnancy test before employing them or to not hire a woman because she is pregnant.

#3 "Poisonous Fumes and Pregnancy"

This improv situation is based on one of my first visits to a maquiladora. Almost all the workers at the plant were women, although our guide was a man, a Mexican supervisor. The maquila had a more informal, almost laid-back feel than others that I'd visited. Many of the women were gluing patches of fabric or other materials into sample books. A few of the women in the factory wore light dust masks. Most wore no protection at all. I asked the supervisor why some workers wore masks and others didn't. He replied that these women were pregnant and so needed more protection. But obviously these little 39-cent dust masks were useless to protect women from toxic fumes. After the visit, one of our guides, Jaime Cota of the Workers' Information Center, told us that his research has found a high rate of deformed babies born to maquila workers. A major culprit, he said, are the solvents used in the electronics industry. Solvents are dissolving agents, and they do their job efficiently, attacking the fatty brain mass and spinal columns in fetuses. Carmen Valadez, former director of the women's support center Grupo de la Mujer - Factor X, said that maquila managers evidenced little concern about worker health and safety, and compared maquilas to a juice squeezer: "They take a lemon, use it, throw it out, take another, use it, throw it out …"

#4 "Sexual Harassment"

The women in this improv are recently arrived from southern Mexico, which is typical of workers in border maquiladoras. One worker teachers met with on a border trip had come from southern Mexico where she had been a farmworker. She told us that when she began work in the maquilas, it was the first time in her life she'd ever worked in the shade. It was an unfamiliar and disorienting world to her. Maquila workers tend to be young — one U.S. owner of a Tijuana maquila told us that he hired women between the ages of 18 and 21 — poor and vulnerable. There are no independent trade unions with contracts in border maquilas, so women are left with little institutional protection from unwanted male attention. Factor X's Carmen Valadez argues that sexual harassment actually helps companies produce docile workers: "Sexual harassment is not just an accident, it's part of controlling the workforce." (Note that the improvisation does not ask students to play out the incident of sexual harassment, but instead to have women talk about how to respond. However, sometimes students decide to act out the harassment incident itself.)

#5 "Police Harassment"

This improv is based on an experience that artist-activist Carmela Castrejón had one evening. As indicated in the improv description, Castrejón saw this incident as part of a pattern of police abuse designed to create widespread fear and compliance. She responded by challenging the policemen who detained her. They asked her for her ID. "I don't have to show you ID," she told them. They said the law had changed and that she did need to produce ID. "No, the Constitution has not been reformed," she shot back. They demanded to know if she used drugs. "Yes, coffee, alcohol, tobacco, aspirin. I'm a terrible addict." Are you married? "None of your business." Carmela told us that the police could have been brutal, but that come what may she was determined to maintain her "dignity" — the one word heard most frequently when talking with Mexicans on the border. Shortly after this incident, Carmela began a major art installation, called "Failed Attempt," commemorating the "failed attempts" to strip women of their dignity.

#6 "Culture and Survival"

This improv is based on a visit to a bilingual Mixtec-Spanish school, Escuela Bilingüe Pipila, during a trip to Tijuana — one of seven indigenous language schools in the area, not including five preschools. The teachers had originally been recruited from Oaxaca. In addition to attending school, many of the children work in Tijuana in the informal sector, selling, begging, performing on street corners as jugglers or singers. In a meeting with our Rethinking Schools–Global Exchange group, teachers told us that the police in Tijuana are especially harsh and regularly assault children. Teachers reported that many parents resisted the use of Mixtec in school because they saw it as a "dead end," not economically helpful to their children. On the other hand, the parents make efforts to stay connected to their indigenous communities, often in rural areas in southern Mexico, and want their children to be grounded in the traditions of these communities. People return home during the year to celebrate holidays such as Día de los Muertos (Day of the Dead), which has indigenous roots.

#7 "Speak Spanish!"

Factories are leaving the U.S.–Mexico border for Asia in search of lower wages, but they are also heading south, where the minimum wage is lower than in the north. As discussed elsewhere in this book, Mexican government policies along with massive U.S. food exports have undercut the position of small farmers throughout Mexico, especially in the south. Corporations take away jobs with one hand and offer them with another — but on their own terms. When we do this improv in class, I give students cards that they can hold up to signal when they are speaking an indigenous language. Students may recognize this linguistic imperialism from other societies and other points in history, e.g., Native American boarding schools, the enforced use of Afrikaans that triggered the Soweto uprising in South Africa, the prohibition of the Irish language and the Anglicization of place names by the British, etc.

#8 "Cheated"

This was a story that a recent deportee at Casa del Migrante told people on one of our border trips. He found himself in this situation at a work site in southern California. The three argued with the U.S. employer and protested until finally the employer called the police, which led to the man's deportation. In this instance, the word of a U.S. citizen was pitted against that of a few "illegal aliens." It highlights the enhanced power granted employers as undocumented workers begin to recognize that to demand their rights can lead to deportation.

#9 "Grandmother Is Ill"

Through 2005, over 3,200 people have died trying to cross into the United States since Operation Gatekeeper began in October 1994. Crossing the border is obviously not a decision to be made lightly. In a context where it is often difficult if not impossible to make enough in Mexico for a family to survive, it is hard to sustain one's family. At Casa del Migrante in Tijuana, I asked the assistant director, Gilberto Martínez, what advice he gives to people like the three individuals in this improv situation. He said, "Do everything that you can to keep your family together." And then he added, "I would tell them, whatever you do, don't trust the smugglers." Before Operation Gatekeeper, it was much easier for migrants to travel home to Mexico for special events — whether an illness of a close relative, such as described in this improv, a wedding, holiday, or Quinceañera (15th birthday, an important milestone in Mexican culture). Ironically, the border crackdown keeps many Mexicans in the United States when they would prefer to spend more time in Mexico.

#10 "Moving to China"

If your class has done the Transnational Capital Auction (see p. 105), students will recognize the kind of extortion exemplified in this improv. And the threat is real. As Sarah Anderson and John Cavanagh of the Institute for Policy Studies point out, from 2000 to 2004, Mexico lost over 230,000 maquiladora jobs — with an estimated 35 percent of these losses because companies moved production to China. Saul Landau discussed this phenomenon in a 2002 *Progressive* magazine article, "The End of the Maquila Era," just as this capital flight was accelerating: "In Juárez, a beginning machine operator earns less than $8 a day, whereas her counterpart in China makes only a quarter of that pathetic wage." This "race to the bottom" plays itself out in shop-floor dilemmas like the one these workers confront. The China option enhances corporations' power vis à vis maquila workers, even if those corporations have no intention of relocating production.

#11 "Neighborhood Organizing"

This is based on the extraordinary work of Lourdes Lujan and others in Colectivo Chilpancingo Pro-justicia Ambiental, described briefly on p. 8 and, as mentioned above, in "Reading Chilpancingo," p. 97, and "A Toxic Legacy on the Mexican Border," p. 102. Lourdes says that out of every 100 or so people they contact in a neighborhood canvass, maybe three respond favorably to the organizers. Some people see no visible negative health effects, some see themselves as there only temporarily and so are unwilling to become active, and many struggle just to survive day to day. According to Lourdes, some residents assume that the women in the environmental organization going door-to-door are religious proselytizers: "'No, we don't want any hallelujahs here,' they'll tell us." However, their tenacity has forced the government to agree to clean up the most egregious toxic site in Otay Mesa, the U.S.-owned battery recycling facility Metales y Derivados, and has given them a large role in monitoring the cleanup process.

#12 "Conflict at Home"

This is a story I heard on my first trip to Tijuana, during a visit to Grupo de la Mujer - Factor X, the support center for working women. As indicated in the situation, it's easier for women than for men to find jobs in the maquilas. Working in a maquila may be unsafe, offer low wages, and subject women to sexual harassment and other humiliation (for example, having to take pregnancy tests and answer personal questions about birth control methods). But it may also offer a workplace camaraderie with other women and a measure of freedom not experienced in one's original community. Women at Factor X told us that they have had to educate their husbands, telling them, "I'm not just someone to clean your mess. I have needs too." Women told us that some men threaten their wives if they even consider looking for work: "You will stay home because I say so." One woman told us that even reading a book could symbolize a new-found independence and could trigger abuse from a male partner. Recently arrived migrants may have no family ties in border communities, so this too can strain a relationship. If both the man and woman in a family have jobs, they may work different shifts and not see each other often. This improvisation is meant to help students begin to explore some of the intimate effects of the maquila system.

#13 "Migrants' Dilemma"

This situation is based on conversations with three men several of us met one evening at Casa del Migrante in Tijuana. Two of the men had been deported from the United States, roughly the proportion of migrants (62 percent) arriving at Casa del Migrante who have been deported. From my conversations with migrants, it seems that U.S. police have been aggressive in apprehending people. Deportees report being picked up for jaywalking, broken taillights, and other minor offenses. Many have left their entire families living in the United States, including children who were born there and are U.S. citizens. Border security measures like Operation Gatekeeper have made a return journey to the United States much riskier and much more expensive. One longtime Tijuana resident told us,

"Before, a coyote was a luxury, now it's a necessity." Migrants may stay 15 days at Casa del Migrante, and then they must find their own place or leave the area. All three of the individuals referenced in this improv planned to head back to the States at the first opportunity.

#14 "Water or Jail"

As a Maclovio Rojas resident told us during one visit, "We are poor people sitting on a ton of gold." This is a highly organized community that has been a thorn in the side of a government that would prefer to have this valuable real estate for its own purposes. Maclovio was first settled in 1988, a land occupation led by the left-wing Independent Confederation of Farmers and Farm Workers. Under the Mexican Constitution's agrarian reform provisions at the time (Article 27, since repealed), the landless were permitted to settle unoccupied land and petition the government for ownership. Since then, it's been a complicated history of repression and struggle. By the time of my first visit, in February 2003, one Maclovio leader, Nicolasa Ramos, was in prison and others, including Hortensia Hernández and Artemio Osuna, were in hiding. All had been charged with illegally taking water from an aqueduct. The community had petitioned the state government for water and was prepared to pay for it. As they waited in vain for the government to take action, the community connected to the water main. As one community activist told us, "This is a human right. Every family has the right to water." Others outside of Maclovio Rojas had tapped into the water as well, but the government was looking for an excuse to crack down on Maclovio's leaders. (A fine summary of the situation at Maclovio is in David Bacon's *The Children of NAFTA*, pp. 130-137, and a wonderful video about community organizing at Maclovio is *Everyone Their Grain of Sand*, see Resources, p. 135).

9. At the completion of the improvs, ask students to take a few minutes and look back over their notes to decide which individual's point of view they would like to write from as an interior monologue. As mentioned, students can write from the point of view of a character they portrayed or one that another group performed. Ask students for some of the situations and dilemmas that made an impression on them. Sometimes prompts are helpful. Read Blake Weber's interior monologue, p. 30, as an example.

10. Circle the class for a read-around. Tell students that as they listen to one another's interior monologues, you would like them to take notes on insights from the "collective text" of the class. On the board or overhead write the questions that you would like students to think about. The ones that I've used include:

   - Which of the situations/circumstances that people wrote about did you find most affecting, moving, poignant?
   - What kind of resistance did you notice?
   - Where can we find hope?
   - What parts of these writings remind you of anything we've studied this year or anything in your own life?

11. See p. 28 for how this assignment played out in my class.

Mexico Border Improvisations

1. Where to Live?

A family has recently arrived in Tijuana from southern Mexico and is living in a neighborhood in the Río Alamar riverbed, about a mile down the hill from Otay Mesa, an area of maquiladoras where the mother and father have found jobs. The Río Alamar "neighborhood" is not desirable for numerous reasons: If it rains, the house (really barely a shack) could flood or even be washed away; there is no running water; there is no garbage collection; the family has to cross a rickety wooden bridge to get to and from work or stores; their home is slapped together out of whatever wood, plastic, and metal they could find; sometimes the authorities come through and dismantle settlements like these. However, residents pay no rent. There is a nearby neighborhood where they could rent a one-bedroom house for $90 to $100 a month. Wages in the maquiladoras average about $6 a day. If they were to rent a home, they would live better but would not be able to save as much for the journey to the United States, where they believe life would be better. The family discusses whether they will rent a house or continue living in the poor area where they are now.

2. Forced Birth Control

A young woman and her husband have recently moved from Oaxaca in southern Mexico to Tijuana, on the Mexico–U.S. border, to look for work. The husband cannot find a job because the maquiladoras prefer to hire young women. The woman finds a job in a factory but the pay is very low. With her wage, she cannot afford even to send money back to her family. Still, it is better than nothing. The factory requires regular health checkups for the women to make sure they are not pregnant. They say it is to ensure their safety, but there have been instances when a worker is "let go" soon after the supervisor learns she is pregnant. (Article 123 of the Mexican Constitution states that in the three months prior to childbirth, women shall not perform heavy labor; after childbirth women are entitled to a month of maternity leave at full pay; and once women return to work they shall be entitled to two paid half-hour breaks a day to nurse newborns.) Some of the women in the factory take the birth control pills offered by the factory doctor even though they are Catholic and it is against their faith. The young woman does not want to lose her job but does not want to take the pills either. She discusses the matter with her husband.

3. Poisonous Fumes and Pregnancy

There is a pregnant woman who works in Tijuana for a U.S.-owned maquiladora that manufactures sample books for department stores. Her family depends heavily on her income from the factory — about $50 a week, slightly over the minimum wage. Workers at this maquila spend much of their time gluing pieces of tile, Formica, or fabric onto the stiff pages of the sample books. The woman is worried about the effects of the fumes on her unborn child. Her co-workers are also concerned. When one of them tells a supervisor that the fumes could be harmful, he brings the woman a thin dust mask that might protect from particles in the air, but not from potentially poisonous fumes. (Article 123 of the Mexican Constitution prohibits "unhealthful or dangerous work by women.") The women talk with the supervisor about the situation.

4. Sexual Harassment

A group of women from southern Mexico — from the states of Chiapas, Oaxaca, and Guerrero — work together in a maquiladora in Tijuana. They left an area of Mexico that is desperately poor and are now working in a factory for the first time in their lives. They hope to save money so that they can pay someone to help them get into the United States, where they have heard that wages are much higher. They have a supervisor at work who has been hinting that if they want to keep their jobs, they should have sex with him. He frequently comes by and puts his hand on their shoulder or arm when they are working. Sometimes, he claims that he needs to show them how to do their jobs better and when he gets closer he rubs up against them. They discuss how to handle this situation. They want it to stop but they are also fearful of losing their jobs.

5. Police Harassment

A Mexican artist has been stopped by the police who have demanded her identification. The artist is a political activist and very knowledgeable about the Mexican Constitution and the rights of citizens. She knows that the police have no right to demand ID from someone who is not otherwise breaking a law. It seems to her that these days, the police are more frequently harassing people whom they decide are potentially threatening or simply not to their liking: poor people, Indians, political activists, gays and lesbians, etc. She has been increasingly fed up with the behavior of the police, but also with the Mexican government in general for taking away so many rights, and for serving the interests only of the rich elites. She values her independence and her integrity. She is also aware that when challenged, the police can be brutal. (Situation: Role-play the confrontation between this woman and the police.)

6. Culture and Survival

Two Mixtec-speaking parents are recently arrived in Tijuana from their home in southern Mexico. Mixtec is an indigenous language spoken in parts of southern Mexico. The parents discuss whether to send their children to a bilingual Mixtec-Spanish language school or to a Spanish-only school — or whether it would be better to have the children work to make money to support the family. They would like their children to continue to speak Mixtec and not to abandon Mixtec culture. However, they know that Mixtec is not a language that will help their children in Tijuana's economy or in the United States, should they choose to go north. They want their children to have good jobs and know that schooling is one route to higher-paying jobs. But getting to the United States is also a route to higher-paying jobs and for this the family will need more money — money that their children could help earn. What will the parents decide?

7. Speak Spanish!

Maquiladoras have been moving from northern Mexico — cities like Tijuana, Mexicali, and Ciudad Juárez — to southern Mexico. Many, probably most, of the workers in the maquilas that move south are indigenous and speak indigenous languages — Mixtec, Zapotec, Nahuatl, etc. Naturally, workers in the factories speak to one another in their native languages. However, factory supervisors speak Spanish and rarely understand indigenous languages. They wonder what the workers are saying. Are they "plotting" something, talking about the supervisors? Some factories have prohibited workers from speaking their native language while at work. This effectively silences many workers, as they speak little Spanish. A supervisor has caught a number of workers speaking in their native language. Just one of them speaks Spanish. The supervisor confronts them on their violation of the Spanish-only language rule.

8. Cheated

Three undocumented Mexican workers are living in southern California. Only one of them speaks English. They have been hired by a man who is a U.S. citizen to help him move furniture and boxes out of a house. They were promised $10 an hour for their labor and they worked a little over eight hours during the day. At the end of the day the man gave each of them $50. He apologized and said it was all he had. "Besides," he chuckled, "that's a lot more than you'd ever make in a day in Mexico." How do the men respond?

9. Grandmother Is Ill

Two brothers from Guadalajara, Mexico, work as day laborers in Austin, Texas. Their family still lives in Mexico. The brothers came to the United States to make enough money to keep their parents fed and their sisters in school. They have lived in Texas for three years and miss their home and family very much. It was hard to cross over. They almost didn't make it. They would love to return home but if they do, they might not be able to return. Stories of people dying during the crossing or getting hustled by coyotes (smugglers) or caught by the U.S. Border Patrol are common. They get a letter from home saying their grandmother is ill and will die soon. She would like to see her grandsons before she dies. The brothers must decide whether to cross back into Mexico.

10. Moving to China

Many thousands of workers in Tijuana have found jobs in maquiladoras, mostly owned by transnational corporations from the United States or Japan. Recently, a number of factories have shut down and moved to China or southern Mexico, where wages are even lower than the roughly $6 a day paid to Tijuana workers. Workers in one typical Tijuana maquila are paid the minimum wage of about $4.54 a day and then if they meet a number of quotas — for example, by producing a certain number of products a day (without any defects), having perfect attendance for the month, arriving early at work — they can make more money. Recently, one of the supervisors called the workers together and said that because of competition the company had decided to increase the production quotas for workers, and people will have to work harder or longer for the same pay. The supervisor said that the company is considering a move to China, so the workers should not complain because at least they still have a job. A number of workers meet to discuss the company's new quotas and its threat to move to China. Some think that they should contact a union, or protest in some other way. Others are worried about losing jobs that are increasingly difficult to find.

11. Neighborhood Organizing

A women's organization is working to clean up the environment in the area of Tijuana called Chilpancingo. This neighborhood has several thousand residents, many of whom work in the maquiladoras in the hills above. It's not a safe place to live. Children have been found to have high contents of lead and other heavy metals in their bodies. Many women have given birth to babies without brains and babies with other birth defects. There is one especially polluted factory called Metales, that used to recycle batteries from the United States. A number of years ago the owner suddenly closed the factory, leaving tons and tons of toxic waste behind, and returned home to his wealthy neighborhood across the border in San Diego. When it rains, these poisons wash down into the Chilpancingo neighborhood. In the dry seasons, the Santa Ana winds blow poisonous dust into people's homes. Several members of the environmental organization are going door to door to try to get others involved. But many people are reluctant to join because they are so busy working and trying to survive. Also, it can be dangerous if the Mexican government identifies someone as a troublemaker. (Situation: Role-play members of the organization going to the home of people in the neighborhood who are reluctant to join.)

12. Conflict at Home

A Mexican family has moved to Tijuana from southern Mexico. In the community where they were living previously, both parents worked very hard, but they did different kinds of work. The man did most of the farming on their small plot of land and sometimes hired himself out to larger land owners in order to make a little extra money. The woman did all the cooking, made clothes, took care of the children, kept up their small house, and at times worked in their herb garden. In order to survive in Tijuana, both need to work. However, most of the jobs in the maquiladoras in Tijuana are for women. She found a job in a box factory but he has not been able to find a job. It seems that he takes his frustrations out on his wife. She comes home from work and he starts bossing her around: "Go make me coffee." "When will dinner be ready?" One day the woman comes home and is especially exhausted. He starts ordering her around and she responds. (As an alternative, you might have a number of women in similar situations meet in a Tijuana women's center, Factor X, and discuss how to respond to their husbands.)

13. Migrants' Dilemma

The Casa del Migrante is a shelter in Tijuana where men stay when they are on the move. Some men are from southern Mexico on their way to the United States. Others have recently been deported to Mexico from the United States. Most of those in the shelter have very little money. Several men discuss what they should do. One was recently deported from San Luis Obispo, Calif. He has two children living with his wife in a small village near Guadalajara, Mexico. They are almost totally dependent on the money that he sent back from the United States. Another man, 18 years old, has never been to the United States. He left Mexico City, where he did a number of odd jobs for little pay. In his last job, he traveled 90 minutes each way to work and made just a few dollars a day. He hopped a freight train to Tijuana. He has no money. A third man was caught by the police in San Jose, Calif., driving without a license. He was deported without being able to say goodbye to his wife or to his two children, who were both born in the United States and are citizens. It is increasingly dangerous to emigrate to the United States and could cost $1200 or more for a *coyote* or *pollero* to bring someone to the States. None of the men has more than $50. On average, more than one person a day dies trying to cross from Mexico to the United States. The men discuss what they are going to do.

14. Water or Jail?

There is an *ejido* just east of Tijuana called Maclovio Rojas. Ejidos are collectively owned communities, provided for in the Mexican Constitution (although this provision was repealed as part of Mexican government "reforms" leading up to the North American Free Trade Agreement). For years, the Mexican government has wanted to move the people of Maclovio Rojas off their land in order to sell it to corporations that would like to expand onto their land. The ejido is sandwiched between two large Hyundai factories. The Mexican government has provided no services for the people of Maclovio Rojas. The community has paid for all its schools and community centers, and even pays the salaries of its teachers. The roads are unpaved. Community members have tapped into electrical power lines that run nearby and have rigged up electrical wiring throughout the community. However, perhaps the most important service the government has refused to provide is water. Nearby is a main water line that is used by large farms and dairies, as well as factories in the area, like Hyundai. Members of the Maclovio Rojas community discuss whether or not to illegally tap into the main water lines. Some argue that this is the only way they've ever gotten any of their rights in Maclovio — by taking them. Others agree, but say that the Mexican government could use this as an excuse to arrest community leaders or even to attack the community and try to bulldoze it and evict residents. They discuss how to handle the water situation.

Resources

More Teaching Ideas

Textbook Critique

In the United States, the war with Mexico is remembered as little more than a sideshow to the tensions building toward Civil War — when it's remembered at all. But in Mexico, the war features prominently in national folklore and is known as the "war of conquest." A huge monument in Mexico City's Chapultepec Park proclaims itself to be "In memory of those who died in the North American Invasion."

Rethinking Our Classrooms, Vol. 1, includes an article that Bob Peterson and I wrote describing a lesson that enlists students in becoming "textbook detectives" and prompts them to ask critical questions about a typical history textbook's treatment of the U.S.–Mexico War. The lesson helps students internalize some of what they have learned from the tea party on the war and from Howard Zinn's "We Take Nothing By Conquest, Thank God." This critical reading activity encourages students to be aware of whose lives and perspectives are missing from a particular text, to think about who benefits and who suffers from different versions of history, and to question the implications of length and detail in a given text.

Metaphorical Drawings

As indicated in "Teaching About 'Them' and 'Us,'" immigration and the border offer rich possibilities for student metaphorical drawings (see p. 32). It's natural to search for metaphors to describe phenomena that we find strange or startling or unfathomable. "The border eats people alive," said labor organizer Jaime Cota on one Rethinking Schools-Global Exchange border trip. On another occasion, Jaime described Mexico as "a poor country rammed up against a rich country." A U.S. Border Patrol agent made a similar comment, that "We have a poor country crashing into a rich country." In her book *Borderlands/La Frontera,*

poet Gloria Anzaldúa imagines the border as "*una herida abierta*" — an open wound — "where the Third World grates against the first and bleeds." A gruesome image on the Mexico side of the wall in Tijuana depicts this wound. "We live next to the mouth of the monster," said a man in the Maclovio Rojas ejido outside Tijuana. "I didn't jump the wall, the wall jumped me," commented one Mexican with a sense of history.

Toward the end of a unit on the border and Mexican immigration, ask students to describe the images that come to mind when they think about the border: "The border is like …" or "The relationship between Mexico and the United States reminds me of …" or "The effect of NAFTA in Mexico is like …." Sometimes it helps to explicitly remind students to think also in terms of hopeful images. For instance, in a workshop Linda Christensen and I led at UCLA, Fresno-area teacher Oscar Hernández drew a car battery representing the toxic Metales y Derivados battery recycling site in Tijuana's Otay Mesa. In his drawing, poisons drain out of the negative side of the battery. But rising from the positive side of the battery, Oscar drew scenes of struggle: residents holding picket signs demanding dignity and a clean environment.

Ask students to list several images, and then to share some of these aloud. Distribute blank paper and colored pencils, markers, or crayons, and allow them to begin their drawings. I ask students to explain in writing the meaning of their drawings, as connecting words to their images can produce some poetic language and can help students further clarify their ideas. As I mention in "Teaching About 'Them' and 'Us,'" the metaphorical drawings can be a good transition to essay writing as the assignment begins to help students identify some of the essential relationships that they've learned in the unit.

SECTION 6 PHOTO: REUTERS/ANDREW WINNING
Mexican farmers protest NAFTA provisions at the U.S. embassy in Mexico City, 2002.

The Women of Juárez

Since 1993, about 400 young women, perhaps more, have been murdered in the Juárez, Mexico area. Most have been workers in foreign-owned maquiladoras. Many have been raped and even tortured. Photographer Connie Aramaki has posted 16 extraordinary photos of a visit to Juárez to document aspects of the community's response to the young women's killings. Her photos can be found at www.conniearamaki.com/HOME.html. (Click on Portfolio and then on Juárez.)

To introduce this issue, put students in small groups throughout the classroom, so each group can see the screen. Distribute questions to each group or write these on the board or overhead:

- Where do you think this photo might have been taken? What clues do you have?
- What do you think is happening here? What clues do you have?
- What questions do you have about the photo?

With a projector connected to a computer, project photos from Aramaki's website one by one and allow time between each photo for students to study details and to discuss. Ask students to list their answers to each question. (Photos I'd recommend using include numbers 1, 2, 4, 6, 7, 8, 9, and 11. There are captions for each photo at the website; in order to allow the lesson to unfold, even if students have access to computers, it's best to project the photos so they cannot see captions.) Ask for a few responses from students about what they think is going on in the photos. Follow this with a reading (or showing) of Amalia Ortiz's slam poem, "The Women of Juárez," see p. 111. (Audio and video of Ortiz performing this poem is at her website, www.amaliaortiz.com, click on Poetry.) And/or show the segment of Saul Landau's video *Maquila: A Tale of Two Mexicos*, about the Juárez murders and the community's response. Some questions for students to explore:

- Why are there so many young women in Juárez? (Look at Juárez on a map and point out its proximity to the United States.)
- How might maquiladoras play a role in what's happening to young women there?
- In her poem, Ortiz says that "the other side allows a slow genocide." Why has so little been done about the murders?
- Why should people in the United States care about this issue?

The Trial of ___

The trial role play format allows students to explore responsibility for a crime or injustice from multiple points of view. Several examples of these can be found in Rethinking Schools books or online. "The People v. Columbus, et al." is in *Rethinking Columbus*, "The People v. Global Sweatshops" is in *Rethinking Globalization*, and "The Case of Cultural Destruction," about the erosion of traditional culture in Ladakh, India, is online at www.rethinkingschools.org/publication/rg/RGLak.shtml. These include models of sample "indictments" and trial lesson plans.

Several situations described in the book lend themselves to a trial format. *Who or what is responsible for the hundreds of deaths every year of migrants crossing the border?* Defendants could include: The U.S. Border Patrol, the Clinton administration for initiating Operation Gatekeeper, the coyotes (smugglers), the migrants themselves, the Mexican government for pushing neoliberal reforms that deprive people of the opportunity to make a decent living in Mexico and necessitate migration as a survival strategy. *Who or what is responsible for the deaths and ailments of children in the Tijuana colonia of Chilpancingo?* Defendants could include: the three NAFTA governments for failing to have environmental enforcement mechanisms included in the treaty, owners of the worst Otay Mesa maquiladora polluters (like Metales y Derivados), the Baja government for neglecting to clean up environmental hazards, Chilpancingo residents for failing to move, corporate and government promoters of the neoliberal strategy that concentrates low-wage, polluting production along the border. *Who or what is responsible for the hundreds of murders of women in Ciudad Juárez?* Defendants could include: Maquiladora owners for refusing to provide safe transportation for workers, Juárez officials for their corruption and failure to pursue the women's killers, Mexican "patriarchy" for creating a climate of misogyny that perpetuates violence against women, and again, corporate and government promoters of an economic strategy that depends most heavily on the labor of poor women, and hence draws them to border maquila zones like a magnet from all over Mexico.

Poems Included in *The Line Between Us*

The first part of Luis Rodríguez's poem **"Running to America"** (p. 3) uses repetition to sketch some of the immigrants "running to America": "They are night shadows. … There is a woman in her finest border-crossing wear. … There is a child dressed in black. …" Students might pattern their own poems on Rodríguez's — "There are … There is … There is …" — and use a similar repetition to describe some of the migrants they have encountered throughout the curriculum: Yolanda Gonzalez-Martínez in *Death on a Friendly Border;* Marco, his father, and any of the migrants in the short story "First Crossing;" individuals in the Border Improvisations; etc. In the second part of the poem, students might describe migrants' experiences after they have "run to America," as does Rodríguez. You might first ask them to list the details that Rodríguez includes to portray immigrants' activities after their arrival here. In his poem, Rodríguez describes "this strange land's maddening ambivalence." Ask students: How is the United States ambivalent about undocumented immigrants? What is the source of this ambivalence?

In the final stanza of **"Heart of Hunger"** (p. 60), Martín Espada turns from critique to hope: "Yet there is a pilgrimage, / A history straining its arms and legs."

Read this stanza aloud with students. What does Espada mean when he talks about a "pilgrimage"? Ask students to list places in the curriculum where they have recognized this pilgrimage — this "inexorable striving," an attempt "to pull a fierce gasping life from the polluted current." Students might use Espada's basic structure — critique of immigrants' treatment followed by "Yet there is …" to craft their own poems. From their study of these issues, what is the "yet" — the hope — that students have discovered?

I suggest one use for Amalia Ortiz's **"The Women of Juárez"** in the lesson above. Another possibility would be to read or watch Ortiz's poem prior to the activity using Connie Aramaki's photographs. Students would then have some background with which to reflect on Aramaki's Juárez images. Some discussion questions about "The Women of Juárez":

- What's your gut reaction to this poem?
- What do you think prompted Ortiz to write it?
- Ortiz writes, "When you fit the profile of a predator's prey / You can't help but take the crimes personally." What does she mean by this? Do you ever feel that you "fit the profile of a predator's prey"? (This could also be the basis of an assignment where students use their own experiences to write a personal narrative. For example, my students of color consistently identify police and store owners who target them for surveillance or harassment because of their race.)
- Ortiz says that the Juárez killings and disappearances "reflect an entire society where young women are expendable." What evidence from your study of the border and immigration issues supports this observation? Is there evidence that refutes it?
- Ortiz describes the "line in the sand drawn between their grandfather and mine." In Ortiz's life, what is the meaning of this line?
- Ortiz says that her mouth is "open in defiance of [the murdered women's] silence," and concludes with the question, "if silenced who would speak for me?" Are there any "silenced" people who you speak for? Are there silenced people you could speak for? This too could be the basis of a personal narrative assignment: Write about a time when you spoke out or acted on behalf of someone or a group who you felt was unable to speak or act on their own behalf. Or alternatively: Write about a time when you felt unable to speak out or defend yourself and someone or some group spoke out or acted on your behalf.
- What questions does the poem leave you with?

Thanks to Portland teacher Heidi Tolentino for suggesting the lesson idea on Connie Aramaki's Juárez photos.

Mexico in *Rethinking Globalization*

The issues explored in *The Line Between Us* are best understood as part of the phenomenon often called globalization — an economic regime driven by transnational corporations who regard the entire globe simultaneously as one big marketplace, labor reserve, resource quarry and, too often, toxic dump. In our book *Rethinking Globalization: Teaching for Justice in an Unjust World,* Bob Peterson and I offer curriculum to engage students in aspects of globalization, from its impact on labor conditions to the environment to food quality. The book includes a number of pieces related to Mexico and Mexican immigration.

"1562: Conquistadores Destroy Native Libraries" (p. 43) is an excerpt from the writer Eduardo Galeano that describes Spaniards' burning of Mayan books. Bob Peterson puts these attacks on indigenous cultures in context in his article **"Burning Books and Destroying Peoples"** (p. 38). It's included in the chapter "Legacy of Inequality: Colonial Roots," which frames today's global inequality as part of the first major globalization that began with Columbus's voyages and the launching of European colonialism in the Americas. In a clever and pointed article, **"The Marshalltezuma Plan"** (p. 93), a Mexican indigenous leader, Cuaicaipuro Cuautémoc, suggests that

the enormous wealth in gold and silver that Europeans extracted from indigenous peoples in the Americas should be considered loans instead of plunder. And now, argues Cuautémoc, it is time to pay back those loans.

A piece that would work nicely with some of the lessons in *The Line Between Us* is **"The Story of a Maquiladora Worker"** (p. 146), David Bacon's interview with Omar Gil of Nuevo Laredo in the Mexican state of Tamaulipas. Gil's biography is a case study in the failure of the maquila model of development to, well, develop. Gil migrates from one dead-end job to another but eventually becomes an activist in the democratic union movement.

AP PHOTO/EDUARDO VEREDUGO

Subcomandante Marcos with Zapatista women and their babies in Chiapas.

Jimmy Santiago Baca's poem **"So Mexicans Are Taking Jobs from Americans"** (p. 149) attacks the "us" and "them" formulation that pits workers in Mexico and the United States against each other, while the higher-ups bathe in "the cool green sea of money."

Some of the people in the United States who harvest our food are children. And some of these children, perhaps most, are Mexican. In **"Child Labor Is Cheap — and Deadly"** (p. 204), Augustino Nieves testifies that he began working in the fields when he was 13 years old. He talks about his working and living conditions — and his dreams. Martín Espada's poem **"Federico's Ghost"** (p. 222) is a haunting description about the effects of pesticides on farmworkers.

In **"The Mystery of the Yellow Bean"** (p. 236), Sandy Tolan describes the strange fate of the mayacoba bean, a traditional Mexican food that was patented by a Colorado entrepreneur, who then denied a Mexican exporter the right to market mayacoba beans in the United States. So much for free trade. It highlights a key issue of globalization: the patenting and private ownership of life forms, legitimated with the high-sounding title, "intellectual property" — more accurately named by indigenous groups as bio-piracy.

"Tomasito's Tour" (p. 240) begins the journey of a typical tomato in Jalisco, Mexico. Its travels take it through a genetic-engineering company, chemical man-

ufacturers, waste disposal sites, and end in a Canadian restaurant. **"Cebolleros"** (p. 250) is Benjamin Alire Sáenz's poignant story of the lives of Mexican onion pickers, that probes deep into the humanity embedded in the food we eat. A lesson on this theme is included in my *Rethinking Globalization* article **"The Lives Behind the Labels,"** where I discuss a classroom lesson using strawberries (p. 130) and the video *¡Aumento Ya!*, about the 1995 strawberry workers strike led by PCUN, the Oregon farmworkers union.

The story of Rodolfo Montiel Flores and Teodoro Cabrera Garcia is featured in **"Mexican Peasant-Ecologists Fight to Preserve Forests"** (p. 280). They resist the arrival of logging companies, whose NAFTA-assisted clearcutting speeded the destruction of some of the last pine and fir old-growth forests in the Americas. Montiel and Cabrera landed in prison, and this recounts their story.

Finally, **"Prayers for a Dignified Life"** (p. 321) is a letter from Zapatista Subcomandante Marcos to schoolchildren in Guadalajara about why the Zapatistas took up arms. As mentioned elsewhere in *The Line Between Us,* perhaps the most frequently heard word from workers and farmers I've met with in Mexico is "dignity." Here, the Zapatista leader describes the conditions in the state of Chiapas that gave birth to their uprising and urges the children to "raise high the dignified flag of peace, to write poems that are 'Prayers for a Dignified Life,' and to search, above all, for equal justice for everyone. ■

Books and Curricula

There are many wonderful books on Mexico, and border and immigration issues — more than can be included here. I've found the following books useful in clarifying the relationship between the United States and Mexico and creating curriculum. Some can be excerpted for use with high school or middle school students.

A Different Mirror: A History of Multicultural America

Ronald Takaki. Boston: Little, Brown, and Co., 1993.

Takaki includes two chapters, "Foreigners in Their Own Land: Manifest Destiny in the Southwest" and "El Norte: The Borderland of Chicano America," that are fine introductions to the unequal relationship between the United States and Mexico. Takaki's writing does not shy away from the exploitative realities of this history, but it has a warmth and an appreciation of human struggle that makes for engaging reading.

The Annexation of Mexico: From the Aztecs to the I.M.F.

John Ross. Monroe, ME: Common Courage Press, 1998.

A writer in the Mexican daily *La Jornada* called Ross "the new John Reed covering a new Mexican revolution." Ross offers an entertaining, irreverent history of Mexico, focusing especially on U.S. domination. It's a good introduction to U.S.–Mexico relations. For Ross, NAFTA and free trade are just the latest iterations of U.S. designs on its southern neighbor.

Basta! Land and the Zapatista Rebellion in Chiapas

George A. Collier with Elizabeth Lowery Quaratiello. Oakland, CA: Food First Books, 1999.

I found this book indispensable in helping grasp some of the roots of the Zapatista uprising and in writing the Chiapas farmer role in the NAFTA role play. It's intricate but clear.

Border Studies Curriculum

Center for Latin American and Border Studies, New Mexico State University, 2004. (www.nmsu.edu/~bsc)

This curriculum includes 20 lesson plans focusing on border life. The lessons here would be of particular interest to students who live in or near border areas. Themes include bilingualism and "Spanglish," borders as metaphors, myths and folklore, poetry, music, and Hollywood depictions.

Bound for the Rio Grande: The Mexican Struggle, 1845-1850

Milton Meltzer. New York: Alfred A. Knopf, 1974.

This is the best student-friendly book about the U.S.-Mexico War. Meltzer weaves story, song, and poetry into a highly readable and accurate account of the U.S.-initiated war that led to the Mexican surrender of half its territory. Several chapters could be used in their entirety with high school or middle school students.

BRIDGE, Building a Race and Immigration Dialogue in the Global Economy

Eunice Hyunhye Cho, Francisco Argüelles Paz y Puente, Miriam Ching Yoon Louie, and Sasha Khokha. Oakland, CA: National Network for Immigrant and Refugee Rights, 2004.

Although aimed at educators working with adults, rather than at classroom teachers, this is an imaginative and critical resource for teaching about immigration. One of the guide's strengths is to ground immigration in the context of race and globalization. The book also has a substantial and helpful section on immigration throughout U.S. history.

The Children of NAFTA: Labor Wars on the U.S./Mexico Border

David Bacon. Berkeley, CA: University of California Press, 2004.

David Bacon is a prolific and astute writer about labor on the border. This is one of the most valuable books I read when preparing my curriculum. Bacon observes that "the border symbolizes the nature of the new economic reality. Production and jobs can move across it easily, but the people who perform those jobs cannot. The border, an imaginary line in the sand for most of its 2000-mile length, enforces vast differences in both standards of living and social and political rights." But this is not a political tract. Bacon fills his book with story and concrete example that brings his analysis to life.

The Circuit: Stories from the Life of a Migrant Child

Francisco Jiménez. Albuquerque, NM: University of New Mexico Press, 1997.

These short stories — connected, but able to be read and appreciated independently — follow a migrant family through its "circuit" of farmwork: cotton, strawberries, carrots, etc. It's a book that Jan Goodman, a Berkeley middle school teacher and traveler on our first Rethinking Schools–Global Exchange border tour, alerted me to and uses as the core of an eighth-grade unit on migrant issues with her students. It's one that could be read in full or in parts at either the middle or high school level. The story that gives its name to the book, "The Circuit," tenderly captures the tension between work and school for the child at the center of these stories. The book is also available on tape and CD.

The Devil's Highway

Luis Alberto Urrea. New York: Little, Brown and Co., 2004.

In this harrowing narrative, Urrea recounts the ordeal of 26 Mexican migrants who entered the scorching "Devil's Highway" in Arizona, simply attempting to find better-paying jobs than were available at home in Vera Cruz. Of the 26, only 12 survived. Although Urrea fails to ask about the broader economic policies that led to this tragedy — the book contains not a single mention of NAFTA — it is a compelling and sympathetic account.

500 Años del Pueblo Chicano/500 Years of Chicano History in Pictures

Edited by Elizabeth Martínez. Albuquerque, NM: Southwest Organizing Project, 1991.

This is a rich and startling bilingual overview of Chicano struggle. Because it covers such a sweep of history, the book doesn't provide great detail about any one episode, but its strength is in its portrait of collective defiance of injustice. I know teachers who have used this book as a course outline to frame units on Chicano history. Also see the video that accompanies the book, described on p. 136.

BOB PETERSON

A young boy from Chiapas, Mexico.

Genders in Production, Making Workers in Mexico's Global Factories

Leslie Salzinger. Berkeley, CA: University of California Press, 2003.

Most accounts of maquiladora work in Mexico begin from the premise that factories go looking for workers who are "cheap, docile, and dextrous" — specimens of "natural femininity." Salzinger focuses instead on how maquiladoras set out to *create* these characteristics in their workers. This is a fascinating ethnography that analyzes the maquiladora phenomenon through a gender lens. It's not a book that could be used with most high school students, but it's full of surprising insights and helpful background.

Hard Line: Life and Death on the U.S.–Mexico Border

Ken Ellingwood. New York: Vintage, 2004.

Ellingwood, a reporter for the *Los Angeles Times,* is a skillful writer with the sensibility of a principled reporter. He has put together a solid overview of life at the border, culminating in two chapters, "The Deadly Season" and "Burying John Doe," that detail the ongoing deaths of hundreds of Mexican migrants every year. Ellingwood also includes an early chapter on the history of the border and the U.S. Border Patrol.

Homage to Chiapas: The New Indigenous Struggles in Mexico

Bill Weinberg. London: Verso, 2000.

This is a long but engaging book that begins with Chiapas's earliest history and moves through the Zapatista rebellion to the movements inspired by that rebellion. Sometimes a history book, sometimes a personal narrative, it's always interesting and worthwhile.

The Late Great Mexican Border: Reports from a Disappearing Line

Edited by Bobby Byrd and Susannah Mississippi Byrd. El Paso, TX: Cinco Puntos Press, 1996.

A collection of short readings about life on the border. It includes the excellent and classroom-friendly story "Exile, El Paso, Texas," by Benjamin Alire Sáenz, about a Chicano man's encounters with the U.S. Border Patrol and his response.

ELEMENTARY BOOKS WITH A CONSCIENCE

I have used the following books in my fourth-grade classroom to help students explore common themes in immigrant children's lives. I find that students who have immigrated to the United States benefit from seeing some of their experiences reflected in books. These stories help all students learn about immigrants' experiences and about xenophobia.

América Is Her Name

Luis Rodríguez; illustrated by Carlos Vázquez. Willimantic, CT: Curbstone Press, 1997. (Spanish title: La llaman América. Willimantic, CT: Curbstone Press, 1998.)

América is a girl from Oaxaca, Mexico, who has moved to Chicago and is floundering in school. She hears her teacher tell another teacher she's "illegal," and gets the idea that she doesn't belong in the United States. After a guest poet visits América's class, she begins to find her voice by writing about her experiences back home; but her father ridicules this work, telling her it's no use since she'll spend her life cleaning, working, and raising kids. América continues to write anyway, and eventually achieves academic success and a sense of belonging. I find this story useful for helping students question immigrant stereotypes and encouraging children to think broadly about their possibilities in life.

My Name Is Jorge on Both Sides of the River

Jane Medina, illustrated by Fabricio Vanden Broeck. Honesdale, PA: Wordsong/Boyds Mills Press, 1999.

This bilingual poetry book shares common themes in immigrant children's lives through the experiences of the narrator, Jorge. Jorge makes friends with English- and Spanish-speaking kids at his new school, tries new foods offered to him by his Anglo peers, and feels proud when he recites poetry to his class. He also wonders why his grades are worse in the United States than in Mexico, feels insulted when a classmate calls his English as a second language class "Mexican dummy time," and leaves the public library without a library card after the librarian insults his mom for being illiterate. A funny, moving, and engaging book that helps students explore the joys and difficulties in the lives of immigrant children.

Friends from the Other Side/Amigos del otro lado

Gloria Anzaldúa, illustrated by Consuelo Méndez. San Francisco: Children's Book Press, 1993.

In this bilingual book, a Mexican-American girl named Prietita befriends a recent Mexican immigrant named Joaquín. She stands up to her cousin and his friends when they tell Joaquín to, "Go back where you came from." When the Border Patrol comes looking for "illegals," she hides Joaquín and his mom so they won't get caught. I use this book to help students learn what xenophobia is and how to be an ally.

The Magic Shell

Nicholasa Mohr; illustrated by Rudy Gutierrez. New York: Scholastic, 1995. (Spanish title: El regalo mágico. New York: Scholastic, 1996.)

When Jaime's family decides to move to New York from the Dominican Republic, his uncle gives him a magic shell that he can use to remember his home. At first Jaime uses the shell often. He is bored in his apartment building and reluctant to make friends with English speakers. Eventually he makes friends at school and in his neighborhood, and starts to enjoy life in New York. In the end of the book he visits the Dominican Republic and uses the shell to recall New York. Although I find this book to be a bit slow-paced, the themes hold students' interest.

—*Kelley Dawson Salas, La Escuela Fratney, Milwaukee*

Lives on the Line: Dispatches from the U.S.-Mexico Border

Miriam Davidson. Tucson, AZ: University of Arizona Press, 2000.

Davidson offers a fine, readable survey of life on both sides of the border in Nogales, Ariz., and Nogales, Sonora, Mexico. It's filled with fascinating, sympathetic vignettes about border life. The entire book could be read by most high school students.

Many Faces of Mexico

Octavio Madigan Ruiz, Amy Sanders, and Meredith Sommers. Minneapolis: Resource Center of the Americas, 1995.

This comprehensive curriculum on Mexico begins with life before the Spanish invasion and includes lessons up to the passage of NAFTA. It offers a range of teaching strategies and a framework for approaching Mexican history.

Mexican Lives

Judith Adler Hellman. New York: The New Press, 1994.

I found this book very helpful in writing the NAFTA role play. *Mexican Lives* offers a portrait of Mexicans from different social groups on the eve of NAFTA ratification. The stories are honest and engaging. Several can be used with high school students. "Adelita Sandoval," pp. 159-171, is one of the readings that we provide travelers on the Rethinking Schools–Global Exchange trips to the border.

The Mexico Reader: History, Culture, Politics

Edited by Gilbert M. Joseph and Timothy J. Henderson. Durham, NC: Duke University Press, 2002.

This is an enormous book that you're not likely to sit down and read start to finish, but it is a lively compendium of documents, articles, stories, and poems, many of which could be excerpted for classroom use.

Occupied America: The Chicano's Struggle Toward Liberation

Rodolfo Acuña. San Francisco: Canfield Press, 1972.

This is a classic history and a book I've returned to over the years as a source for background information and ideas for lessons. Well over 30 years since its publication, the stories and analysis here have still not made it into most U.S. history classes.

Puro Border: Dispatches, Snapshots and Graffiti from La Frontera

Edited by Luis Humberto Crosthwaite, John William Byrd, and Bobby Byrd. El Paso, TX: Cinco Puntos Press, 2003.

A playful and at times poignant collection of border miscellany — as the title suggests.

True Tales from Another Mexico: The Lynch Mob, the Popsicle Kings, Calino, and the Bronx

Sam Quinones. Albuquerque, NM: University of New Mexico Press, 2001.

I approached this quirky book looking for excerpts that I could use with students and came up empty-handed. But I did find a number of these journalistic excursions into Mexican culture to be fascinating and at times enlightening. One of my favorite chapters was on the telenovela, the wildly popular Mexican soap opera phenomenon, whose lessons for women, according to the most powerful television impresario, included: "suffering was purifying and to be borne privately, life is nothing without a man, marriage was required for happiness," etc.

¡Sí, Se Puede!/Yes, We Can!

Diana Cohn. Illustrated by Francisco Delgado. El Paso, TX: Cinco Puntos Press, 2002.

In this excellent children's book, we learn about the 2000 Justice for Janitors strike, involving 8,000 mostly immigrant workers, through the experiences of Carlito's mamá. See Linda Christensen's *Rethinking Schools* article "Justice for Janitors: Making the Invisible Visible" (www.rethinkingschools.org/archive/17_02/Read172.shtml) for ways of working with this story across grade levels. Great for high school students, too.

Voices of a People's History of the United States

Edited by Anthony Arnove and Howard Zinn. New York: Seven Stories Press, 2004.

In his book *A People's History of the United States*, Howard Zinn includes a chapter on the U.S. war with Mexico, "We Take Nothing by Conquest, Thank God," excerpted here on p. 53. *Voices of a People's History of the United States* offers source documents that amplify the themes in *A People's History,* including diary excerpts of U.S. Col. Ethan Allen Hitchcock, a speech and editorial by abolitionist Frederick Douglass, and a handbill from deserting U.S. soldiers.

Women Working the NAFTA Food Chain: Women, Food, and Globalization

Edited by Deborah Barndt. Toronto: Second Story Press, 1999.

In this imaginative book, contributors follow the production of food in North America, examining fast food workers in Canada, supermarket workers, migrant workers, and how globalization is remaking our relationship with food and with each other.

Videos with a Conscience

The curriculum materials in *The Line Between Us* attempt to engage students in the social dynamics surrounding border and immigration issues, and in the lives of the people affected by these issues. Videos and DVDs can be another way to trigger students' social imaginations. Those included below are ones that I either have used with my students or would consider using.

BORDER/IMMIGRATION ISSUES

Death on a Friendly Border

Rachel Antell. 2001. 26 min.

The death in *Death on a Friendly Border* is Yolanda Gonzalez-Martínez's — hers and thousands of others who could not survive the increasingly perilous journey crossing from Mexico to the United States. Yolanda lived with her young child, Elizama, in the village of San Pedro Chayuco, in the southern Mexico state of Oaxaca. She died in the desert attempting to join her husband living in the United States. Miraculously, Elizama lived. It's Yolanda's personal story that helps humanize the thousands of border deaths. Yolanda's mother, now raising Elizama, movingly tells the story.

The video also introduces us to migrants at the Casa del Migrante shelter in Tijuana, border justice activists with the American Friends Service Committee in San Diego, and a U.S. Border Patrol agent. In different ways, all reveal an increasingly militarized Mexico–U.S. frontier.

I've used this video with my students and found it helpful because it offers compelling images of the border and a quick but powerful overview of the effects of U.S. immigration policy. It's less analytically ambitious than, say, *New World Border,* in that it does not discuss the free market reforms that continue to create huge numbers of economic refugees. It offers no further explanation than migrants complaining about a "lack of work, lack of jobs," and farmers lamenting low prices for crops. Nor does the video highlight resistance to the current state of affairs, other than a family on the U.S. side of the border that offers humanitarian aid to migrants, creating water stations in the desert. Despite its limits, this is an excellent classroom resource.

New World Border

Casey Peek. Peek Media, 2001. 28 min.

New World Border is a short, but big-picture look at the causes and consequences of immigration from Mexico to the United States. The video discusses the economic roots of migration, the militarization of the border, and the growing anti-immigrant hysteria in the United States — "Mestizos, go back to the swamps and jungles of your country!" shouts one demonstrator in the video — and ties these together in a way that helps teachers think about how we might frame border and immigration issues in class. As Cathi Tactaquin of the National Network for Immigrant and Refugee Rights comments in one segment, there is a "connection between globalization policies and immigration;" hence immigration is not purely a domestic issue but needs to be approached in a global context. *New World Border* also exposes how the media have conflated illegal immigration with drug smuggling, legitimating the war on immigrants as part of the war on drugs. In the post-9/11 era, the drug threat has been largely replaced by the terrorist threat, but both justify the criminalization of immigrants.

Paradoxically, the video's strength in bringing in so many dimensions of the border issue is also its weakness as a classroom resource. For example, it asserts that "free trade integration" and NAFTA and GATT are responsible for throwing Mexican farmers off the land. We're told that, "NAFTA changed the Mexican constitution so agribusiness could buy up land." This is all crucial background for understanding the exodus of poor farmers to the United States. But it simply goes by too quickly for students to grasp the relationship between economic policy and immigration. This is complicated stuff, and what's here is too thin either to educate or convince.

Still, as an overview that touches so many vital

aspects of the border/immigration issue, this is a very helpful resource.

Everyone Their Grain of Sand

Beth Bird. Women Make Movies, 2004. 87 min.

Years ago, poor people moved onto the dusty hillsides east of Tijuana and established the community of Maclovio Rojas. They paid for the land, but never received formal title. Since then, as Tijuana inexorably sprawled eastward, the Maclovio real estate became more desirable. The Baja government sought to evict this community and set its sights on "development." *Everyone Their Grain of Sand* tells the story of Maclovio residents' difficult but inspiring struggle for land and dignity. The government refuses permission to build a school; the community builds it anyway. The government refuses to pay the teachers; the community organizes to demand full recognition for the school and that teachers be paid. The government refuses to connect electricity or water; the community strings its own power lines and taps into the local aqueduct. The community's leaders are imprisoned or driven underground; the community protests and rallies for charges to be dropped.

At 87 minutes, the video may be too long for most high school classes, although it offers rich teaching possibilities. Producer/director Beth Bird presents the kind of intimate portrait of daily life that a filmmaker can

BETH BIRD

From *Everyone Their Grain of Sand*: Maclovio Rojas community leader Hortensia Hernández, who later went into hiding, addressing community members before a rally to petition for running water.

offer only after spending long hours gaining people's trust. Through her camera, we're in people's homes, in their meetings, with them visiting loved ones in prison, watching parents care for their children. It's spontaneous and authentic.

As one resident explains, "I'm active here — this is a community of resistance, and when you're involved, you come to love your community." The entire video brings these words to life.

Maquila: A Tale of Two Mexicos

Saul Landau and Sonia Angulo. Cinema Guild, 2000. 55 min.

The "two Mexicos" referred to in the title are the countryside and the industrial border zones, home to numerous maquiladoras. Although the video's portrait of maquiladora-centered urban life is much fuller than its depiction of rural life, this is an important resource.

As one observer points out, the maquila boom may represent economic growth, but it is not genuine development. Using as a case study Ciudad Juárez, just across the Rio Grande from El Paso, Texas, the video demonstrates how maquilas cheat workers out of wages, undermine unions, pollute surrounding neighborhoods, offer miserable health and safety conditions, and abuse the largely female labor force. Interviews with workers offer glimpses into the intimate humiliations they confront. One woman maquila worker says that factory managers fire any worker who becomes pregnant; they require women to take pregnancy tests and go so far as to demand to see their sanitary napkins to make sure they are menstruating.

Another startling feature of the video is its investigation into the huge number of disappearances and murders of poor women in Juárez. A crime wave that might be portrayed as horrifying but inexplicable by the mainstream media is here given economic and social context. Be aware that there is an especially gruesome scene of a murdered young woman that could upset some students. But this segment is not unrelievedly grim. The video features a large and inspiring demonstration of hundreds of women waving white handkerchiefs, chanting "Ni una mas!" (Not one more!)

Although we don't learn about conditions in the countryside in as much depth as we learn about urban life, there are effective scenes of peasants in Chiapas resisting the militarization of their lands, and interview segments with the Zapatista leader, Subcomandante Marcos.

Maquiladoras depend on a ready supply of desperate people willing to trade their freedom and sometimes their health for a regular, if inadequate, wage. This video begins to ask why and to locate sweatshops in a broader process of globalization.

The Ties That Bind

Maryknoll, 1996. 56 min.

Divided into three sections, the first of these is too narrator- and interview-dense for most students. But part two, "Just Between Us," and part three, "The Common Bond," are more accessible. Through the story of two women who emigrated from Mexico to the United States, "Just Between Us" humanizes the issue of "illegal" immigration. It points out the contradiction between the rhetoric of openness and so-called free trade on the one hand and the militarization of the border on the other. But it does this concretely, through story.

The final part, "The Common Bond," features the inspiring story of Carmen Anaya, a feisty former teacher from Monterrey, Mexico, who immigrated to the United States and worked in the fields. Anaya became a community organizer and leader of Valley Interfaith, a multi-ethnic, church-community alliance that boasts membership of 60,000 families in the Rio Grande Valley. Through a translator, Anaya narrates a story that recalls the "conductors" on the Underground Railroad of an earlier era:

> It was two in the morning. How can I forget it? The doorbell rang and I saw all these men. "What's the matter?" I asked. They were with Immigration. "Open the door," they said. "Are you Carmen Anaya?" "Sure. How can I help you?" I said. "We want you to go open the church." I asked them, "Why? Do you want to pray?" They said, "We're not joking around. We've been told that you're hiding many undocumented persons in there." I said to them, "I will never open that door if you're going there with any other intention than to pray. So you do whatever you want with me. But I'm not opening that door." And I didn't. — We suffered a lot. Because not everyone agreed with us, but we knew that God agreed with us.

Although it includes the use of Mexican story-songs to effectively illustrate points, the video also features an unfortunate soundtrack with soap-opera-like music that will annoy some viewers, matched by a narration that occasionally dips into the well of God-family-country boilerplate. *The Ties That Bind* is big-hearted but lacks a sustained analysis about why people emigrate from Mexico and what economic and political changes would address the Mexican economic crisis — a crisis that the video largely takes for granted.

Free Trade in Mexico

Segment from *TV Nation, Vol. One.* Michael Moore, 1994. Approx. 15 min. (Available in some video stores and from amazon.com.)

Michael Moore spoofs the era of free trade in this amusing segment of his now-defunct NBC show, *TV Nation*. He travels to Reynoso, Mexico, to pretend to explore the economic benefits of relocating TV production there. In Reynoso, he visits a Whirlpool factory that produces washing machine parts formerly made in Indiana, Arkansas, and Tennessee. The workers there make 75 cents an hour, and don't have Whirlpool machines of their own, because, as the manager tells Moore, "One of the problems is that a lot of the folks don't have plumbed-in water." Moore's Reynoso tour guide shows off life across the border in McAllen, Texas — home to mansions and 20 golf courses — where U.S. managers of Mexican factories can enjoy the quality of life they are accustomed to. The episode is a lighthearted vehicle for Moore to drive home his point that in practice, free trade means freedom for corporations to export jobs to low-wage havens with lax enforcement of environmental protections. However, Mexican workers are as silent in Moore's video as they might have been were this episode produced by a U.S. corporation.

IMMIGRANT WORK AND LIFE

Viva la Causa! 500 Years of Chicano History

Elizabeth Martínez and Doug Norberg. Southwest Organizing Project, 1995. Two parts, 30 min. each.

This is the only video I'm aware of that offers a panoramic history of the Chicano people, stretching from the Spanish invasion to the mid-1990s. "All those faces in the past haunt us," offers the narrator. With 500 years of history to cover in an hour, the video is not able to pause very long on any one episode. *Viva La Causa's* strength is that it offers a compelling framework of *la raza's* resistance to oppression. It's hard to overestimate the enormity of injustice: from the theft of huge swaths of Mexico by the United States after its war with Mexico, to the lynchings of Mexicans in California after the war, to the deportations of Mexicans in the 1930s, to attacks on farmworkers in the 1960s. But this profoundly hopeful video concentrates at least as much on resistance as it does on oppression, surfacing seemingly countless episodes of activism. As the narrator offers late in the second half of the video: "The farmworkers taught us a valuable lesson: Progress is made when people mobilize, organize, and demand change; it doesn't come from the goodwill of the government or the upper classes, but from the strength of the people — *la gente.*"

Viva La Causa is partisan, even polemical, and students who are accustomed to the lifeless narratorspeak of so many school documentaries may find this jarring. In an important respect, this video is as much an artifact of Chicano struggle as it is a chronicle of it.

Fear and Learning at Hoover Elementary

Laura Angelica Simón. 1996. 53 min. (Broadcast on the PBS series POV, and available in some lending libraries.)

On the day that California voters approved Proposition 187 denying "illegal" immigrants public education and access to health care, one of Laura Angelica Simón's students asked her if she was now a "cop" and was going to kick them out of school. *Fear and Learning at Hoover Elementary* is Simón's first-person look at the emotional pain caused by Proposition 187 in one California school: hers. Hoover is the largest elementary school in Los Angeles, enrolling 2,700 kids, 90 percent of them from Mexico, Guatemala, and El Salvador. The video "stars" Mayra, a precocious Salvadoran fifth grader who takes us on a tour of the school and invites us into her home — a one-room apartment across from crime-plagued MacArthur Park that she shares with her mother, uncle, and sister. Mayra and other students we meet represent living criticisms of the dehumanizing term "illegal alien," and their humor and intelligence offer viewers an opportunity to rethink lingering stereo-types. But the video is not content to confront anti-immigrant attitudes simply by introducing us to sweet kids. We also meet Dianne Lee, a seven-year teaching veteran whose grandparents immigrated from Russia; Carmen Arcote, a conservative Mexican-American parent who voted for 187; and Mr. Peakmeyer, the Anglo librarian who engages Hoover students in an impromptu debate about the causes of the neighborhood's decline, and with help from these astute youngsters trips over his own contradictions.

My students enjoyed this personal video essay about immigration issues, and found lots to talk and write about. However, the video can't stand on its own. Although early on, Simón, the narrator, labels the students "economic and political refugees," that's the only hint of the forces that propel so many Latinos to move north. It was beyond the video's scope, but unless students explore the broader economic factors hurting poor countries, they won't be able to think deeply about the wrongheadedness of anti-immigrant crusades. Without this broader context, students may be left sympathetic to immigrants' plights but unaware of how economic and political choices made here create social dislocations throughout Latin America. Limitations notwithstanding, the video is provocative and useful.

Echando Raices/Taking Root

Rachael Kamel/JT Takagi. American Friends Service Committee, 2002. 60 min. (Each videotape contains a Spanish and English version.)

Filled with personal and poignant stories, *Echando Raices/Taking Root* focuses on the struggles of immigrants in different U.S. communities in California, Texas, and Iowa. Many of those interviewed are themselves labor or community organizers, so a hopeful, activist current runs through each of the three episodes, which explore why people came to the United States, their process of adjustment, day laborer and undocumented rights, and tensions between immigrants and longtime residents.

A Mexican immigrant in the first episode describes how Latina and Hmong women have begun to meet together: "There are so many different people from different places living here, but I never stopped to think about why they came, or if their problems were similar to ours or about their way of thinking or living. … And all of us are fighting for a better future." But a Houston day laborer also describes the excruciating isolation, with his wife and five children at home in Mexico: "We're always alone. We see each other once in a while — but what we had as husband and wife, that's all over now. Now we look at each other like a couple of strangers. … And it's all because of the economy. It's destroying our families."

The video's final episode focuses on Perry, Iowa, where a shutdown at a well-paying Oscar Mayer meatpacking plant throws over 800 people out of work. In comes another company, IBP (a subsidiary of the Tyson Foods giant), which starts workers at $6.50 an hour, for dangerous and difficult work. And, surprise, IBP recruits immigrant workers, mostly from Mexico, to fill these jobs. The video lays out the community tensions without trying to suggest simplistic solutions.

A teaching guide can be downloaded at www.afsc.org/takingroot/.

Bus Riders Union

Haskell Wexler. The Strategy Center, 2000. 86 min.

In this extraordinary video, Academy Award–winning cinematographer Haskell Wexler records the several-year-long struggle of the Los Angeles Bus Riders Union (BRU) to win better service and to challenge the race and class bias in city spending priorities. At 86 minutes, it's long for classroom use and drags in a few places for many high school students; but what a rich documentary this is. At the outset, Kikanza Ramsey, a young BRU organizer, explains that the union is "a political, social experiment to see if we can build a multiracial, bilingual, gender-balanced mass movement of working class people that is willing to fight for a set of demands that challenges corporate capital." And this is not mere rhetoric. The remainder of the video brings her words to life, revealing the twists and turns, highs and lows of this struggle as seen through the eyes of participants. We desperately need more classroom resources like this one. First, because in many respects the union is victorious; in the end they win lots more buses — and less polluting ones, at that — to ease overcrowding for their mostly immigrant, poor, people of color, working-class constituency. And students need to learn that struggle matters. But it's how the BRU organizes — especially across lines of race, nationality, and language; with humor; with song; with determination; with an eye on the bigger systemic picture — that will leave a lasting impression. Hope is scarce in some of these "videos with a conscience;" in *Bus Riders Union* it plays a starring role.

A scene from *Salt of the Earth*.

Salt of the Earth

Herbert Biberman. 1954. 94 min.

Set in "Zinctown, N.M.," *Salt of the Earth* uses a combination of actors and nonprofessional community people to tell a great story. Sparked by a mine accident, the workers, mostly Mexican Americans, go on strike. Safety is the issue, but is inextricably linked with racial discrimination as Anglo miners work in pairs, while Mexican Americans are forced to work alone. The film consistently highlights the racial dimension to the class struggle. As one of the white managers says about the workers: "They're like children in many ways. Sometimes you have to humor them. Sometimes you have to spank them. And sometimes you have to take their food away." And the film also addresses racism within the union. The white organizer from the international union is committed to the workers' cause and to union democracy, but his paternalism still creeps in. He is criticized by one of the workers, Ramon Quintero: "When you figure everything the rank and file's to do down to the last detail, you don't give us anything to think about.

Are you afraid we're too lazy to take initiative?"

This is especially a feminist story, as women insist that their issues for indoor plumbing and hot water in the company-owned housing be included as a demand of the all-male union. This is the women's story at least as much as the men's, and they continue to push for equality the more they participate in strike activities. This struggle comes to a head as Esperanza confronts her husband, Ramon, about his determination to keep her in her place:

Have you learned nothing from this strike? Why are you afraid to have me at your side? Do you still think you can have dignity only if I have none? ... Do you feel better having someone lower than you? Whose neck shall I stand on to make me feel superior? ... I want to rise and push everything up as I go.

As effectively as any other film in my curriculum, *Salt of the Earth* celebrates the possibility of people being able to create a very different, very much better society through solidarity and collective action.

When I first showed *Salt of the Earth* a number of years ago, I worried that students would be put off by a black and white film that had quite a bit of amateurish acting and melodramatic music. I was wrong. What the film lacks in polish it more than makes up for in substance. And most students recognize that. (See S. J. Childs' excellent article on teaching with *Salt of the Earth,* "Resistance and Hope," www.rethinkingschools.org/archive/16_04/Hope164.shtml.)

Bread and Roses

Ken Loach. Lions Gate Films, 2001. 106 min. (Rated R for some sexual references and lots of obscene language. Available at video stores.)

This is the fictionalized account of episodes in the Justice for Janitors campaign in Los Angeles. The film opens with Maya's harrowing illegal entrance into the United States from Mexico and follows her travails as she secures a cleaning job in a large downtown office building. Perez, the on-site manager for the cleaning contractor, keeps workers in line through incessant haranguing. Maya bristles at this treatment, and is receptive to overtures from the cocky white union organizer, Sam, but her sister Rosa has learned hard lessons in self-preservation and wants no part of a risky union struggle, especially one led by this guy. "'We, we,' when was the last time you got a cleaning job?" she demands of Sam early in the film.

The best scenes in *Bread and Roses* are the tense conversations between workers about whether organizing is worth the risk. Maya's would-be boyfriend, Ruben, has a law school scholarship waiting, if only he plays it safe and keeps his job. Why would Maya want to endanger her job, Ruben wants to know. She snaps back:

> What was it that you said when they fired Teresa [an older woman who worked with them cleaning the office building]? "She looks like my mother." That's why I'm doing it. I'm doing it because my sister has been working 16 hours a day since she got here. Because her husband can't pay for the hospital bills. He doesn't have medical insurance. .... I'm doing it because I have to give Perez two months of my salary and I have to beg him for a job. I'm doing it because we feed those bastards, we wipe their asses, we do everything for them. We raise their children, and they still look right through us.

Bread and Roses is engaging start to finish and can generate lots of excellent writing and discussion — about treatment of immigrant workers, tensions between immigrant and nonimmigrant workers, risks and benefits of organizing, and many others. But it's not without its flaws. This is supposed to be a struggle to reclaim workers' lost dignity, but the organizer, not the workers, decides every union tactic. They may be in meetings together, but Sam does virtually all the talking — deciding every move, making pronouncements about how he is going to "personally embarrass" the new part-owners of the office building. (Someone in *Bread and Roses* should have criticized him the way the Ramon criticized the organizer in *Salt of the Earth*, above.) And the romance between Sam and Maya was a needless and inappropriate — if predictable — insertion by writer/director Ken Loach. But these are not fatal flaws, and this is a valuable film.

By the way, Loach is a prolific filmmaker, under-appreciated in the United States. Two of his films that would make valuable additions to a global studies curriculum are *Hidden Agenda*, about British repression in Northern Ireland, and *Land and Freedom*, about the Spanish Civil War.

The Fight in the Fields: César Chávez and the Farmworker Struggle

Ray Telles and Rick Tejada-Flores. Paradigm Productions, 1997. 116 min.

This is an excellent film about the life of César Chávez and the history of Mexican-American farmworkers — the best I've seen. *The Fight in the Fields* begins in the California fields in the 1860s and closes with the death of Chávez in 1993. In between is a solid history of the heroic farmworker movement, with a keen eye for the multiracial solidarity that weaves through the long struggle: Mexicans and Okies join forces in the 1930s, Filipinos and Mexicans later; an Arab-American striker was the first person killed in the grape strikes of the late 1960s.

Yes, it's largely a talking head documentary — at times, narrator-heavy. Yes, it's long. And, yes, some students may find it boring. But it's a fine film, rich in details, told mostly from the point of view of the organizers and farmworkers who made the history.

Although later sections on the grape and lettuce boycotts could be excerpted for use in class, the film draws its power from the panoramic view it offers of the farmworker struggle.

¡Aumento Ya! (A Raise Now!)

Tom Chamberlin/PCUN (Pineros y Campesinos Unidos del Noroeste), 1996. 50 min. (In English, some Spanish subtitles.)

"They look at us as if we're their tractor," says one farmworker organizer, describing the white growers' attitudes about their largely Mexican workforce. *¡Aumento Ya!* is the dramatic story of Oregon farmworkers' confrontation with those discriminatory attitudes, and the miserable working and living conditions that accompany them.

The video, presented as the personal narrative of a woman who came to volunteer with the farmworkers union, can be roughly divided into two parts: the first, a short overview of farmworker conditions in Oregon and the farmworkers union Pineros y Campesinos Unidos del Noroeste (PCUN); the second, the story of the strikes held over the summer of 1995 by workers in the strawberry fields. This is not a highly polished video, but its story is compelling, and my students have found *¡Aumento Ya!* engaging and moving. It's one of those "small" videos that allow students to encounter social forces as they manifest themselves in real people's lives.

Workers begin with the simple demand to be paid 17 cents a pound for strawberries rather than the 10 to 12 cents the growers are paying. Beginning with the first walkout from the fields, the video takes us day by day through the strike. A few days into the strike, as workers gain confidence, they add demands about their housing — shacks of blue plastic walls that sleep six or more. Workers call for separate showers for men and women, heat in the cabins, leaking roofs to be fixed, cleaning equipment made available, locks on doors, one telephone for the camp. For my students, the modesty of these demands underscored the wretchedness of farmworkers' living conditions.

It's not easy to find teaching materials that show ordinary people taking action to better their lives. ¡Aumento Ya! is inspiring without being romantic or overstating workers' accomplishments.

Bring some strawberries to class, ask students to write whatever comes to mind about the berries, and then show ¡Aumento Ya! for a different point of view (see p. 130 in *Rethinking Globalization: Teaching for Justice in an Unjust World*).

MEXICO POLITICS/ECONOMY/CULTURE

Granito de Arena (Grain of Sand)

Jill Freidberg. Corrugated Films, 2005. 60 min.

This is an ambitious and wonderful video. Freidberg — who also made *This Is What Democracy Looks Like,* about the 1999 World Trade Organization protests in Seattle — tackles the impact of globalization and neo-liberalism on Mexican education, the history of teachers organizing in Mexico, government and union repression, reform movements within the teachers union and finally reform movements within the reform movements. Without lots of background, this will be tough going for most high school students. But for teachers

JORGE ACEVEDO

From *Granito de Arena*: **Teachers march more than 1,000 kilometers from Oaxaca to Mexico City, 1985.**

considering how our work and lives here connect to teachers' work and lives in Mexico, *Granito de Arena* is unparalleled. As Freidberg chronicles increased privatization, standardized testing, cuts in funding, and curriculum standardization, it's hard to escape the creepy feeling that here and in Mexico all of us are part of the same scheme to turn education into "human capital" development, in the words of Mexican President Vicente Fox.

Freidberg opens with stunning footage of government attacks on a rural teachers college in the state of Chiapas. As one speaker says at a later rally in Mexico City, "All [the rich and the government] want is for schools to prepare a workforce that they can exploit in sweatshops." The video layers interviews with scenes of teacher and community resistance, resulting in a portrait both scary and inspirational.

Toward the end of the video, Eduardo Galeano suggests why, in the era of aggressive global capitalism, teachers of conscience must not merely be good classroom practitioners, but also social activists:

> There is an old proverb that says it's better to teach someone to fish than to give them fish. But what if they sell the river or what if they poison the river? And what good is it to know how to fish if the owner of the river doesn't let us fish? In other words, education is unavoidably, fatally linked to all other aspects of life.

Granito de Arena concludes with activists calling for a "globalization of solidarity" and for the "radicalization" of the teaching profession. Capping a video where we meet so many dedicated teacher-activists but are also confronted with such relentless attacks on public schools, these calls sound more like common sense than rhetoric. As Canadian activist Maude Barlow wonders about today's teachers: "If they don't fight for public education, who will?"

Trading Democracy

Bill Moyers. PBS, 2002. Approx. 60 min.

Bill Moyers calls NAFTA's Chapter 11 provisions "an end-run around the Constitution." Chapter 11 is the science-fiction-like piece of NAFTA that allows corporations to sue governments, before secret trade tribunals, if they believe that a government has taken some action that threatens a corporation's investment. *Trading Democracy* features several Chapter 11 cases, including Metalclad's complaint against Mexico. In 1993, Metalclad bought an abandoned toxic waste dump near the village of Guadalcazar, in the state of San Luis Potosí, Mexico. Metalclad had no experience operating toxic dumps, and the community, suffering high rates of cancer, demanded that before the dump could be reopened it should be cleaned up. Metalclad refused, claiming it had a permit from the national government to reopen

SLAM POETRY

If you've ever been to a poetry slam or watched HBO's *Def Poetry Jam,* then you know what an extraordinary medium this is. Paul Flores and Amalia Ortiz, both of whom have appeared on *Def Poetry Jam,* deliver wrenching performances of poems that can leave an indelible impression on students, and serve as prompts for students' own writing.

Paul Flores's "Brown Dreams" tells a "true story about a brown dream, sinking to the bottom of the Tigris-Euphrates." The dream is U.S. citizenship. A young man is convinced by an army recruiter at his high school to join the military in order to gain U.S. citizenship when he receives his honorable discharge. He is sent to Iraq, where he drowns in a tank accident: "Now his soul is an ancestor in the Euphrates. Chicano blood mixing with Arab soil returning to the garden of Eden by way of the U.S. Army."

On most of our Rethinking Schools–Global Exchange trips to the border, we have met with Fernando Suarez del Solar in San Diego, whose son Jesús, was the fifth U.S. death in Iraq. As Suarez del Solar has told us, a similar promise was made to his son, who had been convinced by a recruiter that for someone born in Mexico, the military would be his only route to a hoped-for career with the Drug Enforcement Agency. Jesús stepped on unexploded ordnance dropped by U.S. forces, most likely a cluster bomb.

As a Mexican-American woman, Amalia Ortiz is haunted by the nearby murders of women in Juárez "who all look like me. I am a dead ringer for an army of the dead." Since 1993, at least 350 women have been murdered in Juárez. Ortiz lives on the "safe" side of the border:

> safe
> yet not quite out of earshot of distant cries
> of families searching ditches and roadsides
> bearing snapshot after snapshot
> …
> I am a symbol of those who survive
> mouth open in defiance of their silence
> spared by a line in the sand
> drawn between their grandfather
> and mine

Flores and Ortiz deliver their poems with passion and conviction. Both are just a few minutes long and can be watched online. "Brown Dreams" is at http://poetrytelevision.com/ptvmembers/paul_video_1.html. "Women of Juárez" is at www.amaliaortiz.com. Click on Poetry. Ortiz's web links offer a long list of articles about the Juárez killings. (Also see p. 111 for the complete poem.)

---

the site. But it had no permission from the state government or from the local community. Denied the "right" to profit from its investment, Metalclad turned to the U.S. embassy to try to bully Mexico into allowing the reopening of the dump. According to the governor of San Luis Potosí, the U.S. ambassador threatened to put his state on an investment blacklist unless the governor relented and allowed the dump to be opened. When he refused and had the region declared a protected ecological zone, Metalclad took its complaint to a NAFTA tribunal.

Trading Democracy deals only with this especially egregious component of the NAFTA treaty, so it offers no discussion of the many other devastating consequences of NAFTA. Nonetheless this is a fine classroom resource. I've used the entire video in class, but at an hour, it may be more Chapter 11 than you have time for. Each segment in the video could be used separately — and the Metalclad piece is an especially accessible and engaging segment. One option would be to show both the first segment, on the Methanex corporation's chal-

lenge to California environmental regulations, and the second, on Metalclad. Examining the Methanex case, in which a Canadian corporation targeted California state environmental legislation, allows students to see that for corporations Chapter 11 is an equal opportunity weapon. A complete transcript of the video can be found at www.pbs.org/now/transcript/transcript_tdfull.html. Documents of the secret Metalclad tribunal have been posted at www.gwu.edu/~nsarchiv/NSAEBB/NSAEBB65/index.html.

Zapatista
Big Noise Films, 1998. 54 min.

"In all the world there are rich and there are poor. In all the world there is injustice and exploitation. This is what we want to end. We want democracy, justice, and liberty. These are our demands." This is the simple, startling, and radical vision articulated by one Zapatista soldier in this video. The strength of *Zapatista,* about the Chiapas-based indigenous guerrilla army and movement, is the eloquence the video assembles. It strings together one powerful, poetic quotation after another. The insights of Subcomandante Marcos, Noam Chomsky, Medea Benjamin, Blase Bonpane, Zack de la Rocha (Rage Against the Machine), and many lesser-known peasants, soldiers, and global justice activists are layered over a hip musical soundtrack and some stunning video clips, culminating in a very sympathetic examination of the Zapatista movement.

But this is not great storytelling and we learn very little about people's lives in Chiapas. This limits the video's usefulness as a classroom resource. If students know lots already about the Zapatista uprising and the conditions in Chiapas that fueled the rebellion, this might be a helpful supplement. But we see so little of ordinary people's lives that, by itself, *Zapatista* is unlikely to hold students' interest or to help them grasp what animates the struggle there.

The Sixth Sun

Saul Landau. Cinema Guild, 1996. 56 min.

Part guerrilla leader, part pop icon, Zapatista Subcomandante Marcos explains a key moment from 1986 in their struggle: "We changed from teachers to students, meaning we didn't enter the communities to teach what a revolution is, but rather to learn what a social movement is." *The Sixth Sun* is a beautifully filmed and mostly captivating video about the Zapatistas and their relationship to the indigenous communities in Chiapas that they serve. It's an effective visual introduction to the land, people, and struggles of this, the poorest state in Mexico.

I wanted the film to slow down and spend more time in just one village, and explore the intimate meaning of "free trade" and the Mexican government's trashing of Article 27, collective land rights, and land reform — and how these macro-policies relate to people's allegiance to the Zapatistas. *Sixth Sun* lists the socioeconomic underpinnings of the revolt, but does not really explore them in much depth. Still, the video offers an unprecedented look at the period before and just after the Jan. 1, 1994, uprising.

Landau saves his most stunning visual for the conclusion, as a determined indigenous community of mostly women and children turns back a heavily armed contingent of the Mexican army. This spirited encounter serves as a hopeful people-power metaphor. *The Sixth Sun* is a resource that could nicely complement the NAFTA role play (p. 63).

VIDEO/DVD DISTRIBUTORS

Some videos may be available at video stores or through Amazon. Additional distributors of videos or DVDs listed below:

Big Noise Films
www.bignoisefilms.com

Cinema Guild
www.cinemaguild.com

Maryknoll Sisters
www.maryknoll.org

Paradigm Productions
www.paradigmproductions.org

PCUN
www.pcun.org

Peek Media
www.progressivefilms.org

Public Broadcasting System

www.shoppbs.org

Women Make Movies
www.wmm.com

Organizations, Websites, Journals

American Friends Service Committee (AFSC), San Diego

www.afsc.org/office/san-diego-ca

P.O. Box 126147, San Diego, CA 92112

tel: 619-233-4114 • fax: 619-233-6247 • sandiego@afsc.org

The American Friends Service Committee sponsors a U.S.–Mexico border program. This program focuses on the defense of migrant human and civil rights as well as farm labor rights, and monitors Immigration and Naturalization Service, U.S. Border Patrol, and local law enforcement policies and practices. Activists in the San Diego office have a wealth of knowledge about the effects of Operation Gatekeeper, the U.S. Border Patrol's seal-the-border initiative in the San Diego sector.

BorderLinks

www.borderlinks.org

620 S. Sixth Avenue, Tucson AZ 85701

tel: 520-628-8263 • fax: 520-740-0242

BorderLinks offers opportunities to learn about economic and social issues along the U.S.–Mexico border. It has an experiential education program for North Americans, with short-term and semester-long immersion programs. Its programs explore economic issues — NAFTA, international debt, microcredit programs, community banking, maquiladoras, labor conditions — as well as women's rights, immigration policy, the U.S. Border Patrol, crime, health and environmental concerns, and human rights.

Campaign for Labor Rights

www.clrlabor.org

1247 E Street SE, Washington, DC 20003

tel: 202-544-9355 • clr@clrlabor,org

Campaign for Labor Rights offers an invaluable email listserv of alerts on sweatshop and solidarity issues. Its website includes past updates, links, resources, and leaflets.

CIEPAC, A.C. (Centro de Investigaciones Económicas y Políticas de Acción Comunitaria)

www.ciepac.org

Calle de la Primavera No. 6, Barrio de la Merced

29240 San Cristóbal, Chiapas, Mexico

tel: (in Mexico) 01 967 674 5168;

tel: (outside Mexico) +52 967 674 5168

CIEPAC is an important research center providing information and analysis to social justice organizing efforts. At its website, click on Boletines from the index and CIEPAC bulletins are listed by year, also indicating which articles are translated into English. An especially helpful bulletin is "In the Crossfire: MesoAmerican Migrants Journey North" (2005). I've relied on CIEPAC's valuable resources for a number of lessons in this book.

Coalition for Justice in the Maquiladoras

coalitionforjustice.info/cjm_website/index.html

3611 Golden Tee Lane, Missouri City, TX 77459

tel/fax: 210-732-8957

A tri-national coalition of religious, environmental, labor, Latino, and women's organizations working to pressure U.S.-based transnational corporations to adopt socially responsible practices. Publishes a newsletter and various reports and alerts on maquiladora struggles.

Environmental Health Coalition

www.environmentalhealth.org

2727 Hoover Ave., Suite 202 National City, CA 91950

tel: 619-474-0220 • fax: 619-474-1210

ehc@environmentalhealth.org

Environmental Health Coalition is a multi-issue coalition working in the San Diego-Tijuana area. In addition to its activist work, it has published a number of valuable reports on NAFTA, globalization and health, that are available at its website. The Colectivo Chilpancingo ProJusticia Ambiental, mentioned throughout the book, is an affiliate of EHC.

Global Exchange

www.globalexchange.org

2017 Mission St., 2nd Floor, San Francisco, CA 94110

tel: 415-255-7296 • fax 415-255-7498

Founded in 1988, Global Exchange is dedicated to promoting environmental, political, and social justice around the world. Global Exchange sponsors excellent "reality tours" to the U.S.–Mexico border and to sites in southern Mexico — and with Rethinking Schools cosponsored the "From the World to Our Classrooms" trips described throughout this book. Global Exchange's online store provides valuable teaching resources and also fair-trade goods from around the world.

Institute for Policy Studies

www.ips-dc.org

1112 16th St. NW, Suite 600, Washington, DC 20036

tel: 202-234-9382 • fax: 202-387-7915 • info@ips-dc.org

An important think tank on global issues from a social justice perspective. The IPS program on the global economy includes resources on NAFTA and globalization in the Americas.

International Relations Center/Americas Program

www.cipamericas.org

P.O. Box 2178, Silver City, NM 88062-2178

tel: 505-388-0208 • info@cipamericas.org

International Relations Center is a policy studies institute based in Silver City, NM, committed to promoting global justice. It provides excellent analysis and policy proposals on immigration, trade, transnational corporations, the environment, and other vital issues. Articles are in Spanish and English.

Maquiladora Health & Safety Support Network

http://mhssn.igc.org

P.O. Box 124, Berkeley, CA 94701-0124

tel: 510-558-1014 • fax: 510-525-8951

A volunteer network of occupational health and safety professionals providing information, technical assistance and on-site instruction regarding workplace hazards in the hundreds of maquiladoras along the U.S.–Mexico border. Its website includes excellent resources and links on maquiladora health and safety issues.

Maquila Solidarity Network

www.maquilasolidarity.org

606 Shaw Street, Toronto, Ontario M6G 3L6, Canada

tel: 416-532-8584 • fax: 416-532-7688

The Maquila Solidarity Network is a Canadian network promoting solidarity with groups in Mexico, Central America, and Asia organizing in maquiladora factories and export processing zones to improve conditions and win a living wage. Its website includes hard-to-find resources on maquilas by country or company, and many articles on sweatshop issues. Valuable links to other Canadian and international organizations concerned with workers' rights issues.

NACLA (North American Congress on Latin America)

www.nacla.org

38 Greene St., 4th Floor, New York, NY 10013

tel: 646-613-1440 • fax: 646-613-1443

NACLA publishes a bimonthly magazine *Report on the Americas,* the most widely read English language publication on Latin America. It features excellent, hard-to-find analyses and over the years has published many articles on the themes in this book.

National Network for Immigrant and Refugee Rights

www.nnirr.org

310 8th St., Suite 303, Oakland, CA 94607

tel: 510-465-1984 • fax: 510-465-1885 • nnirr@nnirr.org

The National Network for Immigrant and Refugee Rights (NNIRR) is an organization composed of local coalitions and immigrant, refugee, community, religious, civil rights, and labor organizations and activists. It serves as a forum to share information and analysis, to educate communities and the general public, and to develop and coordinate plans of action on important immigrant and refugee issues. The NNIRR also publishes valuable reports and curricula.

Resource Center of the Americas

www.americas.org

3019 Minnehaha Ave., Suite #20, Minneapolis, MN 55406

tel.: 612-276-0788 • fax: 612-605-3252

The Resource Center provides information and develops programs that demonstrate connections between people of Latin America, the Caribbean, and the United States. Over the years it has published a great deal of curriculum in this area. Its website includes an online catalog of these and other classroom materials available from their excellent Bookstore of the Americas, along with resources on critical issues about the Americas.

Rethinking Schools

www.rethinkingschools.org

1001 E. Keefe Ave., Milwaukee, WI 53212

subscriptions: 800-669-4192 • fax: 414-964-7220

Rethinking Schools is a quarterly magazine produced largely by classroom teachers with a focus on social

POLYP

justice and equity, as well as a publisher of books on social justice teaching issues, including *Rethinking Our Classrooms, Vols. 1 and 2, Rethinking Globalization,* and *The Line Between Us.* The magazine regularly publishes articles on teaching global issues — including those featured in this book. The website contains this entire resource list with all addresses hot-linked.

Schools for Chiapas

www.schoolsforchiapas.org or www.mexicopeace.org

1631 Dale St., San Diego, CA 92102

tel: 619-232-2841 • fax: 617-232-0500

An organization that works in solidarity with the struggles in Chiapas, Mexico. It mobilizes people and resources to build schools in Chiapas, and sponsors trips there to study Spanish and Mayan language and culture. The website features news articles, historical information, and other resources.

Teaching for Change

www.teachingforchange.org

P.O. Box 73038, Washington, D.C. 20056-3038

tel: 800-763-9193 • fax: 202-238-0109

The Teaching for Change online store is the best source for curriculum materials from a social justice perspective. The organization began in the early 1980s as a network of teachers concerned about issues in Central America, and continues to have a strong interest in Latin America, including Mexico.

United Farm Workers

www.ufw.org

UFW National Headquarters, P.O. Box 62, Keene, CA 93531

tel: 661-823-6250

Affiliated with the AFL-CIO, the UFW is the oldest and most prominent farmworker union in the United States. The union's website includes links, current news articles about farmworker struggles, updates, and background white papers, such as "Fields of Poison: California Farm Workers and Pesticides."

U.S. Border Patrol

www.cbp.gov (follow Border Security links to the U.S. Border Patrol)

This is the website of the U.S. Customs and Border Protection. It includes recent articles about the Border Patrol and sections on Border Patrol history and strategy.

Zapatistas

www.ezln.org.mx

The Zapatistas, based in the southernmost Mexican state of Chiapas, have drawn worldwide attention to the plight of indigenous people in the global economy. Their website is mostly in Spanish, although it does have some English translations. It's a fascinating site and the links will put students in touch with indigenous movements around the world.

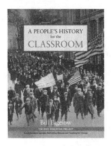
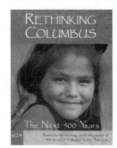

TEACHING FOR JOY AND JUSTICE Re-imagining the Language Arts Classroom
By Linda Christensen
Demonstrates how to draw on students' lives and the world to teach poetry, essays, narratives, and critical literacy skills. Practical, inspirational, passionate.

Paperback • 287 pages • ISBN: 978-0-942961-43-0
Only $19.95!*

READING, WRITING, AND RISING UP
Teaching About Social Justice and the Power of the Written Word
By Linda Christensen
Essays, lesson plans, and a remarkable collection of student writing, with an unwavering focus on language arts teaching for justice.

Paperback • 196 pages • ISBN: 978-0-942961-25-6
ONLY $16.95!*

THE NEW TEACHER BOOK
Finding Purpose, Balance, and Hope During Your First Years in the Classroom
This expanded collection of writings and reflections offers practical guidance on how to navigate the school system and connect in meaningful ways with students and families from all cultures and backgrounds.

Paperback • 384 pages • ISBN: 978-0-942961-47-8
ONLY $18.95!*

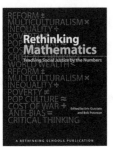

RETHINKING MATHEMATICS
Teaching Social Justice by the Numbers
Shows how to weave social justice issues throughout the mathematics curriculum, and how to integrate mathematics into other curricular areas.

Paperback • 180 pages • ISBN: 978-0-942961-54-6
ONLY $16.95!*

RETHINKING MULTICULTURAL EDUCATION Teaching for Racial and Cultural Justice
Edited by Wayne Au
Collects the best articles dealing with race and culture in the classroom that have appeared in *Rethinking Schools* magazine. A powerful vision of anti-racist, social justice education.

Paperback • 392 pages
ISBN: 978-0-942961-42-3
Only $18.95!*

Rethinking Popular Culture and Media
Beginning with the idea that the "popular" in the everyday lives of teachers and students is fundamentally political, this provocative collection of articles examines how and what popular toys, books, films, music, and other media "teach."

Paperback • 300 pages • ISBN: 978-0-942961-48-5
Only $18.95!*

THE LINE BETWEEN US
Teaching About the Border and Mexican Immigration
By Bill Bigelow
Using stories, historical narrative, role plays, poetry, and video, veteran teacher Bill Bigelow shows how he approaches immigration and border issues in his classroom.

Paperback • 160 pages • ISBN: 978-0-942961-31-7
Only $16.95!*

OPEN MINDS TO EQUALITY
A Sourcebook of Learning Activities to Affirm Diversity and Promote Equity
By Nancy Schniedewind and Ellen Davidson
Activities to help students understand and change inequalities based on race, gender, class, age, language, sexual orientation, physical/mental ability, and religion.

Paperback • 408 pages • ISBN: 978-0-942961-32-4
ONLY $24.95!*

---

* Plus shipping and handling. U.S. shipping and handling is 15% of the total (minimum charge of $4.50). Canadian shipping and handling is 25% of the total (minimum charge of $5.00).

■ **ORDER ONLINE:** **www.rethinkingschools.org**